NEW FRONTIERS OF STATE CONSTITUTIONAL LAW

NEW FRONTIERS OF STATE CONSTITUTIONAL LAW

DUAL ENFORCEMENT OF NORMS

EDITED BY

JAMES A. GARDNER

JIM ROSSI

OXFORD
UNIVERSITY PRESS

OXFORD
UNIVERSITY PRESS

Oxford University Press, Inc., publishes works that further Oxford University's objective of excellence in research, scholarship, and education.

Oxford New York
Auckland Cape Town Dar es Salaam Hong Kong Karachi Kuala Lumpur Madrid Melbourne Mexico City Nairobi New Delhi Shanghai Taipei Toronto

With offices in
Argentina Austria Brazil Chile Czech Republic France Greece Guatemala Hungary Italy Japan Poland Portugal Singapore South Korea Switzerland Thailand Turkey Ukraine Vietnam

Published by Oxford University Press, Inc.
198 Madison Avenue, New York, New York 10016

Oxford is a registered trademark of Oxford University Press
Oxford University Press is a registered trademark of Oxford University Press, Inc.

Library of Congress Cataloging-in-Publication Data

New frontiers of state constitutional law:
dual enforcement of norms/edited by James A. Gardner and Jim Rossi.
p. cm.
Includes bibliographical references and index.
ISBN 978-0-19-536832-1 (hardback)
1. Federal government–United States. 2.Constitutional law–United States–States.
3. Judicial review–United States–States.
I. Gardner, James A., 1959- II. Rossi, Jim, 1965-
KF4600.N49 2010
342.73'042–dc22

2010020544

Note to Readers
This publication is designed to provide accurate and authoritative information in regard to the subject matter covered. It is based upon sources believed to be accurate and reliable and is intended to be current as of the time it was written. It is sold with the understanding that the publisher is not engaged in rendering legal, accounting, or other professional services. If legal advice or other expert assistance is required, the services of a competent professional person should be sought. Also, to confirm that the information has not been affected or changed by recent developments, traditional legal research techniques should be used, including checking primary sources where appropriate.

(Based on the Declaration of Principles jointly adopted by a Committee of the American Bar Association and a Committee of Publishers and Associations.)

CONTENTS

ACKNOWLEDGEMENTS

The seeds for this volume were planted at a watershed conference held in Williamsburg, Virginia, on November 14, 2003. In an unusual partnership of academicians and jurists, the conference was co-sponsored by the Institute of Bill of Rights Law of William & Mary Law School, one of the leading venues for innovative scholarly thinking about federal constitutional law; and the National Center for State Courts, the preeminent organization dedicated to the study and improvement of state judicial systems. The conference, organized by the editors of the present work, brought together some of the most important figures in the field of American state constitutionalism with the goal of catalyzing innovative new responses to the conceptual problems plaguing the field. U.S. Supreme Court Chief Justice William Rehnquist, the Chief Justices of Wisconsin and Indiana, and former Justices of the Supreme Courts of Oregon and South Dakota joined an array of legal scholars to rethink the relation between state and national systems of constitutional law. Neal Devins, the Director of the Institute of Bill of Rights Law, who has contributed a chapter to this volume, played a critical role in facilitating the mounting of the conference, and the editors wish to acknowledge that this volume would not have been possible without Neal's early and energetic efforts.

Many people deserve thanks for helping at every stage of the process by which this volume has been created. The chapter authors wish to extend thanks to numerous and sundry individuals. James Gardner thanks Bob Williams and Hans Linde for valuable comments and suggestions on an earlier draft. Neal Devins thanks his research assistants Adrienne Johnson, Brian Sterling, and Andrea Johnson, as well as Fred Dingledy, research librarian extraordinaire. Robert Schapiro is grateful for the skilled research assistance of Robert McKeehan; Matthew Spivey, Terry Gordon, and Will Haines of the Emory University School of Law Library also provided valuable assistance. Jim Rossi thanks James Gardner, Hans Linde, Greg Mitchell, Robert Pushaw, and Robert Schapiro for comments on a draft; Daniel Norris provided diligent research assistance. Helen Hershkoff thanks John Nichols and Ellison Ward for research assistance; Linda Ramsingh for library support; Stephen Loffredo, Kevin Davis, and Liam Murphy for comments; and the Filomen D'Agostino and Max E. Greenberg Faculty Research Fund.

The editors acknowledge with gratitude the energetic and extraordinarily diligent assistance of Sue Martin in the production of this manuscript.

Some material in Chapters 2, 4, 7, and 8 originally appeared in the *William & Mary Law Review*, Volume 46 (2005) as part of the conference proceedings.

CONTRIBUTORS

NEAL DEVINS is Goodrich Professor of Law, Professor of Government, Director, Institute of Bill of Rights Law and Director, Election Law Program at William & Mary School of Law.

JAMES A. GARDNER is Joseph W. Belluck and Laura L. Aswad Professor of Civil Justice, Vice Dean for Academic Affairs, and Director of the Jaeckle Center for Law and Democracy at the University at Buffalo Law School.

HELEN HERSHKOFF is Anne and Joel Ehrenkranz Professor of Law and Co-Director, Arthur Garfield Hays Civil Liberties Program at New York University School of Law.

JACOB T. LEVY is Tomlinson Professor of Political Theory in the Department of Political Science at McGill University.

DANIEL B. RODRIGUEZ is Minerva House Drysdale Regents Chair at the University of Texas at Austin School of Law.

JIM ROSSI is Harry M. Walborsky Professor and Associate Dean for Research at Florida State University College of Law.

LAWRENCE G. SAGER is Dean, John Jeffers Research Chair, and Alice Jane Sheffield Regents Chair at the University of Texas at Austin School of Law.

ROBERT A. SCHAPIRO is a Professor at Emory Law School.

1. DUAL ENFORCEMENT OF CONSTITUTIONAL NORMS

JAMES A. GARDNER & JIM ROSSI

I. INTRODUCTION

Not so very long ago, the story of American constitutional law was easy to understand and even easier to relate. Constitutional law was a story written by two actors: the framers of the U.S. Constitution and the U.S. Supreme Court. The Constitution provided the content of constitutional law, and the Supreme Court told us what it meant. The framers wrote the script, and the Court directed the show—end of story.

Today although this master narrative still resonates strongly in the public consciousness, it has begun to unravel. Attacks have come from many directions. Observers have begun to recognize and acknowledge that the content and meaning of constitutional law is often influenced significantly by Congress and the U.S. president; by organs of state government; by institutions of international and foreign law such as the United Nations, the European Union, and foreign constitutional courts; and by evolving, contemporary popular opinion. Even within the domestic judicial apparatus, the U.S. Supreme Court is no longer seen as the sole director; instead, the role of state and lower federal courts in shaping constitutional law has increasingly been recognized, even by the Court itself. A story about a fixed, unitary source of law explicated by a single, institutionally privileged, "final" interpreter is fast being eclipsed by a new narrative that treats constitutional law as both the object and the venue of a plural and often remarkably inclusive ongoing conversation about the norms by which we live and govern ourselves.

The seeds of the death of the master unified narrative of American constitutional law are to a great extent sown in its own structure. More than most constitutions, the U.S. Constitution deliberately disseminates power among many actors along both horizontal (allocation of powers) and vertical (federalism) dimensions. In many circumstances, this decentralized power can be used to affect the meaning and content of constitutional law. Moreover, the Constitution creates many distinct spheres of autonomy in which these various actors sometimes enjoy a substantial degree of freedom to contemplate, create, experiment with, and communicate and argue about constitutional law and the foundational norms upon which it rests. The U.S. Supreme Court remains, to be sure, an important, sometimes final, and in many ways preeminent voice in the formal pronunciation of American constitutional law.

But increasingly the Court is understood to share the stage with a plurality of other voices that speak together—sometimes cooperatively, sometimes competitively—in a *collective* enterprise of generating, elaborating, and ultimately applying and enforcing—in the end, living by and under—constitutional norms.

Skeptics might think such an account of constitutional law represents nothing more than a cheap illusion, achieved by redefining what counts as constitutional "law." Sure, a skeptic might say, the United States has a national Constitution and states and other polities have their own constitutions, but the plurality of constitutional documents, constitutional interpreters, and constitutional enforcers shows only that these regimes of constitutional law are precisely what they seem to be: distinct realms of constitutional thought and doctrine, generated and tended autonomously by distinct polities and distinct organs of governance, for distinct purposes, according to distinct sets of values and policy preferences. We disagree. The task of the editors and authors of this volume is not to attempt sophistically to join that which must remain sundered, but to demonstrate how legal spheres that appear distinct are not; that they are, on the contrary, interconnected aspects of a common process that is larger than any of them.

II. THE JURISPRUDENCE OF AMERICAN SUBNATIONAL CONSTITUTIONAL LAW

Provision of a persuasive account of the relation between American national and subnational constitutional law has posed a recurring problem for courts and commentators for more than half a century. Three historical developments have made the interplay between federal and state constitutions fertile ground for jurisprudential development in the twentieth century. The incorporation doctrine has steadily led to the extension of the protections of the Bill of Rights of the U.S. Constitution against states, notwithstanding the fact that many states have similar protections in the texts of their own constitutions.[1] Following the New Deal, the growth of federal power was greatly expanded—sometimes preempting state constitutions and at others allowing federal actors to play a role in the sphere traditionally governed by state constitutions. Finally, particularly in the latter half of the twentieth century, the recognition of new rights by both state and federal courts—sometimes as they moved in the same direction and sometimes as they took conflicting stances—made the relationship between the U.S. Constitution and state constitutions relevant to high-profile social issues.

---

1. Supreme Court decisions applied many of the protections of the First Amendment against the states in the 1930s and 1940s, but protections for criminal defendants were not extended to the states until a series of decisions issued by the Warren Court in the 1960s.

Under the structure of our federal system, state constitutional law is jurisprudentially independent of federal constitutional law and need not follow or even acknowledge it. This independence gives state courts the authority to depart from federal precedent and to construe state constitutional rights provisions differently from, and in many cases more broadly than, the U.S. Supreme Court construes equivalent provisions of the U.S. Constitution. Thus, state courts may construe state constitutional provisions guaranteeing free speech more generously than the U.S. Supreme Court construes the First Amendment.[2] For example, a number of state courts have adopted more expansive readings under state constitutions of the constitutionally permitted treatment of same-sex partnership and marriage than those provided under the U.S. Constitution.[3] Some states also have expanded the generation and enforcement of constitutional rights beyond public actors to include private conduct, an extension that federal courts have never explicitly endorsed.[4]

The amount of discretion available to state courts and other constitutional interpreters is potentially great. To constrain it, state courts require a stock of disciplining jurisprudential concepts. The modern history of American subnational constitutional interpretation is a story about the search for such concepts. Successive generations of scholars and jurists have lurched violently from a dismissive view of state constitutions as documents of purely parochial import, worthy of little serious study by anyone outside of a state's immediate jurisdiction, to an aggressively ambitious approach that understands state constitutions as fundamentally freestanding sources of fully developed, independent legal norms.

Recent decades have seen a growing dissatisfaction with both prior approaches and the emergence of a new, more nuanced one that looks toward a broader, more inclusive, and more integrated transjurisdictional dialogue of constitutional law grounded in the structure of federalism. In this new generation of state constitutional law scholarship, state and national constitutionalism are reconceived as both collaborators and competitors in the production of constitutional norms. This scholarship has co-evolved with judicial decisions that view federalism as requiring state constitutional interpretation to account for a state's position within a larger national system, even where state courts might attempt to characterize issues as grounded purely in state constitutional law.[5]

---

2. *E.g.*, Immuno AG. v. Moor-Jankowski, 567 N.E.2d 1270 (N.Y. 1991).

3. *See* Chapter 6.

4. *See* Chapter 9.

5. *See* Bush v. Gore, 531 U.S. 98 (2000) (holding the Florida Supreme Court's procedure for recounting ballots a violation of the Equal Protection Clause of the U.S. Constitution, notwithstanding the state court's characterization of the issues as based on state constitutional law); Caperton v. A.T. Massey Coal, 129 S.Ct. 2252 (2009) (holding West Virginia's judicial election system violates the Due Process Clause of the U.S.

Such an approach allows scholars and courts to account for and accept common practices of state constitutional adjudication while still subjecting those practices to meaningful normative critique within a framework that transcends any individual state.

Contemporary state constitutionalism was born in the shadow of the federal rights jurisprudence of the Warren Court. During that period, a highly active U.S. Supreme Court not only dramatically expanded the reach and impact of rights protected by the federal Bill of Rights, but also imposed those constraints on state governments. As a result, state constitutional law was widely seen as fundamentally subordinate to national constitutional law. Because the federal Constitution seemed to supply a complete set of hierarchically superior constitutional norms, state courts typically deferred reflexively to the U.S. Supreme Court, looking to it for the solutions to virtually all problems of constitutional law and treating state and national constitutional norms as essentially uniform and thus interchangeable.

This highly deferential approach soon provoked considerable criticism from the bench and the academy, leading to a movement to liberate state constitutional law from its federal counterpart. A counterrevolution—the "New Judicial Federalism"—was born that conceived of state constitutions as independent sources of legal norms arising from organic and entirely local processes of which state constitutions were both the culmination and the embodiment. State courts were thus urged to treat their state constitutions as containing unique and homegrown solutions to commonplace constitutional problems. This approach provided a much-needed justification for state courts to deviate from the path charted by the U.S. Supreme Court during the Burger and early Rehnquist years when the Court adopted an approach to many individual rights that was less expansive than many state judges preferred.

Eventually, however, the independent approach to state constitutional interpretation itself began to show its limitations. It could not plausibly account for the striking similarity of most contemporary state constitutions to one another and to the federal Constitution. Its interpretational methodology sometimes drove state courts to make dubious claims about the social and ideological distinctiveness of their state polities. And it has been seriously undermined in practice by state courts themselves, many of which utterly ignore its prescriptions and continue to look primarily to federal constitutional law and the Supreme Court for guidance. These developments compromised the normative and descriptive appeal of the independent approach, prompting scholars to take another look at state constitutional law, this time focusing on its structural role in the American system of federalism.

Constitution to the extent it allows judges to decide cases for parties who have made contributions to the judges).

III. STATES AS DYNAMIC SUBNATIONAL INSTITUTIONS WITHIN A FEDERALISM FRAMEWORK

Many sophisticated approaches to understanding the role of states within a federal system are now being applied by economists and political scientists and, to a lesser degree, by legal scholars. Although these new approaches draw on the federalism concerns that motivate the new judicial federalism, these efforts are more than just "theories of federalism."[6] That is, they not only provide a defense of both federal and state power, as do dominant understandings of federalism, but also some normative account of how state and national actors understand their respective institutional roles in generating and enforcing legal norms. They also recognize that the roles of national and state actors are not limited to prearticulated spheres of jurisdictional power, but coexist and frequently overlap while being subject to ongoing negotiation.

For several decades, economists have understood the fundamental issues presented by federalism as how optimally to allocate power between federal and state actors. In the 1950s, Charles Tiebout introduced the idea of competitive federalism, in which states serve an important role in the allocation of authority by competing among themselves to attract residents and resources.[7] This line of research focuses primarily on the vertical allocation of power between the federal government and the states, and in particular the importance of national jurisdiction in minimizing the spillover costs presented by state regulation. A later innovation, fiscal federalism, focuses on the ability of states to generate revenue—and emphasizes the horizontal allocation of power between states—but draws on many of the same assumptions while also recognizing the importance of experimentation among the various states.[8]

Both competitive and fiscal federalism see the allocation of authority between national and subnational governments not as fixed and independent but rather as coexisting and evolving to best fit economic resource issues. Although much of this literature sees state governments as better equipped to operate closer to the optimal scale than national government,[9] economists do not view jurisdiction as fixed and isolated, but as adaptive, evolving, and dependent on a variety of factors, including the costs of mobility, the presence of free rider problems, and the likelihood of spillover costs. In addition, an understanding of institutions, behavior, and the incentives of various actors, state and national, is fundamental to the economic understanding of federalism issues.

---

6. For example, one popular theoretical account in the legal academy is *process federalism*, which sees limits on the power of Congress and the U.S. president as largely self-enforcing through the political process.

7. Charles M. Tiebout, *A Pure Theory of Local Expenditures*, 64 J. Pol. Econ. 416 (1956).

8. Wallace Oates, Fiscal Federalism (1972).

9. Gordon Tullock, *Federalism and Problems of Scale*, 6 Pub. Choice 19 (1969).

Another way to understand the structural issues presented by federalism is through the lens of principal-agent theory. Specifically, federalism might be understood as an effort to identify the optimal way by which a principal allocates power to an agent. If the principal is understood as the national polity, i.e., the citizens of the United States, federalism is essentially an effort to allocate power vertically between dual agents, namely the national government and individual states. The allocation of power to dual agents presents a number of economic benefits, as competitive and fiscal federalism reveals, but also presents a number of problems. Two such issues are minimizing monitoring costs (the costs to the principal of ensuring the agents are loyal) and minimizing shirking (the likelihood that an agent will pursue its self-interest over the principal's interest).

In previous work, James Gardner has raised the possibility that the constitutional interpretive space allowed the federal government and individual states may not be entirely symmetrical.[10] The principal-agent framework highlights that it is undesirable for the principal to allocate restrictive jurisdiction to both agents, as this necessitates greater monitoring and amendment costs as the national polity must undertake constitutional adjustments of authority. At the same time, it is undesirable for the principal to allocate broad discretion to both agents, as this enhances the likelihood of shirking. Instead, the optimal allocation of power between dual agents will be to grant one agent considerable discretion, give the other agent limited authority, and charge each with monitoring the behavior of the other. Consistent with this model, in American federalism the national government lacks all powers except those explicitly or implicitly granted to it in the U.S. Constitution. Thus, in contexts where shared jurisdiction exists between state and federal actors, the national polity has arguably delegated only limited power to the national government while leaving the states considerable leeway to generate and enforce constitutional norms.

Yet another way in which federalism can be understood dynamically is as an effort to mediate fluid political identities. Jurisdictional lines that have been drawn around various groups, even those that are drawn for arbitrary reasons, can become meaningful to individuals over time. A nation, as Benedict Anderson maintains, is an imagined political community that takes on meaning to its citizens.[11] To be American differs in important ways from being French or German or Chinese, a difference that may manifest itself in politically salient ways.

The same kind of analysis might be said to apply to subnational political communities such as states. Iowans, for example, might take a sense of collective pride in their practice of small-town democracy, Texans in their frontier individualism, and Georgians in their southern heritage. Federalism might be understood

---

10. *See* ch. 7 of James A. Gardner, Interpreting State Constitutions: A Jurisprudence of Function in a Federal System (2005).

11. Benedict Anderson, Imagined Communities: Reflections on the Origins and Spread of Nationalism (rev. ed. 1991).

as an institutional design feature that requires us to take into account a subnational group's understanding of itself. It is important here, however, to avoid oversimplification, as many differences across subnational groups are not constitutionally relevant, and comparative state constitutional law ought not to devolve into a simplistic exercise in cataloguing different choices or approaches, much as we might identify different approaches to barbeque or wine across regions. Indeed, we can account for differences in the collective political preferences and identities of state polities without presupposing any deeply meaningful differences in political character or culture simply by acknowledging the path-dependency of political identity. People of fundamentally similar character and values may come to diverge along those dimensions not because of who they are, but because of contingent historical events and political choices that cause them to live in increasingly divergent political environments. In either case, however, differences between and across national and state identities may be relevant to the enterprise of constitutional interpretation.

Federalism as an institution provides both a challenge and an opportunity in accounting for and mediating these identities. The challenge is to develop an understanding of subnational identity that fits the social and empirical understanding of contemporary American life without turning state constitutions into oversimplified templates of nostalgic values. The opportunity is for greater legitimacy as a national polity mediates different identities in ways that enrich political participation, provide new understandings of constitutional norms, and challenge a national monopoly over their enforcement.

IV. THE GENERATION AND ENFORCEMENT OF CONSTITUTIONAL NORMS IN A DUAL AGENT FEDERALISM

The approaches to federalism described above all differ from the more traditional views in one highly important respect: they all treat the federal structure of governance as a single system. Instead of beginning from the premise that the federal division of authority between state and national governments creates two (or more) distinct systems of governance or power, these approaches treat federal systems as coherent wholes, albeit complex wholes with many interconnected moving parts. Indeed, these approaches go further, for they conceive of the parts of a well-constructed federal system as moving together in a way that is not only to some degree coordinated, but coordinated in the pursuit of common objectives. These approaches thus stand in especially sharp contrast to the old dual federalism model, which presupposed a federal system to be composed of fundamentally discrete and independent power centers, pursuing the presumptively unrelated and frequently conflicting interests of largely independent political societies.

To be sure, the more nuanced, contemporary approaches, like their predecessors, fully contemplate the possibility that a federal system of government may contain internal tensions, and that such tensions may on occasion be severe and difficult to resolve. These approaches, however, conceive of such internal tensions as controlled and coordinated—as tensions that power the system not toward some ominous and omnipresent risk of fragmentation, but simply forward, in whatever direction the collective parts of the system may contingently permit it to move. In the past, when the federal Constitution was sometimes likened to "a machine that would go of itself,"[12] the dominant metaphor of dual constitutionalism seemed to be a mechanical device such as a gyroscope—an exquisitely balanced mechanism that threatens constantly to topple if the parts fall out of precise opposition.[13] Today, the more apt scientific metaphor for a federal constitution might well be a sustainable ecosystem, a highly complex system that is always in motion, responds adaptively to most external stimuli without ill effect, and is capable of absorbing, disarming, and in all but the most extreme cases surviving all manner of internal tensions and disruptions.

The approach to constitutionalism taken here follows the more contemporary conceptions of federalism. Rejecting both the dual federalism and the new judicial federalism models, the contributors to this volume understand the generation, development, interpretation, and enforcement of constitutional norms to be little different from any other enterprise undertaken collectively by the participants in a complex federal system. Constitutional elaboration at the national and state levels, that is to say, are best conceived as constituent activities of a single, collective enterprise conducted by many actors located in many sites scattered throughout the system. We label this approach *dual enforcement of constitutional norms* as a kind of shorthand reminder that the development and jurisprudential elaboration of constitutional norms and values is not exclusively a property or function of any particular level of government in federal systems of a certain kind.

This last qualification is an important one. The term *federalism* is sometimes applied to a wide variety of power arrangements, and just because a system of governance is decentralized to some degree does not mean that participation in all the major tasks of collective self-governance is meaningfully shared at all levels. Consequently, whether the development of constitutional norms is a shared function in any given federal system depends on the precise arrangement and distribution of power among the different levels of government. In the United States, however, there can be no doubt, as the contributors to this volume emphatically contend, that the generation and development of constitutional norms is to a great degree shared at the national and state levels.

---

12. Michael Kammen, A Machine That Would Go of Itself: The Constitution in American Culture (1986).

13. *See, e.g.*, Immigration & Naturalization Serv. v. Chadha, 462 U.S. 919, 951 (1983) ("power of the Federal government [is to] be exercised in accord with a single, finely wrought and exhaustively considered, procedure").

Although a federal arrangement in which organs of both national and subnational governments share a role in the generation and elaboration of constitutional norms is not unique to the United States, the American brand of federalism is distinctive in the formality with which it creates such a structure. Unlike any other federal nation, the United States possesses a fully developed dual judicial system, state and national.[14] Each judicial system, moreover, has jurisdiction under some circumstances to construe the constitution of the other, allowing multiple voices to speak officially and authoritatively concerning the meaning and content of constitutional provisions throughout the governance system at every level. Even more importantly, however, as the following chapters reveal, each judicial system influences the meaning given to the other system's constitution in numerous informal ways.

In some respects, the fact that the superintendence of American constitutional norms and processes is shared at the state and national levels is so obvious as to amount to an almost tautological truth about the federal system. Paradoxically, though, this very obviousness can also obscure, by hiding in plain view, characteristics of the system that are highly significant. So let us modestly state the obvious: in the American system of dual constitutions, the generation of constitutional norms is shared at the state and national levels. In the most formal sense, this means that state and national polities have independent authority to identify the norms and values they deem worthy of elevation to constitutional status. Were state and national constitutional law entirely distinct jurisprudential regimes, this parallel authority would not in any real sense be "shared." But state and national constitutional law are far from hermetically sealed jurisprudential regimes. In fact, they are connected at numerous points by strong and durable links of shared history and shared politics; pragmatic mutual borrowing; common participation in the development of an evolving body of constitutional common law;[15] judicial comity, deference, and mutual education; and even, at some points, links forged by legal doctrines that look to the meaning of constitutions at one level as a formal source of meaning for the other.[16]

---

14. Ronald L. Watts, *States, Provinces, Länder, and Cantons: International Variety among Subnational Constitutions*, 31 RUTGERS L.J. 941, 955 (2000). Even in federal states such as Australia, Canada, and Switzerland, where the national constitution permits the erection of dual national and subnational court systems, such authority has not been exercised. *Id.* In some other states, such as Mexico, subnational units have well-developed judicial systems, but national courts are supreme with respect to the interpretation not only of national constitutional law, but of subnational constitutional law. Stephen Zamora & José Ramón Cossío, *Mexican Constitutionalism after* Presidencialismo, 4 INT'L J. CON. LAW 411, 434–35 (2006).

15. David A. Strauss, *Common Law Constitutional Interpretation*, 62 U. CHI. L. REV. 131 (1995).

16. Robert Williams describes the problems of federal-to-state lockstepping in Robert F. Williams, *State Courts Adopting Federal Constitutional Doctrine: Case-by-Case Adoptionism*

The interconnectedness of the apparatus of dual *generation* of constitutional norms is only amplified by the associated apparatus of dual judicial *enforcement* of such norms. Enforcement—application—is what gives meaning to otherwise abstract constitutional norms and principles. Again, were the judicial enforcement of constitutional norms at the state and national levels distinct practices completely divorced from one another, we might expect constitutional meaning within the two systems to spin off in unrelated directions, even if they shared a common starting point. Yet judicial enforcement of constitutional norms is a practice that draws upon the same sources of state and national interconnectedness that link the generation of state and national constitutional norms in the first instance. Shared constitutional history, cross-jurisdictional borrowing by drafters of constitutional text, party politics that cut across the formal boundaries of state and national power, common professional understandings of judging and judicial practice—all of these contribute to an enduring overlap between state and national judicial constitutional discourses. As a result, state and national judicial enforcement of constitutional norms is better understood, in many circumstances and for many purposes, as different parts of a single, nationwide process.

On the other hand, to say that state and national practices of constitutional elaboration are strongly linked is by no means to say they are identical. Different institutional strengths and capacities of the state and national judiciaries, distinctive local or regional historical experiences, variations in the nationwide distribution of political opinion or culturally informed preferences, and many other kinds of variability can introduce path-dependent divergences in the development and elaboration of even the most fundamentally shared constitutional norms. Consequently, the best way to think about the regime of dual enforcement of constitutional norms is that it institutionalizes a kind of permanent and highly complex conversation among many actors, each situated somewhat differently from all the others, and each therefore approaching the project of constitutional elaboration from a potentially distinct vantage point.

The idea that constitutional norms may develop within a system of divided power as the result of communication among a multiplicity of official actors is sometimes called a *dialogic* model,[17] a view we endorse, though with an important caution. Because they focus so heavily on the benefits of intersystemic dialogue—talk itself—proponents of the dialogic model sometimes seem to

---

or Prospective Lockstepping?, 46 Wm. & Mary L. Rev. 1499 (2005). James Gardner describes how states serve a resistance role toward the expansion of federal power in *State Constitutional Rights as Resistance to National Power: Toward a Functional Theory of State Constitutions*, 91 Geo. L.J. 1003 (2003).

17. Paul W. Kahn, *Interpretation and Authority in State Constitutionalism*, 106 Harv. L. Rev. 1147 (1993); Lawrence Friedman, *The Constitutional Value of Dialogue and the New Judicial Federalism*, 28 Hastings Const. L.Q. 93 (2000).

suggest that dialogue itself is the point of the system. Clearly though, it is not. No system of governance can exist for the purpose of producing talk; governments exist because of the need for action, indeed for action that is substantively good and collectively beneficial. The value of intersystemic dialogue can therefore only be instrumental; its value, if any, must be that it produces official actions that are better than they would be without the conversation. That is why we believe it is best to focus on dual *enforcement* of constitutional norms as the salient characteristic of American constitutional federalism, for it is through the process of enforcing judicial norms by applying them in concrete cases that the state and national judiciaries participate in an ongoing conversation about the ultimate substance of American constitutional law.

V. THE APPROACH OF THIS VOLUME

Consistent with the framework described above, the authors of this volume begin from the premise that national and subnational systems of constitutional law cannot be adequately understood in isolation from one another—that they are, to the contrary, linked in a web of jurisprudential, social, and pragmatic connections structured by the American system of federalism. The chapters in *New Frontiers* thus present a conception of national and subnational constitutional law as complementary partners in a complex, collective enterprise of constitutional self-governance. Our aim for the book is to advance an understanding of state constitutions in the broader inter-institutional process of constitutional dialogue.

Chapter 2, by Lawrence Sager, begins the individual essays by laying out the broadest implications of a conception of constitutional law as a shared enterprise conducted within a federal system. Sager explores the wider, systemic significance of subnational constitutional law by examining the large-scale movements of the mechanism by which dual constitutionalism, and state-led, rights-based constitutionalism in particular, generates and enfolds moral norms. One of the benefits of a federal system, Sager argues, is its capacity to accommodate and even to encourage moral progress. He envisions this as a continual process in which moral experimentation occurs in a small number of vanguard states, propagates itself within the system through the accumulation of experience and the gradual alteration of public opinion, and finally consolidates itself by migrating to the national level, where formerly cutting-edge moral norms are incorporated, constitutionalized, and then imposed on straggler states to create a new—but only temporary—uniformity.

In Chapter 3, Jacob Levy provides another account of variation in constitutional values and choices within a federation, but grounds it in a conception of federalism as a pragmatic alternative to competing conceptions of the nature of constitutional choice. In what Levy calls the moral-realist tradition, constitutional similarity ought to be the norm because the purpose of a constitution is to operationalize principles of justice that are at bottom universal. In the democratic-positivist tradition, in contrast, constitutional divergence is unremarkable because constitutions embody little more than the contingent choices of one political association or another. Federalism, Levy maintains, charts a middle course. By granting some autonomy to subnational units, federalism permits contingent choice and preference satisfaction, yet by subordinating subnational choices to national ones it sets collectively determined limits on the permissible range of those choices—a kind of "localized universalism," one might say—that results in what Levy calls "bounded variation." The benefits of such an arrangement, Levy argues, include experimentation without instability, diversity without alienation, and the institutionalization of feasible change—although, he adds, this need not always imply "progress" of a moral or any other kind.

In Chapter 4, co-editor James Gardner places the volume's approach in its interpretational context by linking the federal structure of constitutional norm production to the ever-present problem of interpretational methodology. Gardner begins by arguing that previous approaches to the interpretation of subnational constitutions have failed because they improperly attempted to apply the dominant jurisprudence of national constitutional interpretation—constitutional positivism—to the constitutions of the states. Constitutional positivism as a technique makes sense only where subnational units are autonomous, as are independent nations. However, states in a federal system like ours are far from the kind of autonomous sovereigns contemplated by prevailing theories of national constitutional interpretation. Indeed, a state constitution is the product of processes that transcend the state and in which both the state and national polities participate. As a result, the interpretation of state constitutions inevitably will require at least some resort to national norms and sources of constitutional meaning.

Chapter 5, by Daniel Rodriguez, continues the attack on conventional accounts of subnational constitutional interpretation by examining judicial review at the state level in its actual institutional setting. American state constitutions, Rodriguez contends, perform different functions from the U.S. Constitution, functions dictated by their role within a federal system of governance. In this system, governance at the state level is meant to be more active, more comprehensive, and more efficacious than its national counterpart. Because the foundational project, indeed the very *telos* of state and national constitutionalism differs, it makes no sense unreflectively to apply to state constitutions approaches to judicial review worked out in the institutional setting of the U.S. Constitution. Rodriguez goes on to sketch the outlines of an appropriately context-sensitive account of judicial review under state constitutions. Such an approach must, he contends, take account of the contemporary mission of states as agents of active governance; judicial review, in other words, must be "optimized" to serve its actual institutional purposes. Such review should be neither too deferential, thereby leaving broad state power dangerously unchecked, nor too aggressive, thereby unduly restraining state power that is meant to be both broad and effective. The challenge, Rodriguez concludes, is to develop an optimizing account of state constitutional judicial review that facilitates effective governance while simultaneously providing appropriate protections for individual liberty.

The remaining essays in the book turn from the theoretical to the practical by addressing how the federal system of dual enforcement of constitutional norms plays out in particular areas of subnational constitutional law. A practical approach is perhaps most useful in the context of high-profile social issues involving individual rights such as same-sex marriage, the right to bear arms, and constitutional privacy protections. However, as these essays emphasize, even apart from the definition of substantive rights, the dual enforcement of constitutional norms presents structural tensions that also require serious analysis.

In Chapter 6, Neal Devins addresses state constitutional interpretation in the context of same-sex marriage, with a particular focus on its implications for the new judicial federalism. Devins surveys the same-sex marriage decisions under state constitutions, applying an institutional approach to understand their implications within the new judicial federalism framework. He argues that although state supreme courts construing state constitutions should not take into account out-of-state backlash, it is entirely appropriate, and even desirable, for them to consider in-state inter-institutional implications of their decisions when contemplating the recognition of new constitutional rights. Devins's chapter illustrates how state courts simultaneously operate as independent sovereigns while participating in a national conversation about core constitutional values—values that transcend any one state.

Chapter 7, written by Robert Schapiro, a leading theorist of judicial federalism, turns to the complex interplay of state and national judicial power. The unusual dual structure of the American judiciary, Schapiro argues, creates a system of intersystemic adjudication that provides a way for state and federal courts to work together to safeguard important liberties. Elaborating a concept of "polyphonic" judicial federalism, Schapiro takes issue with several well-established principles of federal adjudication that counsel federal courts to avoid construing state constitutions. In fact, he maintains, federal adjudication of state constitutional claims can in many circumstances yield substantial benefits by multiplying the institutional settings in which such claims are considered, generating intersystemic dialogue on the meaning of constitutional principles, and better utilizing available system redundancy to maximize the effectuation of recognized rights. In defending his account of an expanded federal adjudicatory role, Schapiro rejects the view that *Erie Railroad Co. v. Tompkins*[18] requires a complete separation of the state and federal judicial spheres. Nothing in *Erie*'s

18. 304 U.S. 64 (1938).

account of state and national judicial authority, he argues, impugns the legitimacy of intersystemic judicial dialogue and cooperation, which can go a long way toward reducing error in both systems.

In Chapter 8, co-editor Jim Rossi demonstrates the conceptual payoff in the context of the interplay between state and national legislative and executive power by focusing on two recurring problems of cooperative federalism: state implementation of federal programmatic directives and state administrative borrowing of federal regulatory standards. In both of these situations, the state constitution may constrain the ability of state agencies to administer programs in the way they desire, most commonly through a strict nondelegation doctrine purportedly rooted in the state constitutional separation of powers. Rossi here rejects the approaches to these problems worked out by both federal and state courts in favor of one based on comparative institutional analysis informed by the dual enforcement model. On this view, state constitutions should not be construed to bar state administrative compliance with or adoption of federal legal norms because state constitutional nondelegation doctrines are better understood as responses to governance failures peculiar to state-level democracy—failures that have no relevance when a state legislature indirectly delegates power to the national government rather than to an organ of state government. This helps to shed light on the nature of executive power at the state level, particularly where national goals are at issue.

Finally, in Chapter 9, Helen Hershkoff addresses differences in how the U.S. Constitution and many individual state constitutions approach the state action requirement in enforcing constitutional rights. In contrast to the U.S. Constitution, which generally requires state action as a predicate to the adjudication of constitutional rights, some state constitutions do not require the same predicate for the evolution of constitutional norms. Hershkoff describes the practices by which state courts, using common law rather than constitutional law pathways, have extended constitutional protections to private conduct. She grounds this generally in a framework drawn from comparative constitutionalism, and elaborates on its implications for federalism, state courts, and state constitutionalism more generally. The way state courts have developed a convergence between private and public concepts in constitutional law has important implications for the distinct path of state constitutional rights adjudication in the United States, and Hershkoff's chapter provides a descriptive and conceptual grounding for the phenomenon.

2. COOL FEDERALISM AND THE LIFE CYCLE OF MORAL PROGRESS

LAWRENCE G. SAGER

I. INTRODUCTION: HOT AND COOL FEDERALISM

We can divide justifications for federalism-based structures of governance into *hot* federalism and *cool* federalism, with the distinction keyed to the reasons for resorting to a federal structure. By hot federalism, I mean the use of federal structures of governance to solve a type of problem that can arise when relatively settled and coherent social groups seek to create common structures of governance with other groups. Each group, we can imagine, is relatively homogeneous, with sufficient commonalities of experience, belief, commitment, language, and so on, to permit its members to enjoy a fair amount of trust and comfort with each other as members of a political community. But between or among the groups in question, there is substantially less commonality and substantially less trust and comfort with the prospect of becoming members of a single political community. The groups in question, nevertheless, wish to create or perpetuate some form of a trans-group union. This creates a problem in governance: how can such groups work together in the face of the reluctance to concede full and ultimate authority to a trans-group governing entity?

Hot federalism is very important in the contemporary world, and the prospects for its success in various modern contexts are remarkable and exciting. There are reasons, however, to be a bit wary of the capacity of federal structures to overcome problems of the hot federalism variety. In the United States, we certainly began with hot federalism concerns, driven substantially by the issue of slavery. But our federal structure in this regard was a great failure, giving on to the tragedy of the Civil War. Recently, we have seen Canada nearly come apart, and the success of the federal structure there still seems a close question. Europe is moving rapidly to the embrace of a transnational, federal structure of governance—far more rapidly than many would have imagined remotely possible—but it is still too early to assess the ultimate success of this extraordinary transition. The miracle of South Africa's constitutionalized revolution has made important use of a federal structure to permit wary groups to join under a national rule of law; but here too, it is a bit early to draw conclusive lessons. And Switzerland has always seemed too small and quirky to offer lessons for the rest of the world.

In any event, I mention hot federalism only to set it aside. It is cool federalism that interests me here. Cool federalism is substantially less ambitious. It aims not at making it possible for groups to coexist in governance structures that would otherwise be intolerably threatening, but at the more modest goal of making it possible for a political community to govern itself better—to get better, cheaper, or more widely accepted results than would otherwise be possible. The distinction is crude, but the rough idea is that cool federalism supports federal structures of governance in situations where it would be perfectly possible for a unitary structure to operate, but with the hope that a federal structure will improve governance in some salient way.

In this rough dichotomy, it seems reasonable to think in general of functional arguments for federal arrangements in the contemporary United States as claims in the domain of cool federalism. Indeed, I am inclined to the view that the only interesting arguments available to those who want to promote one or another view of contemporary federal arrangements in the United States are functional arguments of the cool federalism variety.

Here, the more precise question I want to reflect upon is the connection between the shape of the overlapping authority of state and federal governments to enforce civil rights and the virtues of cool federalism.

II. THE LIFE CYCLE OF MORAL PROGRESS IN AMERICAN POLITICS

Let us begin with this speculation: it frequently will be the case that moral progress in the project of securing political justice in the United States will follow a common course with regard to the interplay between state and federal sensibilities and consensus. Things will go roughly like this:

- *Invention.* Initially, the ideas that we eventually come to see as representing moral progress will take hold in a small number of states; other states will be less moved by these ideas, or even stridently opposed to them. The concrete form assumed by these maverick ideas in the states where they take hold may be that of state legislation, state constitutional revision, or judicial decision—quite possibly in the name of the state constitution or the U.S. Constitution. We have some obvious contemporary examples of this phase, the most prominent being the moves toward the normalization and acceptance of gay marital union in Vermont and gay marriage in Massachusetts.[1] Oregon's path-breaking concern with the right of the terminally ill to die with dignity[2] and California's experiment with the medical use of marijuana[3] are other examples.
- *Propagation.* Over time, as these minority states begin to act on their commitments, some of these commitments will begin to have wider appeal.

1. For a full account of these decisions see Chapter 6.
2. Oregon Death with Dignity Act, Or. Rev. Stat. §§ 127.800–127.897 (2003).
3. Cal. Health & Safety Code §§ 11362.7–11362.9 (West 2004).

Perhaps experiment and experience will aid their cause; perhaps the political success of what was previously a minority view in the cutting edge states will encourage the spread of political activity elsewhere; perhaps the confluence of related but external events (scientific discoveries, geopolitical trends, governmental steps or missteps, etc.) will extend their influence beyond the boundaries of the cutting edge states; perhaps it will simply be a matter of better moral insights coming to prevail. This is merely a short, suggestive list of possibilities that is not intended to approach an exhaustive rendition. The bottom line is that support for these maverick projects gradually grows even in the face of what may be active opposition.
- *Consolidation.* Eventually, after these once-maverick moral insights have come to occupy a place within mainstream national thought, the federal government may impose those insights on the remaining—now in some salient sense, *outlying*—states. This imposition may assume one of several recognized forms: federal legislation, federal judicial judgment in the name of the U.S. Constitution, or constitutional amendment.

This proposed life cycle of moral progress may seem a figment of an (admittedly liberal) imagination, fueled by events occupying a very thin slice of the historical experience of the United States. Admittedly it is our recent experience with the rights of gays and lesbians to marry that has drawn my attention to this structure of moral development. I am, nevertheless, tempted to think that something like this cycle of events has been characteristic of our most important moral progress. Consider, for example, the abolition of slavery and the much-delayed second abolition of Jim Crow segregation; the recognition of the right of women to vote, and the long-delayed extension of rights to women in other domains; and the protection of children from workplace abuse. It seems not just plausible but likely that we will find recurring instances of the pattern I have sketched from the best historical accounts of each of these progressions away from injustice: early commitments in a minority of states, growing national acceptance, and finally, imposition on the remaining, and increasingly outlying, states.

This should not surprise us, of course, for there are simple and obvious features of federalized governance that make it quite natural for change of all kinds to originate in a minority of states, and if successful, to propagate throughout the nation.[4] The states, by their sheer number and lingering diversity, are going to

4. Because the focus of these brief remarks is minority state invention and experimentation, it is easy to succumb to the temptation to refer to the migration of maverick ideas into national mainstream thought as though it were a matter of conquering other states one by one. Certainly, geographic propagation will sometimes characterize this migration. But there might well be other patterns, as when concrete experimentation in a small number of states supports broad national acceptance that, in effect, bypasses state-by-state development.

include some that develop projects and sensibilities not widely shared in the nation at large. Consider contemporary state ventures: gay marriage (and the constitutional prohibition of gay marriage); the opportunity to die with dignity, even if that requires the assistance of others; and the legalization of the medical use of marijuana. Naturally, we would expect deviations from the status quo on any of these issues to occur in a handful of states before any substantial national support for change was in place. The states have smaller political bases, greater vulnerability to focused political mobilization, a wider range of governing mechanisms (such as legislative initiatives), and somewhat more homogeneous moral sensibilities, religious commitments, cultural predilections, and commercial bases. The blunt consequences of a federal system like ours include breadth of moral imagination and variance in moral judgment.

State courts themselves are promising sources of variation. State constitutions are notably prolix, and state courts have the broad resources of the common law and statutory construction rather than the comparatively narrow substantive portfolio offered by the U.S. Constitution. Even when they are enforcing the federal Constitution, state courts may be encouraged to defect from the leadership of the U.S. Supreme Court. State courts are typically much closer to and involved in the state institutions they superintend—and with familiarity comes sympathy, skepticism, and a willingness to meddle.[5] When state courts want to insulate their dual enforcement of the Constitution from federal judicial review, the adequate state grounds doctrine will easily serve that end.

Are there reasons to be optimistic that from variance will come consensus, and further, that from consensus will come progress? Arguably, yes. The experience of pioneer states can spur moral change in a variety of ways. First, the maverick states by example make the benefits of their moral imagination available to the nation. Second, there are the benefits of experience. Consider the contemporary issues of gay marriage, the right to die with dignity, and the medical use of marijuana. It is particularly true of the right to die, perhaps, but all three of these initiatives are fraught with empirical questions about whether they can work without spawning problems or abuses. The actual experience of states in working with particular regimes of law with regard to physician-assisted suicide, medically prescribed marijuana, or same-sex marital unions is sure to influence the course of events in other states. Third, in those situations where state invention is driven by judicial decision, state court judges are considerably closer to the political and regulatory implications of their justice-driven impulses, and are thereby sometimes more willing than a federal court to undertake and more able to succeed at radical change.

---

5. *See* Lawrence G. Sager, *Foreword: State Courts and the Strategic Space between the Norms and Rules of Constitutional Law*, 63 TEX. L. REV. 959 (1985).

The complex remedial posture of the Supreme Court of Vermont with regard to the rights of gay and lesbian couples and the forthright and tough-minded stance of the Supreme Judicial Court of Massachusetts with regard to the same question are both far more imaginable as state court ventures. Having first served the vital function of thinking and acting upon the heretofore unthinkable, states on the moral frontier then perform the second valuable function of living out the experiments to which their moral lights have led. Justice Brandeis said it famously and well: "It is one of the happy incidents of the federal system that a single courageous State may, if its citizens choose, serve as a laboratory; and try novel social and economic experiments without risk to the rest of the country."[6]

III. WHAT REGIME OF FEDERAL AUTHORITY FOLLOWS?

Suppose we are moved by this picture of our federal structure as an engine for moral progress and want to protect its benefits. What sort of division of authority between state and federal governments follows?

This is a difficult question—and one that ultimately is an invitation to replay most if not all of the debates surrounding questions of federalism, including the overarching question of the degree to which the judiciary ought to rely upon the federal political process to police itself with regard to federalism-based restraints. We can, however, make some speculative gestures toward the ideal shape of federal authority in light of this picture.

Generally speaking, we should seek to restrain premature federal interference during the experimentation stage, but facilitate robust federal enforcement once maverick ideas have worked their way into mainstream judgment. At first blush, this may seem like a contradictory job description for the federalism doctrine, but such an elastic approach may not be entirely out of conceptual or doctrinal reach.

Consider Congress's authority under Section 5 of the Fourteenth Amendment. One way of slowing federal intervention in the name of this authority during the early stages of moral experimentation, but facilitating such intervention later, would be to conceive of Section 5 authority as *narrow* but *deep*. Roughly, the idea is this. We would begin with the basic structure of *City of Boerne v. Flores*;[7] that is, with the Court's view in *Flores* that Congress's Section 5 authority must be targeted at preventing or remedying violations of what the Court would agree were principles of constitutional justice. That would be the narrow part, but once principles of constitutional justice become sufficiently mainstream as to enjoy the allegiance of the Court, Congress should have remedial authority equal to the

6. New State Ice Co. v. Liebmann, 285 U.S. 262, 311 (1932) (Brandeis, J., dissenting).
7. 521 U.S. 507 (1997).

enterprise of ameliorating the entrenched harms of major constitutional deficits. That would be the deep part.

Once the Court has embraced an underlying, basal precept of constitutional justice, Congress's civil rights remedial authority should run deep. Three cases illustrate this view. The first is *Jones v. Alfred Mayer Co.*,[8] which held that Congress has authority under Section 2 of the Thirteenth Amendment to enact legislation prohibiting various forms of private racial discrimination. *Jones* is a radical and important decision that we now take rather too much for granted. The conceptual challenge of *Jones* involves the gap between what the Court sees Section 1 of the Thirteenth Amendment as prohibiting—which is slavery itself, and which emphatically does not include simple private discrimination, however pernicious that may be—and what the Court sees Section 2 of the Amendment as empowering Congress to prohibit,[9] which just as emphatically includes simple private discrimination on grounds of race. The disjuncture is bridged by the Court's view that Congress has authority under Section 2 of the Thirteenth Amendment to eradicate not just slavery, but the pernicious residue slavery leaves behind: its awful cultural relics of distrust and disadvantage.[10] *Jones*, on this view, is fully consistent with *Flores* in that *Flores* restricts Congress to the remediation of recognized constitutional wrongs, while *Jones* speaks to the depth of congressional authority to remedy well-recognized constitutional wrongs.

Two more recent cases bracket the applicability of *Jones* to gender discrimination and Congress's authority under Section 5 of the Fourteenth Amendment. In *United States v. Morrison*,[11] the majority breezily dismissed the argument that Congress had authority to enact the substantive provisions of the Violence Against Women Act, which made private gender-based violence federally actionable.[12] The Court could find no *contemporary* behavior by state or local governments that raised equal protection problems in this regard, and so could find no constitutional peg upon which Congress could hang its remedial hat.

Neither the Court nor the parties, however, considered the argument offered by simple analogy to *Jones*. The argument turns on three propositions. First, there is a long history of state and federal discrimination against women, including exclusion from the franchise, elite public schools, various professional opportunities, and even independent ownership of property when married; and, more pointedly, immunizing husbands from legal oversight of some physical and sexual predations on their wives. Second, this unhappy history, like slavery, has left behind a pernicious cultural residue, which includes the vulnerability of women to violence, particularly at the hands of their husbands. Third, the

---

8. 392 U.S. 409 (1968).
9. *Jones*, 392 U.S. at 439–40.
10. *Id.* at 441–43.
11. 529 U.S. 598 (2000).
12. 42 U.S.C. § 13981 (2000).

substantive provisions of the Violence Against Women Act are reasonably directed to the remediation of this vulnerability. On this account, there is no problem of state action. The relevant constitutional wrongs are part of the historic congeries of federal, state, and local laws that disadvantaged and disabled women in the ways we have just catalogued. If the logic of *Jones* is taken seriously, it would make no sense to demand that state actors be the addressees of a remedy focusing on the residue of these unconstitutional acts, just as it made no sense in *Jones* to insist that the addressees of the antidiscrimination legislation at issue be persons or entities that had held persons as slaves.[13]

More recently, the U.S. Supreme Court decided a Section 5 gender discrimination case that depends arguably, albeit tacitly, on the *Jones* rationale. In *Nevada Department of Human Resources v. Hibbs*,[14] the Court upheld the federal Family and Medical Leave Act of 1993 (FMLA)[15] as an exercise of Section 5 authority. The FMLA requires employers who fall under its aegis to grant employees twelve weeks of unpaid leave each year to attend to family-related exigencies such as the birth of a child or the serious health needs of a child, spouse, or parent.[16] The Court was willing to see the FMLA—at least insofar as it addresses the behavior of state and local government employers—as reasonable legislation addressing discrimination against women in the workplace. Its rationale for so doing ran something like this: first, many employers grant women caregiving leaves but withhold them from men; second, this perpetuates discrimination against women twice over, because it both sustains stereotypes about women as the appropriate caregivers and discourages employers from hiring women; third, merely prohibiting states and other employers from discriminating in this way will not solve the problem, for employers could respond by giving no leave at all, thus excluding women—who in fact do far more of the caregiving—from the workplace.[17]

Prime among the several puzzles surrounding the *Hibbs* decision is this: how could the U.S. Supreme Court—which recently and emphatically insisted that states are not responsible for the mere disproportionate impact of their rational acts as employers[18]—permit Congress to rely on the third proposition, which depends on the disproportionate impact of evenhanded state employment practices?

---

13. For a more expansive account of this argument, see LAWRENCE G. SAGER, JUSTICE IN PLAINCLOTHES: A THEORY OF AMERICAN CONSTITUTIONAL PRACTICE 109–14 (2004).

14. 538 U.S. 721 (2003).

15. 29 U.S.C. §§ 2601–2654 (2000).

16. 29 U.S.C. § 2612(a)(1).

17. *See Hibbs*, 538 U.S. at 735–38.

18. *See Bd. of Trustees of the Univ. of Ala. v. Garrett*, 531 U.S. 356, 366–68 (2001); *see also* SAGER, *supra* note 13, at 117–21.

The most straightforward answer takes us back to *Jones v. Alfred Mayer Co.* If the disproportionate impact of otherwise constitutional state behavior is due to a cultural assignment of roles by gender, which in turn is part of the legacy of the historic legal disadvantaging of women, then Congress can attack that impact as part of its authority to provide a remedy for this structural legacy of historic constitutional wrongs.[19]

In any event, by now the reader has undoubtedly gotten the gist of what I mean by the narrow but deep authority of Congress under Section 5 of the Fourteenth Amendment after *Flores*. What other suggestions for the shape of federal authority are encouraged by our reflections on the life cycle of moral progress?

Obviously, Congress's broad and more-or-less untamable authority under the Commerce Clause is somewhat problematic in this context. Here my suggestions are more skeletal and tentative. It seems both late in the day and improvident in the extreme to seek barriers to congressional regulation of labor and the workplace—and disastrous to ignore the ambient externalities of self-regarding state behavior in matters concerning environmental regulation. More generally, the extended lesson of our experience with the Commerce Clause is one that disfavors ongoing judicial oversight of Commerce Clause authority. But two possible changes in course are suggested by the life cycle analysis.

The first is conditioned on the existence of the deep authority of Congress to remediate entrenched constitutional injustice that I have already sketched above. When such deep authority is firmly in place, it may make sense in extreme cases, far removed from the substantive heartland of Commerce Clause concerns, to apply some form of pretextual analysis to legislation that is fundamentally moral rather than commercial in its aims.

Second, and more interesting, is the possibility that the Court should presume away from the conclusion that federal legislation preempts state legislation in the same domain.[20] An interpretive canon that required a plain statement of preemptive intent from Congress would have two advantages. Given that such a canon would have bite only when a competitive state regulation was at risk, it would select those situations where states were actively working on the problem at hand and make space for state experimentation. Further, such a canon, by making preemptive intent explicit, would give us some reason to suppose that Congress's willingness to preempt state activity reflected national judgment on the question at hand.

Thus far, I have discussed the implications of the life cycle of moral progress hypothesis for the shape of federal legislative authority. There are implications

---

19. *See* SAGER, *supra* note 13, at 124–26.

20. *See* Ernest A. Young, *The Rehnquist Court's Two Federalisms*, 83 TEX. L. REV. 1, 41–51, 115–34 (2004); Ernest A. Young, *Two Cheers for Process Federalism*, 46 VILL. L. REV. 1349, 1377–84 (2001).

for direct exercises of federal judicial authority as well. Here, we do well to attend to Justice Brandeis's reminder that the states are valuable laboratories of social experimentation. His point was that some constitutional judgments depend on facts that we can learn only by social experiment, and that the U.S. Supreme Court should avoid prematurely curtailing useful legislative experiments. Justice Brandeis was concerned with the interruption of state economic regulations in the *Lochner* era. Comparable claims for judicial behavior, however, may be apt to modern experiments in social justice.

Consider the physician-assisted suicide cases in the U.S. Supreme Court.[21] For at least four of the justices in those cases, there was some significant appeal to the claim on behalf of a right to die with dignity. There were, however, substantial practical concerns about protecting the infirm from the mendacious pressures of those who would benefit from their demise; hence the advantages, to which we have already alluded, of state experimentation in this realm. Constitutional questions of this sort, wrapped as they are with practical concerns that can only be addressed by experience, should encourage the Court to find ways of temporizing with regard to bottom-line constitutional judgments rather than foreclosing or inhibiting future judgments informed by the experience in frontier states such as Oregon. This is what we might call the passive case, where the Court confronts practical barriers to what might otherwise be an attractive constitutional mandate, and where the virtues of experimentation should lead to a conditional rather than a final refusal to impose such a mandate.

There is an active case as well, more directly analogous to Justice Brandeis's position in *New State Ice Co. v. Liebmann*. Suppose the Court confronts the constitutionality of the Young Women's Leadership School of East Harlem, a single-sex public school for inner-city young women. Where good-faith experiments of this sort are launched under circumstances of considerable empirical uncertainty, the Court should be hesitant to embrace sweeping constitutional prohibitions that would close down experiments in areas of vital social interest.[22]

IV. CONCLUSION: BREATHING ROOM

During the last half of the twentieth century, we witnessed a massive and desperately important national effort to bring our political community more into conformity with fundamental principles of political justice, particularly with regard

---

21. E.g., Washington v. Glucksberg, 521 U.S. 702 (1997); Vacco v. Quill, 521 U.S. 793 (1997).

22. The claim on behalf of a constitutional jurisprudence that accommodates governmental experimentation has been pressed effectively and explored engagingly in Michael C. Dorf & Charles F. Sabel, *A Constitution of Democratic Experimentalism*, 98 COLUM. L. REV. 267 (1998).

to the historic fault line of race. That effort often arrayed the Supreme Court, Congress, and other federal entities against recalcitrant state and local actors. For those of us who lived through those events directly or who have had occasion to revisit them as a matter of modern history, it is easy to lose sight of an important and obvious feature of American political life: state experimentation on the frontiers of political justice is often an important first step in moral progress.

These brief thoughts have been aimed at remembering this virtue of our federal political structure, to the end of finding breathing room for maverick and majestic state efforts to continue in the pursuit of justice.

3. "*STATES OF THE SAME NATURE*": BOUNDED VARIATION IN SUBFEDERAL CONSTITUTIONALISM

JACOB T. LEVY

> *That the federal constitution should be composed of states of the same nature, above all of republican States.* The Canaanites were destroyed because they were small monarchies that had not confederated and did not have a common defense. This is because it is not in the nature of small monarchies to confederate. The federal republic of Germany is composed of free towns and small states subject to princes. Experience shows that it is more imperfect than the federal republics of Holland and Switzerland. The spirit of monarchy is war and expansion; the spirit of republics is peace and moderation. The only way these two sorts of governments can continue to exist together in one federal republic is by force.[1]

I. INTRODUCTION

After long neglect, questions of state-level[2] constitutionalism and constitutional interpretation have over the past generation increasingly engaged scholars in legal and constitutional theory. The engagement has been significantly less in political theory, not because political theorists and philosophers lack views (sometimes well-informed and sophisticated, sometimes otherwise) on constitutional interpretation but because, for the most part, we have lacked interest in federalism.[3] In this chapter I hope to begin a *rapprochement* between the political theory of constitutionalism and the analysis of *state* constitutionalism. I have sufficiently idiosyncratic views on both constitutionalism and federalism that I do not presume to offer *the* political theory of the dual-enforcement model developed in

1. MONTESQUIEU, THE SPIRIT OF THE LAWS 132 (A.M. Cohler et al., eds. and trans., 1989) (1748).

2. In this chapter, the term *state* refers to the component units of a federation—variously known as states, provinces, Länder, cantons, and so on—and *federation* refers to the overarching polity. Given the subject-matter, there will not be much occasion to discuss non-federated sovereign states such as France, so there should not be much risk of confusion.

3. I have tried to document that inattention in Jacob T. Levy, *Federalism, Liberalism, and the Separation of Loyalties*, 101 AM. POL. SCI. REV. 459 (2007), and to remedy it there, as well as in Jacob T. Levy, *Federalism and the Old and New Liberalisms*, 24 SOC. PHIL. & POLICY 306 (2007), and Jacob T. Levy, *Self-Determination, Non-Domination, and Federalism*, 23 HYPATIA 60 (2008).

several of the other contributions to this volume. Rather, I take advantage of the work done in the dual-enforcement stream of research to set out some political-theory considerations on state constitutionalism, and to offer some reasons of my own for thinking dual-enforcement to be a normatively attractive and promising way to think about federalist constitutionalism.

I have distinguished elsewhere[4] between moral-realist social contract accounts of constitutions and democratic-positivist social contract accounts of constitutions. The latter treat enacted constitutions as holding the place in a real political order that social contracts hold in the idealizations of contract theory—a radically new legal order that consigns all that came before it to a pre-political or pre-legal state of nature, and one that contains within its four corners the whole foundation of the new order for the ages. There is an affinity between democratic-positivist contractarian constitutionalism and originalism as a mode of interpretation: the written constitution enacted at a discrete moment in historical time *is* the social contract to which a people agreed. Moral-realist contractarian constitutionalism reverses this. The real constitution ought to be interpreted in light of what we learn about original agreements from the idealized abstractions of contract theory, whether Lockean or Kantian or Rawlsian. Persons in the correctly idealized moment of choice *would have* entered into a political and legal order that had *these* characteristics, and therefore it would be unreasonable to interpret an extant constitution in ways that diverged (or diverged too radically) from them. In particular, this view ordinarily holds that persons would enter a constitutional system in order to protect their rights (their morally true rights) and therefore that positively enacted bills of rights should be construed as denoting those morally true rights. This is an ideal-typical contrast that does no great justice to the nuances of any particular theory (whether Scalia's democratic-positivist vision or Dworkin's moral-realist one). But I don't think it does great injustice to them, either, and I trust that readers will recognize the contrast.[5] In the context of subfederal constitutionalism, each of these visions yields some familiar implications.

The moral-realist vision is committed to the protection of morally true rights. These are, *ex hypothesi*, the same everywhere, and state-to-state variation can be nothing but a compromise or a second-best.

The democratic-positivist vision could point in a few different directions. To one who holds that the federal constitutional founding is paramount—and that, after it

4. Jacob T. Levy, *Not So* Novus *an* Ordo*: Constitutions Without Social Contracts,* 37(2) Pol. Theory 191 (2009).

5. It will be clear to the careful reader that my "democratic-positivist contractarian constitutionalism" is not quite the same as the "constitutional positivism" described in Jim Gardner's contribution to this volume (see chapter 4). I think that his use of that phrase in chapter 4 encompasses *both* of the branches of contractarian constitutionalism I describe here.

has happened, states are to be understood as creatures of the federation—variation on constitutional fundamentals seems out of bounds or at least undesirable. To one who sees the states as distinct polities with meaningful constitutional foundings of their own, the reverse will hold: We, the people of New Hampshire or Utah or wherever are free to enter into whatever constitutional arrangement we like. And to one who sees the states and the federation as co-foundational, democratic positivism authorizes the states to enact whatever constitutions they like, the federation to enact whatever constitution *it* likes, and for conflicts between them to be adjudicated by agreed-upon rules. These might include, for example, a Supremacy Clause that trumps the operation of state constitutional provisions offending the federal constitution, but that does *not* provide either state or federal courts with a directive to interpret the state constitution so as to avoid the conflict.

In this chapter I offer a defense of the bounded variation in substantive constitutional outcomes to which the dual enforcement model will lead. The extreme positions are the traditionally easy normative ones: there is no reason for state-to-state variation in fundamental questions of constitutional value (because once we know what justice demands, it demands it the same everywhere), or the several states' sovereign peoples may enact any rules they want, because democratic positivism trumps liberal justice. On the second model, states may be constitutionally constrained from the outside, by federal courts enforcing federal constitutions, but as a *domestic* matter their substantive variation could be unbounded. I don't deny that one or the other of these might accurately describe the legal situation in one or another federation. But I will argue that bounded variation is normatively preferable, not just as a middle way but as the right way to attain the benefits of a federal system. And there are at least some good reasons for internalizing at least some of the boundaries within the constitutionalism and jurisprudence of each state.

II. CONVERGENCE AND DIVERGENCE AT THE FOUNDING

It will help to begin by stepping back from the *interpretive* questions that have been most prominent in the legal literature on American state constitutions, namely whether state constitutional provisions ought to be interpreted in light of judicial interpretations of similar provisions in federal constitutions. An account of *constitutional* variation or convergence should precede the theory of *interpretive* variation or convergence.

As Montesquieu maintained and James Madison agreed,[6] successful federalism may depend on some convergence across the constituent political units on

6. See my discussion of Madison and of the Republican Guarantee Clause in Levy, *Federalism and the Old and New Liberalisms*, *supra* note 3. *See also* Madison's 1833 letter, printed under the heading "majority governments," and his 1835–36 document, "On Nullification,"

constitutional fundamentals and political values. For good reason, our discussions of the virtues of federalism often emphasize it as an approach to managing deep political *differences*. But there are deep differences, and there are *deep* differences. The U.S. Constitution declared as a rule what Montesquieu had announced as an aspiration: that the federal system would be made up only of republics. This at least reemphasized the constitutional ban on states granting titles of nobility—hereditary monarchies or aristocracies would be ruled out, and a federal power to intervene in a state's domestic government was envisioned. The clause also probably granted a federal power to prevent violent or anarchic disruptions of orderly republican government; Shay's Rebellion was never far from the Philadelphia framers' minds. The worst excesses of anarchical democratic government were further restrained with the paper money clause and the impairment of contracts clause; core features of constitutionalism and the rule of law were entrenched with the prohibition on ex post facto laws and bills of attainder. The states' internal discretion on constitutional government was constrained; each was to be a constitutional republic, not a democracy, aristocracy, or monarchy.

It is worth noting several reasons for these constraints that were or might have been relevant to the framers. Probably most important to them, but least so for current theoretical purposes, is that the prohibition on titles of nobility and the guarantee of republican government were safeguards of American independence against European meddling. The loyalties of component parts of the Holy Roman Empire were susceptible to the vagaries of external dynastic politics. Indeed, the same was true of independent European kingdoms. Europe's recent history had included: England switching from a position of long-term enmity against the Netherlands to one of allying with them against France (as a result of the Glorious Revolution and William's successful quest to gain the English crown), the War of the Spanish Succession over which dynasty (Hapsburg or Bourbon) would place an heir on the Spanish throne and therefore control Spain's loyalty in international politics, and an additional adjustment in Britain's international position with the Hanoverian settlement of 1720. The latter was particularly noteworthy from a federalist perspective as it joined the Crown to the Hanover and associated possessions within the Holy Roman Empire.[7] To a union whose independence seemed fragile, the risk that one or another state might join with a European royal house was a serious one. Guaranteeing republicanism was in that sense of a piece with forbidding the states to enter into foreign treaties or to make war in an attempt to fuse them into a single entity in international politics. It closed off

---

in 4 LETTERS AND OTHER WRITINGS OF JAMES MADISON: FOURTH PRESIDENT OF THE UNITED STATES (1865), at 326–44 and 395–435, respectively, both citing Montesquieu on the ability of the states to constrain one another's excesses directly, without federal action.

7. The two remained fused for more than a century; they diverged with the ascent of Victoria to the British throne, as women were not permitted to succeed to the Hanoverian possessions in Germany.

a potential avenue by which Britain, France, or Spain might have tried to peel the states off from the union.

Second, the founding generation clearly thought that non-republican governments in some states would be instruments of the subversion of the republican governments of others. While the founders were feeling their way toward a system of democratic republics quite unlike anything in the ancient world, they were keenly aware of the history of political systems in ancient Greece. One central lesson they took away from that history was that the domestic constitution of one state could be supported or undermined by a neighboring state. If a demagogue should rise to power in one state and declare himself a king there, he might certainly attempt to undermine republicanism elsewhere; democratic anarchy *à la* Shay's Rebellion was understood to be virulent and contagious even before its inevitable collapse into demagogic rule by one man. Domestic constitutional orders were understood to have externalities, and thus were legitimate objects of federal supervision.

Third, republicanism at the state level could provide an appropriate civic education for republicanism at the federal level—and, conversely, subjects of a local prince or demagogue could make for poorer citizens of the overarching republic. The voters in and citizens of the federation were also, and in many ways primarily, the voters in and citizens of the several states, and the stability of the union's constitutional order would depend on the commitment to its values on the part of the citizens of the states.

Finally, it is *possible* that the idea given canonical form a few years later in Kant's "Perpetual Peace" was sufficiently widespread as to have an effect: that republics as such were more peaceable than other forms of government. That is, enforced republicanism at the state level might have been considered inherently linked to peace among the states—a central goal of the constitutional framing and not something that was taken for granted. As quoted above, Montesquieu thought that expansion was not in the nature of stable republics, which suggests something peaceable about them. There was a stream in Enlightenment political thought even before Kant that considered war a distinctive disease of monarchy; one can see the idea in Paine. On the other hand, if one believes that Machiavellian and neo-Roman conceptions of republicanism were widely influential in the American 1780s,[8] that idea is hard to reconcile with any proto-Kantianism; the Machiavellian republic was founded on martial virtue, and expansion was in its blood.[9]

---

8. *See*, of course, J.G.A. Pocock, The Machiavellian Moment: Florentine Political Thought and the Atlantic Republican Tradition (1975).

9. And I interpret Montesquieu to have thought that republics *were* prone to militarism and expansionism. That this undermined their republican constitutions was no contradiction, but rather a reason to doubt republics' longevity. I discuss this in Jacob T. Levy, *Beyond*

All of these concerns are compatible with considerable state-to-state variation in constitutional orders. And in fundamental and sometimes radical ways, the constitutional orders of the original thirteen states *did* diverge from one another. Whether and how the state constitution was entrenched, the extent of the franchise, terms of office, the independence of the judiciary, the structure of bicameralism, the establishment of a church (and of *which* church), and other basic structural questions differed dramatically from one state to the next. Even setting aside the divergences among the states concerning the fundamental question of slavery—divergences that were not so great at the founding as they would be two decades later—it seems to me that constitutional variation among the thirteen states at the founding was much greater than is common in federations today.

This, then, was the American constitutional settlement, supported by Montesquieu's theory and reiterated by, among others, Madison in his theoretical writings: a republican federal order in which constitutional variation at the state level could be wide, but would be mutually constrained through the enactment of a federal constitution that assured each state that the rest would abide by fundamental republican constitutional norms.

III. HOW MUCH CONSTITUTIONAL VARIATION?

At a more abstract level, consider three perspectives on state-constitutional design.

(1) From the perspective of the state's own original enacters and ratifiers, that is to say its citizens at the time of constitutional adoption, it is desirable to be able to *make constitutional choices*. Whether because the state populace is unified around some substantive political commitment (say, a strong individual right to keep and bear arms that could survive the vagaries of federal gun politics and jurisprudence), or because a heterogeneous state populace needs to be able to make some distinctive choice to reach a locally appropriate constitutional compromise (the large local Catholic minority will not endorse the new order unless it is clear that nonestablishment does *not* constitutionally prevent aid to parochial schools), or for some other reason, initial drafters and ratifiers want to be able to choose from a relatively wide range of substantive constitutional commitments. In addition, with respect to procedures and institutions, a wider choice set seems valuable as such, because any constraints on the set will have been put in place by some fallible institution or person.

(2a) From the perspective of those who, in the future, may move into the state, matters are a bit more complicated. On the one hand, they have reason to want

---

Publius: Montesquieu, Liberal Republicanism, and the Small-Republic Thesis, 27 HIST. OF POL. THOUGHT 50 (2006).

states to be able to differentiate themselves—and to do so clearly. States offer a range of legal and political climates from which to choose, and the possible migrant wishes for choices. Some states offer high levels of social spending in exchange for high taxes, others the reverse. Some offer the freedom of no-fault divorce, some the security of stronger protections for marriage. Some, through zoning, urban planning, and transport policy, prioritize the entertainments of urban life, some the large-family affordability of exurbia. These ranges of choices are a mix of ordinary political choices and constitutional- (or at least potentially constitutional-) level principles. And potential migrants have an interest in the existence of a wide range of possible choices.

(2b) But this is not their only interest. They also have an interest in easy, low-cost mobility, in the ability to follow a job to one state or a spouse to another or a dream to another. Although some of their reasons may be related to policy or legal choices (there are jobs to follow because one state has chosen business-friendly policies, there is a dream of theatrical success to follow because another has cultivated the arts), many are not, or are so only very indirectly. Potential migrants have an interest in making the choice for reasons relevant to them without waking up one morning in the new state and discovering that rights they took for granted do not apply there.

(2a) and (2b) add up to a serious ambivalence. Potential migrants have an interest in states being different from one another so that there is a range of meaningful available choices. But they also have an interest in the states not being *so* different from one another that some are effectively *unavailable* due to their alienness. In a way, this is just the banal point that trade-offs involve, well, trade-offs, and naturally enough people have an interest in being able to have their cake and eat it too. But it is not *only* that. Sometimes the logic of trade-offs means that the middle position will leave us neither having our cake nor eating it; moderation sometimes offers all the costs of both extremes and few or none of the benefits. In this case, however, (2a) and (2b) jointly mean important interests are served by a constrained variation in state constitutionalism and political systems—they point to the middle position rather than to a tragic choice between the two extremes.

From the perspective of the federated constitutional system, the political order, there is a similar ambivalence.

(3a) The existence of a wide range of constitutional choices enables productive competition and experimentation among the states to discover the virtues and vices of various legal regimes. The variation in basic political cultures also facilitates one of federalism's important constitutional features: partisan opposition. No matter how complete one party's dominance at the center may be, in a large federation the opposition party is sure to govern *somewhere*. This prevents the out-party from degenerating into irresponsibility; it offers governing experience to opposition politicians who will return to power someday; and it provides institutional weight to oppositional politics that is unavailable to an outvoted parliamentary minority alone.

(3b) However, state-level radical divergence in fundamental political values can be destabilizing, leading to a profound alienation between some states and the rest of the country. Serious divergence at an earlier time (perhaps but not necessarily the time of constitutional enactment) can become radical divergence at a later time, as dissidents from the local view move out and those attracted to it move in.[10] If the outlier state is allowed to persist in its radical deviation, it may come to view the rest of the country as foreign—and vice versa. If it is not—if the federation's government (judicial or otherwise) blocks the deviation—then a sense of being ruled by alien forces and values can set in. Ultimately, perhaps, the house divided against itself cannot stand.

Moreover, states with political or constitutional cultures that are radical outliers from the federation's norms are likely to fail to provide the benefits provided under (3a). The opposition party holding power in an outlier state that is hostile to and viewed hostilely by the rest of the system is unlikely thereby to gain any plausibility as a governing party in the center. It may entrench itself as marginal, or it may devote its energy in the political system entirely to the non-generalizable interests of the outlier. (Think of the southern Democrats for the first two-thirds of the twentieth century.)

I have thus described one group with an interest in maximum permissible divergence—those who live in a state at the time of constitutional foundation—and suggested that both the future potential residents and the constitutional order as a whole are better served by moderated or constrained variation. Why should the interests of the nonresidents or the system as a whole matter?

The strong democratic-positivist contractarian might deny that they should. But they will have to resort to question-begging to do so. If we understand the relations of states to the center to be a constitutional question *about the federation as a whole,* then the relevant constituent power would seem to be the people of the federation as a whole.[11] Now, some state constitutions predate the U.S. Constitution,[12] and one could think that this ruled out an appeal to any extra-state source. But this

---

10. I am a New Hampshire native, and a lifetime of people confusing broadly-libertarian New Hampshire with represented-by-an-avowed-socialist-in-Congress Vermont stimulated some reflection on the divergence between them. Wherever the initial distinction came from, it was reinforced and exacerbated for two generations as people moved from one state to the other, and as migrants from Massachusetts chose between them by prioritizing either low taxes or environmental protection and social spending.

11. I should emphasize that this paragraph is written in an as-if voice; it is written as if democratic-positivist contractarianism is a good constitutional theory, and argues that it would not have good reason to be confined to a state-level demos. But I do not actually believe that it is a good constitutional theory.

12. Though not many. New Hampshire and Massachusetts have constitutions that have been in continuous effect since before 1787 and have never been replaced wholesale, though

seems implausible: the ratification of the federal constitution by the people of those states reshaped at least to some degree what the states legally *were*. Either the new federal order was understood to be compatible with the preexisting state order (making the federal order a legitimate source of information about the content of the state order) or it was not, but by virtue of coming later and being "supreme law," it must be understood to have reshaped what state constitutionalism could be about. And of course the ratifiers of later state constitutions that were explicitly part of a federal constitutional order, many of whom had to submit their constitutions for congressional approval, cannot be understood to have been wholly self-contained contractarian peoples.

IV. HOW MUCH INTERPRETIVE VARIATION?

I turn now to the problem that animates the contemporary literature—the problem of constitutional *interpretation*. Bounded variation, the space between the democratic-positivist self-contained enacted social contracts and the moral-realist one-right-answer hypothetical contracts, might be the right way to understand federated constitutionalism, but still not bear directly on the interpretive question.

On the one hand, it could be that "bounded divergence" is precisely what one would get with similar texts and divergent interpretations. On the plausible thought that there are only but so many reasonable interpretations of a given piece of text describing a given right (i.e., that the text or the rights-claim exercises a kind of gravitational pull on interpretive creativity), perhaps the argument so far gives us good reason to allow *more* interpretive divergence just to the extent that the texts converge.

But there is an important countervailing consideration. Of the interests and arguments described in the previous section, (2b) in particular seems related to the topic of divergent or convergent interpretation. Unpleasant surprises are probably inevitable if there is any degree of interstate mobility and states have any divergence at all in their legal systems. But they are especially likely and especially unpleasant if similar clauses mean very different things from state to state. The in-migrant who does all the due diligence that could be expected of a nonlawyer–reading the constitution itself and finding phrases he or she has grown up knowing from the federal Bill of Rights—would have especially strong grounds to complain if he or she later discovers that the words jurisprudentially mean something very different in the new home state. Of course, expectations are in part endogenous to rules that are adopted; perhaps a well-established practice of

---

of course they have been amended many times. I would judge the constitution of any state that seceded during the Civil War to be discontinuous by definition.

divergent state constitutional interpretation would mean that in-migrants would not be surprised. But this seems unlikely given realistic assumptions about public information and ignorance on constitutional questions.

In practice, the substantive question—how closely should state constitutionalism track federal constitutionalism?—and the interpretive question—in the event of a close tracking of constitutional values or constitutional text, how closely should state courts track the interpretive lead of federal courts—may be less distinct than they first appear.

The modern state holds a massive grip on the political imagination and political culture of its citizens. The European Union has repeatedly found out how hard it is to compete with that grip, to the dismay of some of its officials and architects. As for provinces and states, consider the massive isomorphism of governmental forms within federations. Parliamentary federations have parliamentary provinces; presidential federations have provinces with independently elected governors. The United States has only one state without a bicameral legislature—even though post-*Reynolds v. Sims*[13] state senates lack any of the differentiation from lower houses that traditionally justified bicameralism (e.g., that the upper house represented the nobility, the propertied class, the states corporately, or distinct geographic regions within the states partially independently of their population sizes). The image of the shape of government formed by a nation-state is so powerful that those forming provincial governments find it difficult to shake off, or indeed do not even try to do so.

If this is true of the shape of government—something that is rarely very emotionally important, something about which one could easily imagine people understanding that there are costs and benefits on both sides and that, perhaps, yielded a difference balance of benefits in one state than in another—it is likely to be much more true of constitutionally protected rights. A radical or unbounded divergence cannot help but be shocking because the substance of the federally guaranteed rights cannot help but occupy an outsized place in the political imagination.

Of course "surprising" and "shocking" are not tantamount to "illegitimate." What I offer here is one set of normative reasons for bounding divergence, not a dispositive argument for eliminating it. Choice and variation remain valuable as well. They are useful as sources of information and experimentation: often an interpretation is staked on an implicit hypothesis about the bad consequences of a rival interpretation ("allowing state funding of sectarian education will generate religious-political conflict, therefore our establishment clause should be interpreted to prohibit such funding"; "an absolute exclusionary rule will hamper police work and impair public safety"; etc.). Allowing the hypothesis to be tested

13. Reynolds v. Sims, 377 U.S. 533 (1964). The Court held that state legislative districts for upper and lower houses alike had to be roughly equal in population.

in some jurisdiction adds information. Sometimes there are balances to be struck among values, and the balances are not dictated or even much guided by textual provisions, so seeing different balances tried out can illuminate the trade-offs at stake.

The case for divergent interpretations varies in an unusual way with citizens' awareness of, interest in, and knowledge of constitutional questions. If constitutionalism is purely a matter for judges and lawyers, and citizens know nothing about their state-constitutional rights, then the unpleasant surprise never occurs because the citizen never notices. Wide variation can occur without the cost described here ever arising. If citizens are extremely knowledgeable and well-informed, they could find out in advance that constitutional law differs in fundamental ways from place to place. Again, wide variation could exist without unpleasant surprises occurring; people could consider state constitutional law in their package of considerations about where to live. But if, as is probable, most people are and will remain solidly in the middle—they care about constitutional rights when they arise, but do not know very much about constitutional law—then divergent interpretations of the same text are somewhat unattractive because unpleasant surprises are likely to be too common.

V. TURNABOUT

It is apparent that the position described here allows federal constitutional norms to have some weight in a state's domestic constitutional interpretation. It is perhaps less apparent, but noteworthy, that it also allows sister-state constitutional norms and jurisprudence to have such weight. And, perhaps most surprisingly, it allows state-level norms to have weight at the federal level.[14] Perhaps the gravitational weight of federal constitutional interpretation is greater than that of the interpretation of any one of the states, but gravity is mutual, and planets pull on the sun as well as being pulled by it.

This should be less surprising than it is, at least in some cases. The original U.S. Constitution and Bill of Rights often drew on language used in one or more pre-1787 state constitutions. The Fourteenth Amendment federally constitutionalized both the equal protection of the laws and the privileges and immunities of citizens of the several states—phrases well-known to and in the latter case substantially drawn from state-constitutional jurisprudence of the preceding

14. Although it should go without saying throughout that the views expressed in this chapter are my own and not necessarily shared by the volume's editors or other contributors, I suspect that it is particularly important to stress it at this point. I think that this mutual influence is a necessary and attractive feature of the "dual enforcement" approach studied in this volume, but I would be surprised if the editors or my fellow contributors shared this view.

half century. As Howard Gillman has shown,[15] there was a lively and vibrant antebellum state-constitutional jurisprudence on equal protection and privileges and immunities that centered on a thick conception of the rule of law and a hostility to what was understood as class legislation or legislation for partial interests and privileged groups:

> The requirement that legislatures demonstrate a legitimate public purpose became a standard limitation on the taxing power and the power of eminent domain, thereby voiding subsidies to private businesses. . . . But "public purpose" as a limit on the powers of government did not mean "laissez-faire"; it meant, by and large, class-neutral legislation. . . . Judges upheld inspection and public health laws, ordinances restricting dangerous or unhealthful businesses to certain locations, regulations of weights and measures. . . .[16]

On any theory of federal constitutional interpretation that accords even a minor place to originalism, this jurisprudence is surely relevant to the interpretation of the Fourteenth Amendment, and provides a model for the exercise of a non-pro forma rational-basis review under its protections. I want to suggest that this jurisprudence is *also* relevant to the interpretation of, say, the Fifth Amendment's "public use" clause. It seems to me that the willingness of the state judiciaries to inquire into whether state power was being exercised for the private benefit of a partial interest, and to distinguish such benefit from "public purposes," points the way to a path not taken in *Kelo v. New London.*[17]

Other examples of possible state gravitational pull on federal jurisprudence might lack that historical pedigree but still be of potential importance. In non-originalist jurisprudence, there is already plenty of precedent for treating trends in state constitutional law as relevant. For example, consensuses, emerging and otherwise, at the state level about whom to execute and for what crimes have been explicitly taken into account in the Supreme Court's interpretation of the Eighth Amendment. But this willingness to look to the states has been confined for no particularly clear reason. The interpretation of constitutional provisions addressing legal and especially criminal proceedings have mostly been innocent

---

15. Howard Gillman, The Constitution Besieged: The Rise and Demise of Lochner Era Police Powers Jurisprudence 19–39 (1993).

16. *Id.* at 55.

17. 546 U.S. 807 (2005). I should note that I also think taking this history seriously might improve research on state constitutionalism, which has been too prone to take "the new judicial federalism" as entirely new. The leading scholar of state constitutionalism, in the leading book on the subject, held that "state courts' recurrence to and reliance on state rights guarantees in the 1970s was, quite literally, unprecedented." Alan Tarr, Understanding State Constitutions 178 (1998). Tarr briefly discusses the Jacksonian-era jurisprudence, at, for example, 100, 111–113, so "unprecedented" reflects what I take to be a mistaken judgment that the earlier jurisprudence is not sufficiently like the later Bills-of-Rights jurisprudence to be instructive.

of such examinations. But even today, most criminal law is a state enterprise, and state courts have vastly more experience than do federal courts with the balances among competing considerations needed, for example, in interpretations of search-and-seizure protections. Moreover, state constitutions routinely replicate the substantive commitments and even the language of the federal Bill of Rights in these matters. I have offered reasons above for thinking that this is a good area of law to hope for constrained variation, but the constraints need not be unidirectional, flowing from the federal government downward. It seems to me that the state courts could be constitutional interpreters of first resort, unpacking the meaning of criminal justice protections through their tens of thousands of cases—and that consensuses reached at the state level could exert some gravitational pull on subsequent federal interpretation of the federal guarantees, which in turn of course bind the states.

Indeed this is an added attraction of a constrained-variation model that understands the constitutional orders of the states and the federation to be normatively linked. On a model of separate foundings, one wherein the state constitutions could enact just anything and be subject to external constraint by the Supremacy Clause, there would be no reason to expect the states or the state courts to provide useful information about the meaning of the federal constitution. But if state constitutional orders are understood to be (to *have* to be) somewhat like the federal order, then their jurisprudence ought to be at least somewhat relevant to it.

However, it is important to note—against the more Panglossian suggestions one sometimes sees about the new judicial federalism—that it is impossible for the states to pull the federal courts only in a "more" rights-protecting direction. Because states are not permitted to transgress federally protected constitutional rights, it is often assumed that a wider scope for state judicial interpretation or experimentation must mean that some states will protect more rights, or will protect rights more strongly, than do the federal courts. But this view is basically incoherent. When a state protects freedom of speech "more" by relaxing the state action requirement, insisting that a private actor (say, a shopping mall) must be bound by the same constraints as a state, it reallocates rights; it does not expand them. It infringes on rights of property owners to exclude and to determine the kinds of activities allowed within their space. Rights of educational finance and rights of local self-government, rights to expansive procedural protections for accused criminals and rights of crime victims—all of these have been given varying state interpretations, and all involve balancing rights-claims. If state constitutional interpretation can reshape federal interpretation, then it cannot be only in a "more" rights-protective way, and eventually we will need a jurisprudence about permissible and impermissible variation.

VI. CONCLUSION

Constitutions are not social contracts, either of the positivist or the realist sort, and the hybrid constitutionalism of a federal order cannot be understood just with reference to its founding or moral truth. This leaves us in the domain of non-dispositive reason-giving and argument about the scope for constitutional variation. It typically does not count as much intellectual progress to say that answers will lie at some indeterminate point in the middle. But the claims of federal supremacy and of state sovereignty have been such that the middle has sometimes seemed squeezed out; there has been a perceived need to resolve the *logic* of state constitutionalism to a greater degree than the nature of the problem permits.

The work of Walter Murphy and the Princeton School on constitutional exposition outside the judiciary, the return to departmentalism, and the intellectual turn from the courts have meant that federal-level constitutional theory in the United States is somewhat less concerned with the logic of finality and somewhat more concerned with ongoing arguments among interpreters than it has been in some decades. State constitutionalism could fruitfully be considered in the same light: the question of constitutional divergence is a question of the constitutional culture of a federation and what it means to live in a compound constitutional system, not only a question of legal or interpretive logic. The research agenda associated with the dual-enforcement model holds out the promise of focusing attention on the vast middle ground, where it belongs.

4. WHY FEDERALISM AND CONSTITUTIONAL POSITIVISM DON'T MIX

JAMES A. GARDNER

I. INTRODUCTION

Ever since state constitutional law arrived as a field of study twenty years ago, its most pressing and contentious problem has concerned how state constitutions ought to be interpreted, and in particular whether the methods appropriate for interpreting a state constitution differ from those commonly employed in analyzing the U.S. Constitution.[1] In the course of this ongoing debate, it has frequently been argued that state constitutions ought to be interpreted using a methodology of strict constitutional positivism. I shall define *constitutional positivism* more formally below. For now, it is sufficient to say that constitutional positivism is, broadly speaking, a familiar and commonplace theory of interpretational legitimacy that requires courts to approach a constitution as an authoritative expression of the will of the people who made it, and to interpret that constitution strictly in accordance with the popular will as it is expressed in the document. I shall argue in this chapter that the interpretational methodology of constitutional positivism, which furnishes the dominant approach to the interpretation of the U.S. Constitution, cannot simply be lifted from federal constitutional law and applied willy-nilly to state constitutions. Although it is possible, and perhaps desirable, to adapt the methods of constitutional positivism to the interpretation of state constitutions, substantial modifications must be made before such methods can be used successfully in this very different setting.

In their strongest statements, advocates of a state constitutional jurisprudence of constitutional positivism sometimes argue that only the narrowest positivist approaches to constitutional interpretation, such as textualism[2] or originalism,[3] should be applied to state constitutions. But even in its most general and moderate formulations, advocates of strict positivist approaches are

1. For an overview, see G. ALAN TARR, UNDERSTANDING STATE CONSTITUTIONS, ch. 6 (1998).

2. *Textualism* holds that in most cases and for most purposes, the meaning of a constitutional provision can and should be discerned by examining the text alone. *See, e.g.*, Paul Brest, *The Misconceived Quest for the Original Understanding*, 60 B.U. L. REV. 204, 205–17 (1980) (examining the method and rationale of textualism).

3. *Originalism* holds that the meaning of a constitutional provision can and should be adduced by examining the intentions of the provision's framers and ratifiers. For a good overview of originalism, see Daniel Farber, *The Originalism Debate: A Guide for the Perplexed*, 49 OHIO ST. L. J. 1085 (1989). On the link between originalism and constitutional positivism, see

united by a methodological belief that the job of the interpreter is, essentially, to pay *really close* and *exclusive* attention to the state constitution and its unique and exclusive interpretational props—its text, the intentions of its framers, its relevant history, and so on. Certainly, an interpreter proceeding in the strict positivist mode would have no business relying on the text, framers' intentions, or founding history of any *other* constitution; the central tenet of constitutional positivism is that the only constitution relevant for purposes of interpretation is the one under consideration, along with its unique associated body of interpretational aids.

Sometimes a jurisprudence of state constitutional positivism is justified on the ground that, because state constitutions are so easily and frequently amended, it is often possible actually to discern "the framers' true intent"[4] in a way that is sometimes impossible when interpreting the U.S. Constitution due to its age. Thus, the argument goes, whatever its potential flaws as a tool of federal constitutional interpretation, a jurisprudence of original intent can be effective when applied to state constitutions. Others have argued that the tendency of state constitutions to regulate a wide variety of governmental activities in great detail makes many provisions of state constitutions unsuitable for any kind of analysis other than a purely textual one.[5] More generally, though, constitutional positivism is typically defended on the ground that it is the only sound methodology for interpreting any constitution, whether state or national. This is the view taken by adherents of what has come to be known as the "primacy" approach to state constitutional interpretation.[6] It is the view that I wish primarily to dispute.

A frequently expressed frustration in the field of state constitutional law is that state courts often fail to follow the prescribed methodology of constitutional positivism: they ignore subtle (and sometimes not-so-subtle) cues contained in the state constitutional text; they fail to inquire into the views of the state constitution's framers; and they undertake no meaningful investigation into the history of

---

James A. Gardner, *The Positivist Foundations of Originalism: An Account and Critique*, 71 B.U. L. REV. 1, 6–9 (1991).

4. Hon. Vito J. Titone, *State Constitutional Interpretation: The Search for an Anchor in a Rough Sea*, 61 ST. JOHN'S L. REV. 431, 460 (1987). To the same effect is Tarr, *supra* note 1, at 196.

5. William F. Swindler, *State Constitutions for the Twentieth Century*, 50 NEB. L. REV. 577, 593 (1971). For similar views, see Tarr, *supra* note 1, at 195; James Gray Pope, *An Approach to State Constitutional Interpretation*, 24 RUTGERS L.J. 985, 1004–05 (1993).

6. Some of the leading works in this school of thought include Hans Linde, *First Things First: Rediscovering the States' Bills of Rights*, 9 U. BALT. L. REV. 379 (1980); Hans Linde, *E Pluribus—Constitutional Theory and State Courts*, 18 GA. L. REV. 165 (1984); Robert F. Williams, *In the Supreme Court's Shadow: Legitimacy of Rejection of Supreme Court Reasoning and Result*, 35 S.C.L. REV. 353 (1984); Robert F. Williams, *Methodology Problems in Enforcing State Constitutional Rights*, 3 GA. ST. U.L. REV. 143 (1987).

their state or the development of its constitution.[7] Instead, state courts frequently look to federal constitutional law for guidance: they examine the text of the U.S. Constitution and the writings of Madison, Hamilton, and other key framers of the federal Constitution and rely heavily on decisions of the U.S. Supreme Court.[8] Sometimes state courts seem to assume that the meaning of state constitutional provisions is given more by national sources of constitutional meaning than by any distinctive attributes of the state constitution itself, and they thus incorporate federal constitutional doctrine wholesale into state constitutional jurisprudence. Although this practice has been the subject of frequent and intense criticism,[9] I shall argue that it is in fact often a logical response to the situation in which judicial interpreters of state constitutions find themselves, in large part because orthodox constitutional positivism simply is not a viable interpretational methodology for subnational constitutions in a federal system.

The application of constitutional positivism to state constitutions has been criticized before, most often by invoking interpretational models that challenge the conceptual foundations of constitutional positivism itself. Critiques by Paul Kahn and Lawrence Friedman, for example, proceed from a dialogic model of constitutional meaning,[10] and Robert Schapiro has offered a theory of state constitution-making that abandons reliance on an intentional correspondence

---

7. For examples of state courts ignoring textual differences, *see, e.g.*, Reid v. Gholson, 327 S.E.2d 107 (Va. 1985) (ignoring considerable textual differences between the religion clauses of the First Amendment and Va. Const. art. I, § 16); State v. Ceci, 255 A.2d 700 (Del. Sup. Ct. 1969) (ignoring the fact that Del. Const. art. I, § 5 protects only the freedom of the press, and treating it as though it also contained a speech clause); Ramada Inns, Inc. v. Dow Jones & Co., Inc., 1988 Del. Super. LEXIS 29; 15 Media L. Rep. 1586 (Del. Sup. Ct. 1988) (same). On the failure of state courts to inquire into the intentions of the framers or make other historical inquiry, see James A. Gardner, *The Failed Discourse of State Constitutionalism*, 90 MICH. L. REV. 761, 793–94 (1992). On the inept analysis by state courts of constitutional history, see Jack L. Landau, *A Judge's Perspective on the Use and Misuse of History in State Constitutional Interpretation*, 38 VALPARAISO U. L. REV. 451 (2004).

8. Linde, *First Things First*, *supra* note 6, at 387–92; Linde, *E Pluribus*, *supra* note 6, at 186–88; Todd F. Simon, *Independent but Inadequate: State Constitutions and Protection of Freedom of Expression*, 33 KAN. L. REV. 305, 308 (1985).

9. See *especially* Williams, *In the Supreme Court's Shadow*, *supra* note 6, at 389–97; Tarr, *supra* note 1, at 180–82; Robert F. Williams, *In the Glare of the Supreme Court: Continuing Methodology and Legitimacy Problems in Independent State Constitutional Rights Adjudication*, 72 NOTRE DAME L. REV. 1015 (1997).

10. Paul W. Kahn, *Interpretation and Authority in State Constitutionalism*, 106 HARV. L. REV. 1147 (1993); Lawrence Friedman, *The Constitutional Value of Dialogue and the New Judicial Federalism*, 28 HASTINGS CONST. L.Q. 93 (2000). Similar points are made in Ann Althouse, *Federalism, Untamed*, 47 VAND. L. REV. 1207, 1219–20 (1994); Rachel A. Van Cleave, *State Constitutional Interpretation and Methodology*, 28 N.M. L. REV. 199, 203–05 (1998). For an earlier related example, see Robert M. Cover & T. Alexander Aleinikoff, *Dialectical Federalism: Habeas Corpus and the Court*, 86 YALE L.J. 1035 (1977).

between a self-conscious polity and its governing constitutional document.[11] Although these critiques are useful and potent, the one I offer here is different in that it preserves the basic assumptions and conceptual structure of constitutional positivism, which is after all a very good theory—in our time, the preeminent one—on which to sustain and legitimize indirect republican democracy. What I wish to show, however, is that the premises of constitutional positivism cannot, except with substantial modification, be coherently applied to the constitutions of the American states.

Part II of this chapter sets out the political theory of constitutional positivism and its attendant ideology of interpretation. Part III turns to the federal structure of American government, and argues that the status of subnational units in a true federal system violates the conditions necessary to justify the interpretational methods of constitutional positivism. Part IV draws out some of the implications of this disjunction for state constitutional interpretation, Part V examines some potential complications of my analysis, and Part VI concludes.

II. CONSTITUTIONAL POSITIVISM

The basic theory of constitutional positivism is Lockean, and it tells a familiar story about the significance of constitutions and the source of their legitimacy as fundamental law. According to this story, autonomous individuals, self-ruling in the state of nature as a matter of natural law, agree voluntarily for their own mutual security and advantage to band together into a civil society.[12] In so doing, each member of the society gives up his or her natural right of self-rule to the collective group. Having thus entered into a self-governing society, society's members—now known as "the people"—generally find it advantageous to create a government to handle the chores associated with collective self-rule. The government, on this view, is thus no more than a servant or agent of the people, and can exercise only the powers that have been delegated by the people, and then only in a way that the people have authorized.[13] A government that has been duly appointed by the people and acts within the bounds of its delegated powers is "legitimate"—it has the right, not merely the power, to make laws binding on society. A constitution, on this view, is simply a positive statement of the instructions of the principal (the people) to its agents (the government), and that is why government officials must strictly obey and implement the will of the people as

11. Robert A. Schapiro, *Identity and Interpretation in State Constitutional Law*, 84 VA. L. REV. 389 (1998).

12. JOHN LOCKE, THE SECOND TREATISE OF GOVERNMENT (Thomas P. Peardon ed., Bobbs-Merrill 1952) (1690), §§ 4, 87, 89 at 4, 48–50.

13. Id. §§ 134–142, at 75–82.

it is expressed in their constitution.[14] This is, of course, the familiar story of the American founding—one that is told and retold in the canonical texts of American law.[15] It provides, in Eugene Rostow's words, "the prevailing political theory of modern times and the only modern rival for the doctrine that power proceeds from the barrel of a gun,"[16] and it furnishes the theoretical foundations of constitutionalism itself. To a very great extent, we are all constitutional positivists.

The political theory of constitutional positivism also provides an accompanying theory of legitimate constitutional interpretation. Because a constitution contains the positive and binding instructions of the people, judges, who are themselves only specialized public servants, must construe the constitution consistent with the will of those who made it. Consequently, according to constitutional positivism, judicial review consists in the main of an attempt to discern and faithfully to enforce the will of those who made and adopted the constitution.[17]

Nevertheless, just because constitutional positivism provides the central narrative account of the U.S. Constitution does not necessarily make it the best account of state constitutions. Constitutional positivism makes a number of critical assumptions about the nature of the polity and its relation to its constitution, three of which are relevant here. Under constitutional positivism, the polity that creates the constitution must have three characteristics: it must be (1) unique, (2) determinate, and (3) self-constructed.

The uniqueness requirement assures a one-to-one correspondence between a polity and its constitution. Under the constraints of Lockean political theory, there can be only one people, one government (or perhaps one collection of governments), and consequently one set of instructions from principal to agent. By definition, on this view, it is not possible for one people to give binding instructions to another people's government, nor would a government be acting legitimately were it to obey instructions issued by some people other than the one that created it and to which it owes obedience. Thus, we would not expect the Supreme Court of Canada to obey commands contained in the U.S. Constitution, nor could Americans legitimately harbor any expectation that Canadians will obey the U.S. Constitution, either in lieu of or in addition to their own.

The closely related determinacy criterion requires that it be clear who comprises the polity that is entitled to issue binding commands to any particular

---

14. Originalism, for example, is only one very strong account of what is necessary for judges to assure their obedience to the popular will. *See* Gardner, *supra* note 3, at 21–22.

15. Declaration of Independence (U.S. 1776); U.S. Const preamble; McCulloch v. Maryland, 17 U.S. 316 (1819).

16. Eugene R. Rostow, *The Rightful Limits of Freedom in a Liberal Democratic State: Of Civil Disobedience, in* Is Law Dead? (Eugene R. Rostow ed., 1971).

17. Alexander Hamilton, The Federalist, No. 78 at 466–69 (Clinton Rossiter ed., 1961); Marbury v. Madison, 5 U.S. 137, 174–76 (1803).

governmental agent. In a regime of constitutional positivism there must be one and only one principal—but who is it? For constitutional positivism to function effectively, a government must be able to identify with some precision who is and who is not a member of the unique polity entitled to issue it instructions, knowledge that permits it to know exactly where—that is to say, in what constitution—its unique set of binding instructions may be found.[18] It is not enough for a court to know that it is, say, the agent of the people of Italy, or of Argentina, if there is any significant question about who comprises the members of those polities. The most familiar kinds of indeterminacy problems appear when nations begin to break down; for example, officials of the Yugoslavian government in the mid-1990s might have known they owed obedience to the Yugoslavian people and their constitution, but have been thoroughly confused as to who comprised that people and just which constitution contained the instructions that Yugoslavian officials were required to obey. Similar problems have arisen in some of the Commonwealth countries as they have gradually disengaged themselves from British oversight.[19]

Finally, according to constitutional positivism, a polity must be self-constructed, meaning that its members, and they alone, must be the ones who decide to form an independent civil society and to create constitutional rules for

---

18. The kind of uncertainty I refer to must be distinguished from the normal kinds of uncertainty that, in Lockean theory, nearly always accompany any attempt to identify with precision the membership of a given polity. For example, in- and out-migration, the status of resident aliens, and problems arising from the intergenerational transmission of consent may all complicate questions of political membership. But these kinds of problems are endemic in contractarian political theory and are not generally thought to pose insurmountable problems.

19. A particularly acute example of this problem arose upon Southern Rhodesia's unilateral declaration of independence from Britain in 1965. Courts sitting in the former colony owed their existence to a 1961 colonial constitution conferred by Britain, yet were permitted to continue to sit pursuant to Rhodesia's 1965 revolutionary constitution. This presented difficult problems of constitutional pedigree for the judges. *See* F. M. Brookfield, *The Courts, Kelsen, and the Rhodesian Revolution*, 19 U. TORONTO L.J. 326 (1969). The same problem, though in a very different context, has arisen in Canada, for which there is no clearly identifiable event marking the moment when it ceased to be a British colony and became an independent nation. Instead, it has acquired independence from Britain in a slow, evolutionary process. Moreover, Canada has never formally adopted a constitution; the Canadian Constitution consists of a mix of statutes, common law, and customary practices, many of which, including the constitution's centerpiece, the 1867 British North America Act, date to the era of British rule. Canadian constitutional history is well recounted in Peter H. Russell's excellent book, CONSTITUTIONAL ODYSSEY: CAN CANADIANS BE A SOVEREIGN PEOPLE? (1992). According to Russell, as recently as the 1960s, when the Canadian Constitution was still formally the product of British statutory law, "Canadians had not yet been able to agree on the locus of constitutional sovereignty in the nation they were endeavouring to build." *Id.* at 57.

their collective self-governance. A basic premise of Lockean theory is that a group forms its own civil society to take itself *out* of the larger world, to create a self-contained enclave of complete self-sovereignty. For such a transaction to be meaningful, the decision of the members to constitute themselves a polity must be voluntary and rational—done, that is, on their own volition, and not, say, at the instigation of some other group. Operation of this requirement may occasionally be seen in the international community's refusal to recognize new nations when it suspects that they have been formed less than fully voluntarily, for example under pressure from outside forces. The former South African Bantustans fit this description,[20] and the same principle helps explain why American Indian reservations are not understood to be truly independent nations.

The conditions of uniqueness, determinacy, and self-construction, then, are necessary to justify interpreting a constitution using the methods of constitutional positivism. These are exactly the conditions, however, that American state polities fail to satisfy, and which indeed cannot be satisfied by any subnational unit in a system of true federalism, as in the American case.

III. FEDERALISM AND SUBNATIONAL UNITS: WHOSE CONSTITUTION IS IT?

A. Subnational Autonomy

In any multilevel system of governance—in any system, that is, other than a completely centralized and unitary one—the relationship between the national and subnational units of government may range across a potentially broad spectrum of subnational autonomy. At one end of the spectrum, a subnational unit may possess complete or very nearly complete autonomy and consequent independence from the national government. This is the arrangement that might prevail in a treaty league or a confederacy, such as existed in the United States under the Articles of Confederation. At the other end of the spectrum, subnational units may occupy a status of complete or very nearly complete subordination to the national government, and thus enjoy virtually no meaningful autonomy. This would be the situation in a highly centralized government with a system of strict hierarchical decentralization, as for example with the *départements* of France.[21]

---

20. John Dugard, *South Africa's "Independent" Homelands: An Exercise in Denationalization*, 10 J. Int'l L. & Policy 11, 11–16 (1980); Brian Bunting, The Rise of the South Africa Reich 309–16 (1964).

21. Norman Dorsen et al., Comparative Constitutionalism: Cases and Materials 387 (2003).

Federalism, at least when it is genuine rather than merely nominal,[22] sits uneasily in the middle of this spectrum. In a truly federal system, subnational units are partly dependent and partly independent, partly autonomous and partly subordinate. A subnational unit's autonomy may be restricted territorially or by area of competence, or both; residuary powers may be allocated to the national government or to the subnational units.[23] Whatever the precise arrangement, in all such cases the people of the subnational unit have the authority to govern themselves as they see fit in some instances, but not in all. They are autonomous sovereigns for some purposes but not for others, or with respect to some subjects but not others. A subnational unit in a federal system is thus simultaneously an independent, autonomously self-governing entity, guided solely by the independently formulated wishes of its own polity, *and* a hierarchically subordinate dependency of the national government, required to adhere to decisions made by a national polity that is essentially external to it, even when its own polity would, if given the chance, choose some other course.

B. Joint Ownership of State Constitutions

The indeterminate status of subnational units in a federal system calls into question the extent to which their constitutions can be viewed in the positive sense. A useful heuristic for framing this inquiry is to consider the question: *whose* constitution is it? If constitutional positivism is to be available as a theoretical framework for an interpretational methodology, the answer must be that a state's constitution "belongs"—uniquely, determinately, and by virtue of a process of independent and voluntary self-construction—to the people of that state, and to them alone. Yet it is clear that the constitutions of the American states cannot satisfy this definition. If we ask to whom does the constitution of an American state belong, we must conclude that the best answer, at least from the point of view of constitutional positivism, is that a state constitution belongs jointly to the polities of both the state and the nation.

This property of joint ownership shows up most obviously in the very basic fact that the U.S. Constitution establishes the outer boundaries of the constitutional space that any state polity may lawfully occupy by imposing direct, binding limitations on the content of state constitutions.[24] Thus, no matter how earnestly

---

22. The charge is sometimes made that American federalism has degenerated from a system of genuine federalism to a merely nominal one that is much closer to a centralized national system. *E.g.*, Robert F. Nagel, The Implosion of American Federalism (2001).

23. For overviews of subnational autonomy in federal systems around the world, see Chester James Antieau, States' Rights under Federal Constitutions (1984); Ronald L. Watts, *Foreword: States, Provinces, Länder, and Cantons: International Variety among Subnational Constitutions*, 31 Rutgers L.J. 945 (2000).

24. For a comparative overview, see Robert F. Williams & G. Alan Tarr, *Subnational Constitutional Space: A View from the States, Provinces, Regions, Länder, and Cantons, in*

a state polity may desire them, a state constitution may not validly contain provisions violating equal protection or due process, limiting the privileges and immunities of American citizens from other states, impeding interstate commerce, establishing a state currency, or erecting an aristocratic form of government, and so on.[25] These restrictions place significant limitations on the state polity's agency—limitations that are severely in tension with the premises of constitutional positivism, especially the requirement of political self-construction. Moreover, the partial subordinacy of states in a federal system means that instructions to the state government come from two different constitutions, state and national, and by implication from two different polities, also state and national. State governments thus serve two masters simultaneously, violating constitutional positivism's uniqueness requirement.

Another difficulty arises from the fact that under the U.S. Constitution, state polities are legally disabled from unilaterally defining and constructing themselves. Article IV of the U.S. Constitution provides specifically that new states may be admitted into the union only with the permission of Congress, and prohibits the creation of a new state within the territory of any other state without the permission of the states concerned as well as of Congress.[26] Furthermore, it is the Constitution of the United States, and not of any state, that establishes the system of federalism in the first place, and it is to that decision of the national polity, and not to the decision of any existing or putative state polities, that states owe their existence.[27] The presence of these constraints means that the decision to form a state, to say nothing of the decision to include it in the federal union, is one made not by the state polity in question, but jointly by the state and national polities acting together. These considerations further undermine both the uniqueness and self-construction requirements of constitutional positivism.

The problems with applying constitutional positivism to the states, however, go deeper still. Although it is the reigning theory of American constitutionalism, constitutional positivism is somewhat limited by certain Enlightenment-era assumptions about human nature on which it is based.[28] According to more

---

FEDERALISM, SUBNATIONAL CONSTITUTIONS, AND MINORITY RIGHTS (G. Alan Tarr et al. eds., 2004).

25. U.S. Const. amend. XIV, § 1 (equal protection and due process), art. IV, § 2 (privileges and immunities), art. I, § 8, cl. 3 (commerce), art. I, § 10, cl. 1 (currency, titles of nobility).

26. U.S. Const. art. IV, § 3.

27. SAMUEL H. BEER, TO MAKE A NATION: THE REDISCOVERY OF AMERICAN FEDERALISM 1–2, 20–21 (1993); WILLIAM P. MURPHY, THE TRIUMPH OF NATIONALISM: STATE SOVEREIGNTY, THE FOUNDING FATHERS, AND THE MAKING OF THE CONSTITUTION (1967).

28. Constitutional positivism derives from classic liberalism, which is often said to rely on an unrealistically atomistic theory of individuals. *See, e.g.*, Charles Taylor, *Atomism*, *in* ALKIS KONTOSED, POWERS, POSSESSIONS AND FREEDOMS: ESSAYS IN HONOR OF C.B. MACPHERSON 39–61 (1979); MICHAEL J. SANDEL, LIBERALISM AND THE LIMITS OF JUSTICE

recent political theories that take a more realistic view of how constitutions function in the political and social world, constitutions are more than sets of exogenously generated instructions issued by rationally self-constructed collections of individuals; they also form a crucial part of the social matrix that shapes the individuals and societies that live according to constitutionally decreed rules.[29] In other words, the arrow of causality points in both directions: constitutions do not merely reflect political choices made by polities, but also in significant ways help to frame those choices by establishing a social context in which political preferences are conceived and formulated. In this way, it is true not only that a people creates a constitution, but also that a constitution helps create a people.[30]

On this view, the fact that an American state polity must live not only under its own state constitution but also under the national Constitution has significant consequences for its identity. If a constitution not only reflects but also reciprocally constitutes the identity of the polity that lives under it, then the polity of an American state is constituted simultaneously by both the state and national constitutions. As every state polity is partly constituted by the U.S. Constitution, every state polity necessarily shares to some extent the national polity's values, commitments, and history—in short, its identity.

To make matters even more confusing, this sharing of identity occurs not only on the level of collective political identity, but on the individual level. In the American political system, every citizen of a state is also automatically a citizen of the nation,[31] and consequently all Americans are members simultaneously of both their state and national polities. This dual social membership necessarily contributes to a uniting, or at least a substantial blurring, of the two identities, and suggests strongly that they are mutually constraining through principles of individual personal integrity. As the philosopher Alasdair MacIntyre has explained, human life is embedded in narratives: we explain ourselves to ourselves and to

---

9 (1982) (in liberal theory, the individual is conceived to be "prior to and independent of experience" and thus "prior to its ends").

29. This view is often associated with communitarianism. Leading works include ALASDAIR MACINTYRE, AFTER VIRTUE (2d ed. 1984); Sandel, *supra* note 28; BENJAMIN BARBER, STRONG DEMOCRACY: PARTICIPATORY POLITICS FOR A NEW AGE (1984). It is also associated with the law and literature movement. *See* JAMES B. WHITE, HERACLES' BOW (1985); JAMES B. WHITE, JUSTICE AS TRANSLATION (1990); Richard Delgado, *Storytelling for Oppositionists and Others: A Plea for Narrative*, 87 MICH. L. REV. 2411 (1989). In state constitutional law specifically, see Gardner, *supra* note 7, at 815–22; Schapiro, *supra* note 11, at 393 ("The constitution does not reflect a preexisting community of value, but rather creates its own community.").

30. See BENEDICT ANDERSON, IMAGINED COMMUNITIES: REFLECTIONS ON THE ORIGIN AND SPREAD OF NATIONALISM (rev. ed. 1991) (arguing that nations do not necessarily reflect coherent preexisting communities, but rather result from collective leaps of imagination, often stimulated by artifacts in the shared environment).

31. U.S. Const. amend. XIV, § 1.

others, and from such accounts acquire our identity.[32] But because personal identity is based on an intelligible narrative account of oneself, identity can never be wholly unconstrained; one's identity cannot be just anything one wishes it to be, but rather is inevitably constrained by the bounds of narrative plausibility: "personal identity is just that identity presupposed by the unity of the character which the unity of a narrative requires. Without such unity there would not be subjects of whom stories could be told."[33] Because of this narrative drive toward unity in personal identity, individual membership in distinct communities becomes difficult to sustain the more the communities are understood to differ in important respects. One way to resolve this tension is to choose between communities,[34] but where choice is not an option, the only alternative is to attempt to hold things together by intellectually minimizing the differences between the communities to which one belongs. For Americans, this very likely means that there are important social limitations on how different our state and national communities, and thus our state and national identities, can ever be.

If a constitution reflects the identity of the polity that creates it, the identity of a state polity in a federal system is yoked in a significant way to the national identity, and thus cannot differ greatly from it. But this seepage of identity from state to nation and from nation to state is in considerable tension with the premise of constitutional positivism holding that the authors of a constitution have a political identity that is determinate. In the American system of federalism, it is difficult to tell where national identity ends and state identity begins. Again, then, the more realistic position is to conceive of state constitutions as the joint product of the state and national polities.

To put the point another way, it may be possible to preserve constitutional positivism as an interpretational methodology for state constitutions, but only by radically reconceiving the nature of the polity that creates them. Orthodox constitutional positivism requires that we conceive of a state polity as a unique, voluntary, distinct, and self-defined civil association, but that is clearly far from accurate. If constitutional positivism is to be retained, it must be adapted to recognize that the polity that makes a state constitution is fuzzy and ill-defined; its membership at any given moment includes elements of both the state and national citizenries. Moreover, the locus of the polity to which the state constitution is attributable is not necessarily settled, as constitutional positivism requires, but may wander

---

32. MacIntyre, *supra* note 29, ch. 15.

33. *Id.* at 218. Charles Taylor has made a similar argument; *see* CHARLES TAYLOR: SOURCES OF THE SELF: THE MAKING OF THE MODERN IDENTITY 27, 47–52 (1989).

34. This was the option chosen by Southerners upon seceding from the union, and it was typically justified on the ground that the differences between Southerners and the rest of the nation had become too great. For an account, see James A. Gardner, *Southern Character, Confederate Nationalism, and the Interpretation of State Constitutions: A Case Study in Constitutional Argument*, 76 TEX. L. REV. 1219, 1252–55 (1998).

between the two conventionally defined poles of state and national citizenries depending upon the particular issue or constitutional provision in question. In a federal system, then, a state polity simply is not a fixed, unique, and determinate entity—a problem that greatly complicates the application of the methods of constitutional positivism to the interpretation of state constitutions.

IV. IMPLICATIONS FOR INTERPRETATION

The foregoing analysis permits us to draw some rough conclusions concerning the circumstances in which constitutional positivism is capable of furnishing a valid justificatory theory of constitutional interpretation. First, constitutional positivism clearly makes sense for national constitutions; they furnish the paradigm case, and undoubtedly the foundational premises of constitutional positivism make their closest approach to reality when a national polity frames and lives under a national constitution. To invoke the heuristic of ownership mentioned earlier, a national constitution thus "belongs to" the national polity in the strongest possible way.

Second, in the case of subnational constitutions, constitutional positivism makes the most sense at the extreme ends of the spectrum of subnational autonomy referred to earlier. In a treaty league or confederacy, where subnational units enjoy nearly complete autonomy, constitutional positivism again furnishes a good description of the relation between polity and constitution at the subnational level. Here, because the subnational unit has a degree of autonomy that approaches closely the autonomy enjoyed by independent nations, the subnational constitution is created by, and thus belongs to, the subnational polity, which is therefore the source of the complete or nearly complete stock of constitutional norms. In such a governmental structure, interpreters of the subnational constitution may confidently apply the interpretive prescriptions of constitutional positivism.

Conversely, at the other end of the autonomy spectrum, subnational units are merely decentralized hierarchical subordinates of the national government; they lack any independent agency and are bound to implement authority that is merely delegated from the central government, much like an administrative agency. Here, too, constitutional positivism furnishes a useful conceptual framework, for it tells us that subnational constitutions in such a system must be interpreted solely in light of national rather than subnational norms and interpretational aids. In a highly centralized system of governance, subnational governments are essentially servants of the national government, so their constitutions will be fully determined by norms established at the national level. The subnational constitution, in other words, belongs to the national polity.

In a federal system, however, neither subnational nor national sources of meaning are likely by themselves to tell the whole story. Because the state polity has considerable independent agency in a federal system, subnational sources of meaning will clearly be highly relevant to interpretations of the state constitution. At the same time, however, national norms in such a system are part of the constituting matrix of the state polity and, by implication, its constitution; the state polity, as we have seen, cannot be neatly separated from its national counterpart. Consequently, ownership of a state constitution in a federal system is shared to some degree,[35] and constitutional positivism is thus at its least effective in describing the constitutional document and in prescribing a suitable methodology of constitutional interpretation.

If constitutional positivism does not adequately capture the situation of the American state constitution, how, then, ought such documents to be interpreted? This is not the place to attempt a comprehensive answer,[36] but it seems clear, if constitutional positivism is to be preserved as a guide to interpretation, it must be adapted to take account of the fact that the state constitution is not solely a product of the state polity, but is rather the outcome of more comprehensive processes in which both the state and national polities participate. At a minimum, then, to interpret a state constitution in these circumstances inevitably will require at least some resort to national norms and sources of constitutional meaning. Interpreters of state constitutions thus will need to search for the meaning of the document not only in state sources of meaning, such as the text and history of the state constitution, the intentions of its framers, and the precedential decisions of state courts, but in corresponding national norms, history, experience, and precedent.

To look solely at state sources of meaning,[37] as advocates of strict constitutional positivism demand, is to exclude from the analysis potentially useful or even critical information upon which to base a meaningful interpretation of the state constitution. To be sure, national sources of constitutional meaning may not always significantly illuminate the meaning of the state constitution; doubtless some provisions of state constitutions owe their contemporary meaning to influences and processes so overwhelmingly local that an examination of national history, precedent, or values will yield little information of relevance.[38] At other

35. The degree of sharing may differ from system to system; *see, e.g.*, Martha A. Field, *The Differing Federalisms of Canada and the United States*, 55 Law & Contemp. Prob. 107 (1992), or even from state to state within a single federal system. *See* G. Alan Tarr, *Creating Federalism in Russia*, 40 S. Tex. L. Rev. 689 (1999) (describing asymmetrical federalism in Russia).

36. I attempt a more complete, though still far from comprehensive, answer in James A. Gardner, Interpreting State Constitutions: A Jurisprudence of Function in a Federal System (2005).

37. Paul Kahn refers to this body of information as "unique state sources." Kahn, *supra* note 10, at 1147–50.

38. *See* Pope, *supra* note 5, at 991–94 (identifying several instances in which state constitution-making has been informed by deliberate and distinctive local choices).

times, however, national sources of constitutional meaning may entirely on their own provide a complete and satisfying account of the meaning of a provision of the state constitution, while in other cases the construction of a satisfactory account may require resort to some combination of state and national sources of meaning. At bottom, then, a sound approach to state constitutional interpretation requires a willingness to examine both kinds of sources, state and national.[39]

This is, of course, precisely what state courts already do. One of the most common phenomena in state constitutional law is so-called "lockstep" interpretation, in which state courts construe provisions of state constitutions to have precisely the same meaning as similar provisions of the U.S. Constitution.[40] In conducting a lockstep analysis, or even in conducting more sophisticated "adoptionist" analyses in which federal constitutional law is first consulted and then voluntarily incorporated into the body of state constitutional law,[41] state courts frequently examine the text, founding history, and federal judicial interpretations of the U.S. Constitution. In so doing, state courts apparently recognize that the meaning of the state constitution can be illuminated by looking to national sources of constitutional meaning. For this they have been routinely criticized.

---

39. A similar argument might be made about the interpretation of state statutes, although it would be significantly more attenuated, mainly because legislative positivism rests on a legitimating theory that is further removed from the identity-blurring problems I have been discussing. According to the prevailing theory of legislative positivism, statutes are the product of a duly-appointed legislature possessing the delegated authority to make laws binding within the relevant political jurisdiction. In consequence, the touchstone for all statutory interpretation is the intent of the legislature. Legislatures, however, are emphatically not self-created, nor do they ordinarily suffer from structural ambiguities of uniqueness or determinacy. It is conceivable that such problems could arise, but one would expect them to result from some kind of political crisis rather than from a permanent structural feature of the legislative system, as is the case with subnational constitutions in a federal system. Nevertheless, one might still say that state legislatures partake of ambiguities like those that characterize state polities because the ambiguities that exist in a state legislature's constitutional environment are necessarily ramified within the legislature itself, so that the intentions of state legislators must occasionally be construed by reference to national constitutional or statutory norms. While there is something to this argument, I am inclined to think that about the furthest one might plausibly go in this direction would be to say that national norms are relevant to the interpretation of state statutes only insofar as the interpretation of a state statute requires examination of principles embodied in the state constitution. In any other situation, the intentions of a state legislature are probably better viewed for all practical purposes as a sufficiently strong intervening cause to overwhelm the much more attenuated connections to national norms.

40. For an overview, see Robert F. Williams, *State Courts Adopting Federal Constitutional Doctrine: Case-by-Case Adoptionism or Prospective Lockstepping?*, 46 Wm. & Mary L. Rev. 1499 (2005).

41. *Id.* at 1505–20.

My argument here suggests, however, that this criticism is not always well-founded.

V. COMPLICATIONS

Having laid out my basic position, I now turn briefly to some potential complications of my analysis. First, I want to clarify the difference between the approach I have been defending and two commonplace practices of American courts. The first occurs when courts interpreting one constitution consult the decisions of other jurisdictions as an aid to interpretation. The second involves the interpretation of what we might call constitutional "wormholes": provisions in constitutions that deliberately incorporate concepts or values developed by, and borrowed from, other polities. In each of these situations, courts deliberately examine the constitutional law of a jurisdiction other than the one whose constitution they are construing, yet neither practice has ever been thought to be inconsistent with the premises of constitutional positivism. I conclude by discussing the possibility of including in a state constitution positive meta-instructions to the judiciary to ignore "outside" sources of constitutional meaning.

A. Consulting Decisions from Other Jurisdictions

American courts have a long tradition of consulting related rulings from other jurisdictions when analyzing issues arising under the law of their own jurisdictions. Although the process of interjurisdictional consultation is probably most familiar in common-law fields,[42] where courts are free from the kinds of decisional constraints imposed by the obligation to obey positive law, it also occurs in constitutional law despite the fact that the answers to constitutional questions are in principle to be found exclusively within the four corners of the relevant constitution.[43] So, for example, in taking up a question arising under the search and seizure provisions of the U.S. Constitution, the U.S. Supreme Court might consider how state courts have construed similar provisions of state constitutions,[44] and a state court facing a similar question might consult the

42. *E.g.*, Bradley Canon & Lawrence Baum, *Patterns of Adoption of Tort Law Innovations: An Application of Diffusion Theory to Judicial Doctrines*, 75 AM. POL. SCI. REV. 975 (1981).

43. I include here the set of unique interpretational aids conventionally associated with every constitution, such as the founding history and framers' intentions, for example. Although it has been persuasively argued that constitutional decision making has much more in common with common law decision making than is generally recognized (*see* David A. Strauss, *Common Law Constitutional Interpretation*, 62 U. CHI. L. REV. 131 (1995)), that is a complication I wish for present purposes to set aside.

44. *See, e.g.*, Mapp v. Ohio, 367 U.S. 643 (1961).

constitutional search and seizure jurisprudence of other state courts or of the U.S. Supreme Court.[45]

This kind of interjurisdictional consultation, however, has not typically been thought to be inconsistent with the principles of constitutional positivism.[46] Indeed, some of the leading exponents of state constitutional positivism have maintained that there is no basis for objecting to state judicial consultation of federal constitutional rulings, provided those rulings are given only the weight to which their persuasive value entitles them.[47] But if constitutional positivism permits this kind of routine interjurisdictional consultation, then does not constitutional positivism provide a suitable method for interpreting state constitutions after all?

The answer is no: subnational constitutional interpretation in a federal system contemplates a closer relationship between state and national constitutional law than is captured in the kind of interjurisdictional consultation approved by proponents of state constitutional positivism. When state courts merely "consult" similar decisions from other jurisdictions, they are conventionally understood to be doing something optional, and the consulting court typically considers itself equally free to attend to or to ignore the consulted opinions; consultation, in other words, is not premised on a belief that judicial rulings from other jurisdictions are in any sense binding within the consulting jurisdiction. Rather, courts

---

45. Examples of both kinds of consultation appear in Commonwealth v. Edmunds, 586 A.2d 887 (Pa. 1991) (consulting both state and federal rulings in determining whether to read a "good faith" exception into the state constitution's protection against unreasonable searches and seizures); State v. Oakes, 598 A.2d 119 (Vt. 1991) (same). In its stronger forms, of course, consultation shades into adoption, prompting complaints about lockstep analysis. *See* Williams, *supra* note 40.

46. A recent exception is Justice Scalia's vociferous objection to the U.S. Supreme Court's consultation of decisions from foreign jurisdictions in the course of construing the federal Constitution. *See* Lawrence v. Texas, 539 U.S. 558, 586 (2003) (Scalia, J., dissenting); Atkins v. Virginia, 536 U.S. 304, 347–48 (2002) (Scalia, J., dissenting).

47. *See, e.g.*, Tarr, *supra* note 1, at 182 ("if a state court decides to conform its interpretation of a state provision to the Supreme Court's interpretation of an analogous federal provision, this decision has to be based on the persuasiveness of the Court's argument"); Williams, *In the Supreme Court's Shadow*, *supra* note 6, at 403 (noting that U.S. Supreme Court opinions are entitled to weight as "persuasive authority in state constitutional interpretation," but observing that they deserve less weight than "decisions of sister state jurisdictions"); Linde, *First Things First*, *supra* note 6, at 392 (quoting with approval statement by the Hawaii Supreme Court in State v. Kaluna, 520 P.2d 51, 58 n.6 (1974) to the effect that U.S. Supreme Court decisions are "to be afforded respectful consideration"); Linde, *E Pluribus*, *supra* note 6, at 179 ("Of course we pay attention and respect to Supreme Court opinions on issues common to the two constitutions"); William J. Brennan, Jr., *State Constitutions and the Protection of Individual Rights*, 90 HARV. L. REV. 489, 503 (1977) (state judges should follow federal court decisions "only if they are found to be logically persuasive and well-reasoned").

seem to consult rulings from other jurisdictions more to educate themselves than to inquire into any authoritative constraints on how they themselves may rule. In consulting other decisions, then, judges seek only to gain the benefit of relevant human experience for the purpose of sharpening their own decision making; the consulted ruling carries no more intrinsic weight than would a work of history, say, or a law review article.

Once again, the point may be clarified by considering the relationship between state and national constitutional law as ranging across a spectrum. At one end of the spectrum, state constitutional law is completely controlled by the content of national constitutional law, and state judges are thus required not only to consult but to follow national law because it fully determines the meaning of state constitutional provisions. This is the kind of unreflective lockstep analysis that commentators have properly criticized. The criticism is warranted because, in a genuinely federal system, the state polity has some degree of independent agency in the formulation of its constitutional rules of self-governance and courts cannot assume, except upon the strongest evidence, that the state polity has chosen entirely to forgo any exercise of that agency.

At the other end of the spectrum, state and national constitutional law are completely independent, such that national constitutional law has no formal relationship whatsoever to state constitutional law; they are jurisprudential strangers. This is where interjurisdictional consultation comes into the picture. Here, state courts may educate themselves by consulting similar decisions from other jurisdictions, but they are not required to do so, and when they do consult such decisions they may do as they please with whatever information they might happen to acquire. This is the position taken by proponents of the primacy approach. This position, however, simply makes a mistake that is the mirror image of unreflective lockstepping, for it assumes, wrongly as I have argued above, that a state constitution in a federal system is the product solely of the state polity. On this view, the national polity has no agency in the construction of the state constitution, and the national polity's constitution, history, identity, values, and judicial precedents can therefore be treated as though they were entirely external to the state constitution. Consequently, if consultation of federal decisions does happen to prove useful, that utility results more from good luck and happenstance than from any systematic structural relation between the two documents.

My argument here is for a middle position between these two extremes. In a genuinely federal system, state constitutional law is partly independent from national constitutional law, but also partly dependent upon it. State courts cannot assume the identity of state and national constitutional law because states are not administrative subdivisions of the national government, but neither may the courts assume the kind of complete independence from national constitutional law that constitutional positivism requires, because states in federal systems are not fully independent sovereigns. As a result, state courts must do more than merely "consult" federal constitutional law in the hope that such a chance encounter might yield useful ideas or arguments. Instead, state courts must approach the state constitution with the understanding that national constitutional law may, in many though perhaps not in all cases, provide information necessary to comprehend its meaning. Resort to national sources of constitutional meaning is, then, an integral part of the process of elucidating the meaning of the state constitution, not an optional consultation to be undertaken by judges who happen to have the time and inclination.

B. Wormholes

Another instance in which constitutional positivism permits judges to look to the constitutional law of other polities when construing their own constitution is where the constitution in question contains provisions that have been deliberately copied from other constitutions.[48] In these situations, it is often said that the borrowed provision must be given the same meaning as it had under the constitution from which it was borrowed at the time of the borrowing.[49] The borrowed provision thus contains a constitutional anomaly, a "wormhole" to another constitutional dimension: stick your hand into this constitutional provision and it emerges somewhere far away, in the constitutional universe of an entirely different jurisdiction. For example, the framers of Article I, § 6 of the Delaware Constitution, a provision protecting individuals from unreasonable searches and seizures, self-consciously copied it in 1792 from the Pennsylvania Constitution of 1791.[50] As a result, courts of Delaware to this day interpret the provision by looking to decisions of the Pennsylvania Supreme Court that construe the provision of the Pennsylvania Constitution from which the Delaware one was borrowed.[51]

---

48. For a useful overview, see Tarr, *supra* note 1, at 50–56.

49. *E.g. id.* at 207 ("one chooses not only the text but the consequences of that textual formulation, as indicated by the judicial decisions interpreting the text"). Sometimes the much stronger (and untenable) claim is made that the borrowed provision must be construed in tandem with the source provision even when the meaning of the source provision evolves as a result of judicial rulings made in the source jurisdiction subsequent to the borrowing. This position, however, results in a kind of constitutional lockstep that is inconsistent even with the premises of constitutional positivism. *See* John Devlin, *State Constitutional Autonomy Rights in an Age of Federal Retrenchment: Some Thoughts on the Interpretation of State Rights Derived from Federal Sources*, 3 Emerging Issues St. Const. L. 195 (1990); Tarr, *supra* note 1, at 207.

50. Jones v. State, 745 A.2d 856, 860 n.12, 865–66 (Del. 1999).

51. *Id.* at 866. The Pennsylvania Constitution is also a source for some provisions of the Kentucky Constitution, and decisions of the Pennsylvania courts construing the source provisions carry special weight in Kentucky. Commonwealth v. Wasson, 842 S.W.2d 487, 498 (Ky. 1992). Even federal constitutional jurisprudence occasionally invokes a wormhole jurisprudence. For example, the Supreme Court has interpreted the Seventh Amendment's

On the surface, this approach to borrowed provisions seems to violate the uniqueness requirement of constitutional positivism because it requires a court construing the borrowed provision to consult the will of a polity other than the one to which it owes constitutional obedience. In fact, however, the conceptual integrity of constitutional positivism is preserved in these situations by assigning to the founding polity itself responsibility for requiring the interpreting court to look for the meaning of a constitutional provision in the constitutional law of another jurisdiction. Consequently, when a court of state A interprets a provision of A's constitution by examining the constitutional text, history, framers' intentions, and precedent of state B, it does so because the polity of state A has so instructed it. Because the court is merely obeying the binding instructions of the polity to which it owes obedience, it is not violating but rather complying with the tenets of constitutional positivism.

The problem that I have addressed in this chapter, however, is not simply a wormhole problem writ large. My argument is not that a state court should look to national sources of constitutional meaning because the state polity has instructed its courts to do so, or should be understood tacitly to have permitted the use of national sources. My point is rather that a state court attempting to adhere to the protocol of constitutional positivism will in some cases find it impossible to arrive at a complete and satisfying understanding of certain provisions of the state constitution without looking to national sources of constitutional meaning. Reference to national sources is thus in many circumstances required regardless of whether the state polity has authorized it.

C. Meta-Instructions to Ignore "Outside" Sources

The final complication I wish to address is the possibility that a state polity might affirmatively forbid state courts to consult national sources of constitutional meaning. That is, the state polity might include in the state constitution meta-instructions to the judiciary concerning how to interpret the document. What would happen if such an instruction required state courts to interpret the state constitution by relying solely on state sources of meaning, such as the state constitutional text and history and the intentions of the state constitution's framers, and to ignore national sources of meaning?[52] Would this be sufficient to negate my analysis?

---

guarantee of a right to jury trial to incorporate by reference the state of the common law right to a jury trial as it stood at the time of the adoption of the Bill of Rights, in 1791. Baltimore & Carolina Line, Inc. v. Redman, 295 U.S. 654, 657 (1935). The Seventh Amendment is thus a wormhole that directs interpreters to the common law of the eighteenth century.

52. This is not a wholly speculative possibility. Provisions in the constitutions of Florida and California, for example, require that certain rights guarantees in the state constitution be construed solely in accordance with federal constitutional norms. Cal.

I think not. In fact, such an instruction would in many cases prove impossible to obey because of the ambiguous identity of the state polity, and would do nothing more than shift the locus of ambiguity from one place to another. I argued earlier that the unsuitability of constitutional positivism for the interpretation of state constitutions is demonstrated by asking the question "whose constitution is it?" A meta-instruction to ignore non-state sources of constitutional meaning attempts to answer this question by fiat, in essence by claiming "this constitution belongs to us—the polity of this state."

The general futility of attempting to solve interpretational ambiguities by definitional fiat ought to be apparent.[53] In any event, here the relevant ambiguity would simply be referred to the next level of inquiry. Instead of asking "whose constitution is it?", the court would have to confront different but equally intractable questions: Who is the "you" of which the state polity consists? Which sources of constitutional meaning are "yours"—and which are "theirs"?

For example, would it be permissible for a state court operating under such an instruction to consult the Declaration of Independence? The Declaration is generally thought to be a "national" source of constitutional meaning, but it so deeply influenced the thinking of generations of drafters and ratifiers of state constitutions that to exclude resort to it might seriously compromise a state court's ability to make sense of certain provisions of the state constitution, or certain episodes in the state's history, or certain important statements by the framers of the state constitution. Thus, the challenge that federalism poses to subnational constitutional positivism cannot be made simply to disappear, but must be confronted at some point or another in the process of interpreting state constitutions.

VI. CONCLUSION

Constitutional positivism is a powerful and widely accepted political theory of governmental and constitutional legitimacy, and there are consequently good

---

Const. art. I, § 7; Fla. Const. art. 1, § 12. Conversely, a different provision of the California Constitution and a provision of the Rhode Island Constitution permit, but do not require, courts to construe state constitutional rights provisions according to norms other than those informing the U.S. Constitution. Cal. Const. art. I, § 24; R.I. Const. art. I, § 24.

53. The critical problem is that it is impossible for a principal, whether an individual, a polity, or a legislature, to control by fiat the way in which its agents construe its instructions. This is because interpretation always takes place in a context, and it is impossible for any actor within that context to exercise complete control over the context in which it issues its instructions, much less to control the way in which that context is understood (interpreted) by others acting within or upon it. William N. Eskridge, Jr., *Spinning Legislative Supremacy*, 78 Geo. L.J. 319 (1989). But there is no need to press this position here, as the more modest argument given in the text is sufficient to rebut the contention.

and tempting reasons to rely upon it for the purpose of legitimizing judicial interpretation of constitutions. It is important, however, not to confuse the power of a theory with its applicability; political theories derive their power in part from their plausibility in the settings in which they are applied. In particular, it is tempting to think that because constitutional positivism supplies a plausible account of interpretational legitimacy for judicial review of the U.S. Constitution, it is capable of doing the same for judicial review of American state constitutions. But this appropriation rests on a faulty premise: it assumes, wrongly, that constitutional positivism applies just as straightforwardly to subnational constitutions as it does to the paradigm case of national constitutions. Although constitutional positivism may, without modification, provide useful guidance for construing subnational constitutions in certain kinds of multilevel systems of governance, in a genuinely federal system it does not. This is because subnational polities in a federal system lack several characteristics that constitutional positivism deems them to possess, making it an unsuitable method, at least in its conventional form, for application to the constitutions of the American states.

Constitutional positivism can, however, be retrieved as a useful methodology for interpreting state constitutions, but only by relaxing some of its methodological prescriptions. In particular, we must abandon the idea that the meaning of a state constitutional provision is determined solely by reference to sources of meaning associated with that constitution. Instead, interpreters of state constitutions must recognize that elucidation of the meaning of provisions of state constitutions may from time to time require them to consult not only state sources of constitutional meaning, but also corresponding national sources. That is, the meaning of the state constitution may be determined not only by the state constitutional text, state constitutional history, intentions of the framers of the state constitution, and prior state constitutional precedent, but also by the history, values, experience, and precedent associated with the U.S. Constitution.

Despite a steady stream of academic criticism, state judges have often looked to federal constitutional law to guide their interpretation of the state constitution. The analysis here suggests that academic commentary would be better directed not to criticizing state judges for resorting to national sources of constitutional meaning, but to educating them about how best and in what circumstances to do so.

5. STATE CONSTITUTIONALISM AND THE SCOPE OF JUDICIAL REVIEW

DANIEL B. RODRIGUEZ

I. INTRODUCTION

In early 2006, the Florida Supreme Court issued a major decision in the continuing controversy over education financing in the state. In *Bush v. Holmes*,[1] the court considered the constitutionality of an "opportunity scholarship program" that used public funds to send underperforming students to private school. The court struck down the statute, holding that it violated the education clause in the Florida Constitution. In dissent, Justice Bell insisted that the majority had failed to follow the "fundamental principles of state constitutional jurisprudence." First, "the people are the ultimate sovereign." Second, "unlike the federal constitution, our state constitution is a limitation upon the power of government rather than a grant of that power." Lastly, "because general legislative or policy-making power is vested in the legislature, the power of judicial review over legislative enactments is strictly limited."[2] The first two axioms are accurate statements of the general theory of state constitutionalism.[3] They express the underlying framework shaping positive and normative perspectives on state constitutional law. The third principle, however, is another matter entirely. Why does it follow from the first two principles of state constitutionalism that the state judiciary's role in constitutional review is strictly limited? This is the topic of my chapter.

Despite the mechanical, even syllogistic, quality of the reasoning in the good justice's opinion, a careful consideration of the issue of judicial review in state constitutional law requires attention to some of the functional aspects of state constitutionalism and the judicial role. Indeed, if there is a predicate theme to my argument it is this: state constitutional law is a product of distinct choices made by state judges grappling with complex issues of state constitutionalism. Although there is much to learn from the general architecture of constitutional theory at the national level, state constitutional law and theory is properly focused on the written constitutions of the states. Moreover, state constitutionalism can be understood only by resort to deeply functional considerations. We lack, to put it mildly, a comprehensive founding history of state constitutions, documents

---

1. 919 So.2d 392 (Fla. 2006).

2. *Id.* at 54–56.

3. *See generally* ROBERT F. WILLIAMS, STATE CONSTITUTIONAL LAW ch. 1 (4th ed. 2005); Walter Dodd, *The Function of a State Constitution*, 30 POL. SCI. Q. 201 (1915).

enacted, after all, over the course of 220 years; thus, state constitutionalism as an "ism" makes sense only if we can draw smart conclusions from theories and perspectives generally applicable to state constitutions taken as a whole. These theories, as I have argued elsewhere,[4] are necessarily functional.

In this chapter, I consider one piece of the larger puzzle. The question of what ought to be the courts' approach to judicial review in state constitutional law is a surprisingly open one. On the one hand, we have the view reflected tersely in Justice Bell's opinion that courts should be particularly circumspect when reviewing state legislative enactments. I will call this the "deferential" view. In other state cases, judges take the opposite tack, suggesting that it is precisely because state legislative power is so broad under principles of state constitutionalism that active judicial interventions are necessary to keep the system in some balance. I will call this the "aggressive" view. And, finally, there is the approach that looks at constitutional review through what is essentially the same lens as in federal review, a view that I will call "neutral" in that it captures the idea that the scope of judicial review should not turn on the broad principles of state constitutionalism. To unravel these competing approaches, we must wade into the waters of state constitutional theory more generally. In particular, to gain traction on this issue we must consider two large questions, both of which are viewed most helpfully by attention to functional considerations. First, what are the basic objectives of state constitutions? Next, what are the objectives of judicial review? Marrying the two answers to these questions will shed light on the competing perspectives on the role of courts in constitutional review at the state level.

II. STATE CONSTITUTIONS AND THE DILEMMAS OF GOVERNANCE

The functions and structure of our fifty state constitutions must be understood in the shadow of the jagged history of state political development and constitution-formation over the lifespan of the American republic. The early state constitutions, documents that garner perhaps a disproportionate share of scholarly attention in the historical literature on state constitutionalism in the United States, were designed primarily to restrict the scope of political power within the states, particularly the power of the executive branch.[5] Fresh from heroic struggles with the English monarch and steeped in the conflicts of the constitution-making process at the national level, the architects of the early state constitutions limited the power of governors, crafted structures for the exercise of regulatory power by

---

4. Daniel B. Rodriguez, *State Constitutional Theory and Its Prospects*, 28 N.M.L. Rev. 271 (1998).

5. *See generally* Christian G. Fritz, *Rediscovering the Lost Worlds of America's Written Constitutions*, 68 Alb. L. Rev. 261 (2005); Gordon Wood, *Foreword: State Constitution-Making in the American Revolution*, 24 Rutgers L.J. 911 (1993).

state legislatures, and delineated certain individual rights—rights that, not surprisingly, either presaged or mirrored those contained in the Bill of Rights of the U.S. Constitution.[6]

More interesting as a matter of novel political architecture—and ultimately more revealing for what we ought to think about state constitutionalism today—were the bursts of constitution-making and revising in the aftermath of the Civil War and Reconstruction.[7] Of course, the states of the vanquished South reconstructed nearly from scratch their respective constitutions; in so doing, they followed, rather slavishly in fact, standard templates of constitutions developed in the rest of the states. Key northern states, including Pennsylvania and Illinois and, somewhat later, California, reconstructed their constitutions in the shadow of rapidly growing mistrust of state legislatures. Presaging the Progressive and Populist eras, these constitutions limited in important ways the powers of state government, creating, for instance, restrictions on special legislation and debt financing.[8] This plethora of key anti-legislative constitutional innovations forged a new administrative movement in American public governance, a movement that took shape in the Progressives' pitch for neutral expertise over partisan politics and, ultimately, in the creation of an alphabet soup of new regulatory agencies.

Less conspicuous, but nonetheless important in late nineteenth century new state constitutionalism, was the emergence of municipal power under the rubric of constitutional home rule. State constitutions were amended to include new guarantees of municipal power, specifically, an *imperium in imperio* framework in which cities could act free of state intervention so long as these cities acted with regard to "local affairs." This home-rule movement was of a piece with the Progressive Era's efforts to limit in various ways the powers of state legislatures to act in "political" ways.

Yet perhaps the most striking development in this era of significant constitutional revisionism was the creation of direct democracy through constitutional structures of initiative lawmaking. To be sure, this development was not universal; the western states, states with considerably less constitutional tradition and, moreover, entrenched political interest groups, proved fonder of this new constitutional development. For these states, however, this development was critical in creating a rather distinctive approach to intrastate governance. State government would thereafter be regulated not only by a deliberate separation of powers and

6. *See, e.g.*, Judith S. Kaye, *Foreword: The Common Law and State Constitutional Law as Full Partners in the Protection of Individual Rights*, 23 RUTGERS L.J. 727 (1992).

7. *See generally* DANIEL J. ELAZAR, THE AMERICAN CONSTITUTIONAL TRADITION (1988); Christian G. Fritz, *The American Constitutional Tradition Revisited: Preliminary Observations on State Constitution-Making in the Nineteenth-Century West*, 25 RUTGERS L.J. 945 (1994).

8. *See, e.g.*, Frank E. Horack, *Special Legislation: Another Twilight Zone*, 12 IND. L.J. 108 (1936); *see generally* WILLIAMS, *supra* note 3, at 802–23.

a detailed list of individual rights, but also by the people directly through their power to upend the processes of state government.

The busy activity of constitutional reform in the early twentieth century was directed mostly toward reworking in modest-to-moderate ways the structure of state government. Fundamental changes to state constitutions were few and far between. Where state power was reconstructed, as in California in 1978 with Proposition 13,[9] it was because of a popular uprising among the voters, who used their initiative powers to place new reins on their public officials. In the main, the basic underpinnings of state constitutionalism in the United States can be described today in largely the same terms we might have used a century ago. To be sure, the nature and scope of the issues confronting state governments have changed in many ways, but the project and predicament of state governance under state constitutions remains intact.

What, then, is this project? As the written document establishing the fundamental law of the state, the state constitution is the template for the administration of political power by state government and its subordinate entities.[10] It delineates the institutions of state governance and the content of individual rights. Every state constitution regulates the processes of governmental decision making at the subnational level. These broad-bush principles are expressions of general constitutional characteristics. As a matter of particular legal consequence, they are rather banal; they tell us what state constitutions are intrinsically about as primary legal documents, as charters of governance. However, they do not tell us, at anything other than a wholly theoretical level, what state constitutions are expected to accomplish. The more interesting question is this: what are the functions of state constitutions?

State constitutions accomplish three critical objectives. First, they create the structures of state government; they establish the branches that exercise legislative, executive, and judicial power and, unlike the federal constitution, they often delineate the structure and powers of distinct government institutions. In California, for example, the regents of the University of California are provided for expressly; in Ohio, the director of the state penitentiary is expressly provided for in the state constitution. Second, state constitutions establish the regulations and restraints on the exercise of power by state government and its instrumentalities. Most typically, such limitations are established through express rights or separation of powers. These two objectives—structuring power and regulating power—are hardly unique to state constitutionalism; indeed, these roles are

9. *See* Williams, *supra* note 3, at 945–55; Heather Marie Hayman, *The Legal Ramifications of Proposition 13: Protecting State Fundamental Rights in Federal Court*, 30 Syracuse L. Rev. 937 (1979).

10. Significantly, these "subordinate" entities include municipalities. *See* Hunter v. Pittsburgh, 207 U.S. 161 (1907). They also include various administrative agencies and special purpose governments.

characteristic of every authoritative document described as a constitution, as fundamental law of a polity. Third, and somewhat more distinctly, state constitutions are legal means of facilitating the means and ends of state governance. This third role requires some additional explanation.

Most public policy in the United States is made by officials at the state and local level. This is not to judge the relative significance of national policy making versus state- and sub-state-level policy making. National defense and the ubiquitous war on terrorism jump to mind as overlapping areas that are within the primary scope of national decision makers and are crucial elements of our well-being as citizens, regardless of the state in which we happen to reside. However, the basic range of policies and policy choices made by state and local officials dwarf—indeed, *always have dwarfed*—national policy activity.

The comparatively larger amount of policy activity is not accidental; rather, it reflects the fundamental allocation of roles and responsibilities under our constitutional system of federalism. The federal government's role is a limited one; to be sure, not nearly so limited as the framers originally expected or as would be gleaned from a review of national authority in the latter part of the nineteenth century, but limited nonetheless. The main principle of national constitutionalism—that the U.S. Constitution is a document of grant—reinforces the idea that federal power is limited. By contrast, state power is incomparably broad. The police power, a concomitant of the principle that state constitutions are documents of limit, illustrates the breadth of state power. Simply put, we expect our state and local officials to protect our "health, safety, and welfare." Wherever we turn, we see officials doing exactly that. Regulations establishing speed on the roads, curfews, standards of adequate housing and basic education, designations of where we can smoke, sleep, urinate, meet, or park—these far-flung rules of everyday life are by and large the product of subnational decision making. The federal government's role, although admittedly growing since the time of the founding, has always, *always* been interstitial and episodic.

The inherent activism of state governments is reflected not only in the power to restrict our liberties through regulatory mandates and "police" regulations, but importantly in the responsibility of state governments to secure certain positive rights.[11] For the past generation or so, a bevy of creative legal scholars has drawn elegant critiques of American constitutionalism based primarily on the grounds that our constitution fails to protect adequately positive rights, including, for example, the rights to education, housing, and a suitable level of welfare.[12] Within this critique, scholars compare this lack of protection with the ambitions of other non-U.S. constitutions, noting the impressive ambitions of

---

11. *See generally* WILLIAMS, *supra* note 3, at 545–63.

12. *E.g.*, Frank I. Michelman, *In Pursuit of Constitutional Welfare Rights: One View of Rawls' Theory of Justice*, 121 U. PA. L. REV. 962 (1973); Frank I. Michelman, *Welfare Rights in a Constitutional Democracy*, 1979 WASH. U.L.Q. 659.

nations such as Canada, Israel, and South Africa along with the European Union to turn the government's role toward the assurance of certain affirmative rights. Curiously, these scholars have usually neglected to look within the United States to the various state constitutions that, in fact, establish positive rights. These commonly established rights exist in state constitutions rather than in the national Constitution primarily because of the comparatively different objective of state constitutions. State and local governments are expected to be more activist not only in the restriction of our liberties for general public aims, but in the protection of our affirmative rights established in constitutional mandates. Where, for example, the state constitution establishes a right to adequate education, the state government is charged with—and provided suitable legal authority to undertake—the responsibility of securing actively this positive right of its citizens. This responsibility will usually include the power to enact rules that would be anathema if enacted by the federal government, such as the imposition of a tax or the setting of a level of suitable funding. These positive rights and the constitutional means for the protection of these rights represent well this third objective of state constitutionalism, what I will call *active governance*.

The state constitutionalism project is, as I have sketched it, distinct from national constitutionalism. To be sure, we ought not and could not understand that state project in isolation from American constitutionalism more generally. The states are, after all, part of the *United* States, and state constitutions must be understood in the broader context of American political and legal development. My emphasis in this section, however, has been on what is usually neglected: state constitutions indeed have different sorts of objectives than does the U.S. Constitution. In particular, state constitutionalism is concerned with setting the conditions for active governance, and the various doctrines of state constitutional law should be considered in light of this overarching concern. Before returning to this insight in earnest, I take a short detour by focusing on the practice and objectives of judicial review. Although the broad questions of judicial review and its proper role is beyond the scope of this chapter, I must at least dip my toe into these waters to best frame the question: what ought to be the scope of judicial review in reviewing state enactments?

III. OPTIMAL (OPTIMIZING?) JUDICIAL REVIEW

Judicial review is an entrenched part of American constitutional doctrine and thought; it has been so since the time of the founding of the republic; and no American court, whether federal or state, now seriously questions the authority of judges to review the constitutionality of enactments and actions of local, state, and national officials.

But what objectives does judicial review serve? Two, broadly speaking. First, judicial review endeavors to correct legislative mistakes, what Alexander

Hamilton in *Federalist No. 78* called the "infractions of the Constitution."[13] By mistakes, we mean simply choices made by the legislature (I will leave aside here matters of executive or administrative actions) that are inconsistent with the fundamental law. When we say they are in error, we are really saying the enactments are beyond the scope of the legislature's proper constitutional authority. The U.S. Supreme Court, for reasons explained most famously by Chief Justice Marshall in *Marbury*, implements the Constitution by correcting these errors. The utility, then, of judicial review is found primarily in the capacity of courts to assess accurately whether and to what extent the legislature acts erroneously. In a recent essay, Yuval Eylon and Alon Harel characterize the conventional view of the judiciary's review function as that of a watchdog: "Just as the police fight crime, and the Holy Inquisition protected the faith, the institution of judicial review supervises the decisions made by the political branches."[14] Courts act as watchdogs to make sure the legislature does not overstep its bounds.

Viewing the courts' role as correcting legislative mistakes helps—but only a little—in clarifying the proper scope of judicial review. Whether courts should be more or less activist in scrutinizing legislative actions for mistakes depends on the extent to which we predict that the legislature will err; it depends, separately, on how successful we believe that courts will be at sorting out erroneous from correct decisions. More than a century ago, James Bradley Thayer framed this basic function of judicial review concisely.[15] For Thayer, Congress would ordinarily be expected to make decisions consistent with the Constitution. More pertinent, though, was the risk attendant to judicial intervention. Courts' capacity for careful, thoughtful scrutiny was limited. For these reasons, the courts should exercise their review authority only where there are clear mistakes.

In the end, we need a theoretically and empirically more informed sense of the likelihood of legislative errors and how successful courts will be in combating these errors in order for us to develop and sustain a particular approach to judicial review. Once the justification for judicial review is squarely set, we are left with the monumental task of establishing a measure of review—what scholars of administrative law in another context usefully call a "mood" or an "attitude"—for courts to implement. Though monumental, this task has been undertaken by a large collection of influential constitutional scholars. The figures are new (or at least new-ish), the perspectives are often novel, and the methodology more eclectic than in the past, but the questions are the old ones: how interventionist should courts be in reviewing legislative enactments for potential "infractions?"

---

13. THE FEDERALIST, No. 78, at 544–45 (Hamilton) (H. Dawson ed. 1891).

14. Yuval Eylon & Alon Harel, *The Right to Judicial Review*, 92 VA. L. REV. 991, 994 (2006).

15. James Bradley Thayer, *The Origin and Scope of the American Doctrine of Constitutional Law*, 7 HARV. L. REV. 129 (1893).

A second, and arguably distinct, function of judicial review is the promotion of good incentives for improving governance. Courts can facilitate democracy and representative government by requiring the legislature to follow certain processes. These processes ensure that congressional activity will facilitate objectives that the people believe are essential or at least important. For example, we may be concerned with the structure of representation in Congress, fearing that the powerful advantages of incumbency and party-driven hierarchies may make it difficult for legislators adequately to represent the social interests of the nation.[16] Or we may be concerned, as the Supreme Court was in *Lopez*, with the extent of legislative deliberation and fact-finding in the lawmaking process. In any event, we may see the courts' role in reviewing legislative enactments as not merely error correction, but as a strategic effort to improve democratic lawmaking. Certainly there is evidence in the Supreme Court's constitutional decisions over the course of the past several decades that judges worry about the structure and performance of Congress.

This process-improving function need not be wholly distinct from the error correction function described above. In the work of John Hart Ely and Cass Sunstein, for example, there is an intellectually complex and interesting marriage between the argument for active judicial intervention to protect disadvantaged groups and the argument for interventions to improve the capacity of governments to govern effectively. For Ely, the sine qua non of review is the facilitation of democracy and democratic decision making through closer scrutiny of the outputs of our representative political processes at the national level. For Sunstein, we ought to be concerned as well with the efficacy of these processes and therefore ought to intervene in more deliberate ways to improve democratic decision making.

Attention to governance incentives has been especially prominent in the emerging influential paradigm of positive political theory (PPT).[17] For scholars in the PPT tradition (myself among them), deep understanding of the strategic incentives of lawmakers and institutional matrices of modern lawmaking is essential in evaluating legal doctrines. More ambitiously, PPT scholars of public law aim to develop legal instruments to better incentivize political decision makers—that is, to take account of strategic behavior in order to channel these behaviors and intra-legislative structures in more fruitful directions. From the vantage point of judicial review and constitutional law, PPT stresses this second,

---

16. *See, e.g.*, Daryl Levinson & Richard Pildes, *Separation of Parties, Not Powers*, 119 HARV. L. REV. (2006).

17. *See, e.g.*, Daniel B. Rodriguez & Barry Weingast, *The Positive Political Theory of Legislative History: New Perspectives on the Civil Rights Act of 1964 and Its Interpretation*, 151 U. PA. L. REV. (2003).

incentive-promoting function. It looks at particular approaches to judicial review for what they have to offer in facilitating useful patterns of legislative behavior.[18]

Optimal (or optimizing) judicial review is that approach to review that succeeds in realizing whatever *objective* we associate with review. More fundamentally, however, optimal judicial review realizes objectives that are at the heart of constitutionalism more generally. In other words, the scope of judicial review must be consistent with the general values underlying the particular constitution at issue. The utility of judicial review cannot be measured by resort to the goals and values of judicial decision making. We should be interested primarily in how close judicial review gets us to the aims we associate with constitutionalism, and it is this measure—the connection between review in practice and in the constitution's objectives—that frames the normative argument for one or another approach.

I return to the formulation of the three alternative "moods" of judicial review described earlier in this chapter. One mood is deferential. Courts might be especially deferential to legislative judgments. Certainly Thayer and Learned Hand expressed an informed skepticism about the value of activist judicial review. The thumb on the scale favored legislative judgments and thus only rare judicial intervention. Later, scholars in the legal process tradition ranging from Bickel to Kurland to Choper charted interesting strategies for limiting judicial review to particular questions. Such paeans to narrow review inform some of the fashionable popular constitutionalist theory so prominent in the law reviews today. But although these deferential theories aim to tie questions concerning the proper role of courts in our constitutional system to the efficacy of legislative decision making, there is not much insight to draw upon for a deeper understanding of judicial review in the distinct state context. To put it simply, a century's worth of elegant, eclectic constitutional argument has been centered mostly around the interpretation of the federal Constitution.

Likewise, influential theories that urge a more activist role for courts in construing a constitution and in implementing constitutional values—think here of the recent work of Ronald Dworkin, Jed Rubenfeld, Bruce Ackerman, Robert Post, and Lawrence Sager—are preoccupied with questions concerning the Constitution of the United States. Significantly, the synthetic arguments mobilized in this work for a particularly aggressive approach to interpretation draw mainly from qualities, characteristics, and historical developments pertinent to the U.S. Constitution. When Ackerman, for example, calls for a fuller-bodied approach to understanding constitutional change, the relevant episodes concern matters of national historical importance, such as the adoption of the Reconstruction amendments and the New Deal. And in scholarship that avowedly

18. *See* Matthew C. Stephenson, *Legislative Allocation of Delegated Power: Uncertainty, Risk, and the Choice between Agencies and Courts*,119 Harv. L. Rev. 1036 (2006).

emphasizes the expansion of national power and the imperative of courts embracing this expansion through their interpretations of, say, the Commerce Clause or the Privileges and Immunities Clause, it is not surprising that the connection between this interpretive strategy at the national level and the possible strategies of interpreting state constitutions is neglected. *It is not that connections are utterly lacking; rather, it is that state constitutionalism and constitutional interpretation are simply not the subjects of the analysis.* We can say about both the "deferential" and "aggressive" views that they are tethered mightily to theories of constitutionalism as they play out at the national level. At their best, these theories of judging and judicial review are fueled by comprehensive, historically sensitive theories of American constitutional and political development. Therefore, they aim explicitly to connect the strategy of optimal judicial review to constitutional text, structure, and values. To be sure, comparative analyses inform their work (although some would argue not nearly enough), but their project is American constitutionalism as framed by the U.S. Constitution and its distinct history and architecture.

So, in essence, we are back where we started. Having bracketed the most interesting debates about constitutionalism and judicial review at the national level, I have now previewed the question at the heart of the chapter, namely, what should state judges do in reviewing legislative enactments under their respective state constitutions? The purpose of the last part of this essay is to bring the question back to where it belongs: to state constitutionalism as a distinct project.

As we shift our attention to the proper role of state courts in creating state constitutional law, we return to what is essentially the same project. What function does judicial review serve in constructing the parameters of governance? Are the functions described above—correcting errors and improving the legislative process—distinctly national? Or are they equally relevant to state constitutionalism and its predicaments? The answer to this question in the state constitutional context requires connecting the process of judicial review to the foundations of state constitutionalism.

IV. SCOPE OF CONSTITUTIONAL REVIEW REVISITED

The constitutions of U.S. states contain various provisions, some rather common to all state constitutions—for instance, powers distributed explicitly to the legislative, executive, and judicial branch, and, save for Nebraska, a bicameral legislature—and some distinct. The distinctions are important and, indeed, any effort to speak confidently about state constitutionalism as a trans-state "ism" must confront these distinctions in ways beyond the scope of the present chapter. That said, a common theme fundamental to state constitutionalism is the idea referred to earlier that state constitutions are documents of limit, not grant. All state constitutions recognize broad legislative power such as the police power, and all state constitutions regulate the exercise of this power in essentially the same two ways: through the structuring of governmental power (e.g., the creation of legislative, executive, and judicial institutions/separation of powers) and through the delineation of certain individual rights. This commonality enables us to talk fruitfully about state constitutionalism as a sensible project.

A. State Constitutionalism as Focal Point

To understand the distinctive project of state constitutionalism, an understanding that must precede any conclusions about the scope of judicial review, we must sort out the elements of state constitutionalism. These elements can be categorized into powers, rights, and institutions.

1. Powers As I have suggested, the powers of government within the American states are quite broad. State constitutions are charters of active governance. The lion's share of policy making, and thus policymaking powers, exists at the subnational level; and the terms and structure of state constitutions, in particular the police power, support this distribution of responsibility under principles of American federalism.

Precisely because these powers are broad, mechanisms to channel the effective exercise of these powers, along with carefully designed legal and political constraints on government, are essential. The structure of state governance, by and large, reflects this fundamental insight. Consider that some state constitutions, unlike the federal Constitution, contain express provisions assuring a separation of powers.[19] The framers of the U.S. Constitution had available to them the text of state constitutions that expressly delineated a separation of powers, but declined to do so in the U.S. Constitution. An oversight, perhaps? More plausibly, the drafters of state constitutions were more concerned with ensuring that there would be a strong, judicially enforceable separation of powers among the branches and therefore spelled out this separation in express, even cumbersome, terms.

Likewise, consider that many state constitutions, particularly those that were either adopted or significantly reconstructed in the latter part of the nineteenth century, have a critical external constraint on the exercise of power by their elected representatives through mechanisms of direct democracy. Initiative lawmaking, whether statutory or constitutional, limits in politically salient ways the exercise—some would say the *abuse*—of governmental power. Not only does direct democracy give to the state's citizens an avenue for creating public policy without representative intermediaries, but also an important weapon with which to defend themselves against liberty encroachments by government authorities.

---

19. For a comprehensive overview, see Jim Rossi, *Institutional Design and the Lingering Legacy of Antifederalist Separation of Powers Ideals in the States,* 52 VAND. L. REV. 1167 (1999).

On the one hand, the powers of state government are immense and the threat of encroachment upon our liberties by state and local officials is great. On the other, the mechanisms that have emerged to restrain governmental officials who might otherwise overreach are, while obviously imperfect, important in ameliorating the dangerous consequences of a state constitutionalism that favors active governance. A theme that emerges is that of balance: we expect and want our processes of state governance to be in rough balance with one another and also *in balance* with the imperative of assuring a sphere of liberty and freedom. Although we will return to this point later, I will say now that balance as a constitutional value is particularly important in state constitutional analysis given the distinct principle—what the Florida justice described as a "fundamental" principle—of plenary state legislative power.

2. **Rights** State constitutional rights have always presented a puzzle for American constitutional theory. The record of state judicial enforcement of individual rights, including rights expressly provided for in the constitutional document, is a rather dismal one.[20] For much of American history, state judges contented themselves with construing state constitutional rights protections in lockstep with the federal Constitution.[21] And although state constitutions contained rights not found in the federal Constitution, state courts often neglected to acknowledge or to enforce these rights. Lawyers contributed to this neglect; seldom did they make effective arguments for the enforcement of distinct state constitutional rights or for distinct interpretations of their state's rights. State constitutional law reflected, in the main, a sort of junior varsity American constitutional law, with thinly reasoned opinions articulating a state constitutional jurisprudence yoked mainly to constitutional jurisprudence at the federal level. There were, to be sure, conspicuous counterexamples, but these were the exceptions, not the rule.

The clarion call for a new state constitutionalism emerged in the 1970s with Justice Brennan, a handful of influential state supreme court justices (Hans Linde of Oregon at the top of this list), and a few constitutional scholars.[22] These lawyers argued for a state constitutional law that would be distinct from federal constitutional law; in particular, they appealed to state judges to interpret their

---

20. *See, e.g.*, Paul W. Kahn, *Interpretation and Authority in State Constitutionalism*, 106 HARV. L.REV. 1147 (1993); James A. Gardner, *The Failed Discourse of State Constitutionalism*, 90 MICH. L. REV. 761 (1992).

21. *See generally* WILLIAMS, STATE CONSTITUTIONAL LAW, *supra* note 3, at 368–426.

22. *See* Hans A. Linde, *Are State Constitutions Common Law?*, 34 ARIZ. L. REV. 215 (1992); William J. Brennan, Jr., *State Constitutions and the Protection of Individual Rights*, 90 HARV. L. REV. 489 (1977); Robert F. Williams, *In the Supreme Court's Shadow: Legitimacy of State Rejection of Supreme Court Reasoning and Result*, 35 S.C. L. REV. 353 (1984); Frank P. Grad, *The State Constitution: Its Function and Form for Our Time*, 54 VA. L. REV. 928 (1968).

state constitutions differently (and, as there were important ideological motivations underlying this appeal, more liberally) than federal courts were interpreting the U.S. Constitution.[23] At around the same time, some state courts developed doctrines that turned express positive rights in their state constitutions into engines of enormous, albeit controversial, engines of social change.[24] The New Jersey and California Supreme Courts were particularly ambitious in this regard, developing a far-reaching policy apparatus in the areas of education and education finance.[25] These same courts, and other state courts, similarly expanded the scope of public policy through activist judicial interpretations of positive rights.

These twin developments—independent constitutional interpretation and the development of a muscular positive rights jurisprudence—have begun to frame a very distinct and exciting state constitutionalism for a new century. New, of course, is not always salutary, and it remains unclear whether the emerging state constitutional law will be a movement of legal progress or, instead, a cacophony of rebel voices acting out one or another view of proper public policy through interpretation of "unique" constitutional provisions. In any case, the principal venue for this new state constitutional jurisprudence is the interpretation of state constitutional rights. Thus, the project of state constitutionalism, of which state constitutional law is one crucial part, must take suitable account of the key role of state courts in interpreting in this rather new way the rights provisions of their respective state constitutions.

3. Institutions State constitutions empower state governments to act; they simultaneously regulate state governmental actions. Yet public policy making at the subnational level does not happen by virtue of these constitutional instructions. Governments act through institutions. To understand the contours of state governance under state constitutions and principles of state constitutionalism, we must understand the structure and incentives of these institutions.

Without surveying some landscape of state governmental institutions, let us pick through the structural detail to highlight key characteristics of three central state governmental institutions, one from each of the legislative, executive, and judicial branches. To begin with the legislature, we observe that each state (save for Nebraska) establishes a legislature of two houses, each of which meets the federal constitutional requirement of equal apportionment.[26] This arrangement

---

23. *See, e.g.*, Robert A. Schapiro, *Identity and Interpretation in State Constitutional Law*, 84 VA. L. REV. 389 (1998); Thomas Morawetz, *Deviation and Autonomy: The Jurisprudence of Interpretation in State Constitutional Law*, 26 CONN. L. REV. 635 (1994).

24. *See* Helen Hershkoff, *Positive Rights and State Constitutions: The Limits of Federal Rationality Review*, 112 HARV. L. REV. 1131 (1999); Burt Neuborne, *Foreword: State Constitutions and the Evolution of Positive Rights*, 20 RUTGERS L.J. 881 (1989).

25. *See, e.g.*, Serrano v. Priest, 135 Cal. Rptr. 345 (1977); Robinson v. Cahill, 62 N.J. 473 (1973).

26. Reynolds v. Sims, 377 U.S. 533 (1964).

is often taken for granted, but is rather significant in framing and structuring state legislative power. When state legislators act, they do so in the service of a large collection of constituents, yet each group of constituents sends precisely two representatives to the capital to act on its behalf. Nearly every representative of every state is elected in a single-member district; every representative is elected through a majority electoral system with only those voters who are residents of the district attached to that legislator authorized to vote; and every representative, as just noted, represents a roughly equal number of constituents.

Contrast this legislative system with alternatives that exist in local governments in the United States. Many city council members are elected at large; as a result, they are incentivized (we would not want to say necessarily "obliged") to represent the interests of a wide group of constituents. Indeed, we might suppose that this is precisely the reason that they are elected at large rather than through single-member districts. While any state is free to construct either house of its legislature in accordance with an at-large electoral mechanism, none does. Why not? Because the state constitution says so.

The "says so" answer similarly explains why no state legislative assembly is constructed around different electoral principles, whether cumulative voting, proportional representation, or any other scheme. The uniform mechanism for electing state legislators is especially striking when we consider that very different mechanisms have been adopted by other public and private organizations within the United States. Justice Brandeis labeled states "laboratories of experimentation," yet few states have experimented to any great degree with electoral structure.

The federal Constitution and its interpretation in the classic reapportionment cases of the 1960s explain why no state is permitted to create a legislative institution that looks like the U.S. Senate. Although states of course face no demands of federalism that would counsel a Senate-like institution, they are made up of important cities and counties. It would not be inconceivable that the citizens of a state would want the interests of their respective municipalities suitably represented in the state legislative process. However, municipal representation in the state legislature would be flatly unconstitutional, as the U.S. Supreme Court has made clear in its "equal apportionment" cases.

At least two other qualities of modern state legislative institutions might affect constitutional governance. One is the existence in many states of a so-called professional legislature. When legislators serve as full-time governmental officials and sit in more or less continuous sessions, they have greater opportunities for extensive deliberation along with political machinations. Simply put, there is more time and room for governance in those states in which legislators are professionalized; the scope of public policy in those states is predictably wider.

Another is the recent rise (and, in three states, fall) of legislative term limits. The effect of term limits on legislative governance is a widely studied area among political scientists, yet, interestingly, the conclusions drawn are controversial. Term limits ensure greater legislative turnover, and the incentives on the part of experienced, ambitious legislators would seem to drive legislatures away from broad-scale public policy making toward narrower and more parochial strategies—indeed, this was one of the primary motivations behind the term limits movement. Yet, the record appears to be more complex. Without the persistent pressures of campaigning and attendant fund-raising, legislators may prove more amenable to actual governance activities. Moreover, the new structure of legislative rewards and incentives may lead to the election of legislators who come into the legislature with bold agendas and more grass-roots interests.

Let us move on to the executive branch. It is tempting at first glance to consider the role and place of the governor in state constitutional government as analogous to the U.S. president, although without the vast scope of powers and prerogatives that are uniquely national. Upon closer inspection, however, the analogy mostly dissolves. State constitutions typically divide executive power among separately elected officials. The state attorney general is ordinarily elected by the people directly; therefore, law enforcement responsibilities are undertaken by an executive official with his or her own electoral base and, correspondingly, distinct political pressures. Not surprisingly, governors and attorneys general frequently come into conflict—conflicts that are occasionally resolved by state courts. Other state executive officials (in California, for example, a fairly large number, including an insurance commissioner elected statewide) are similarly separated from the direct control of the state's governor.

Just as we might conclude that the governor's power is incredibly weak, we see other constitutional structures that enhance the executive power of the state's chief executive. For example, state governors typically possess the line item veto power, a power thus far denied to the U.S. president. This power is exercised routinely and to rather large policy effect by U.S. governors.[27] Even more remarkable is the power of the governors in six states (Alaska, Illinois, Massachusetts, Montana, New Jersey, South Dakota, and Virginia) to amend statutes unilaterally through the power of the so-called "amendatory veto."[28] These powers, and other key powers of governance, protect to a greater or lesser degree the general executive powers of governors. And, as any political scientist or pundit might predict, the degree to which governors act as effective checks on the power of the legislature turns on the presence and persistence of these powers in a particular state. Indeed, we have available to us a great natural experiment in comparatively assessing executive power, as state constitutions structure the executive branch and executive power in different ways.

We come, finally, to the judiciary. The most important characteristic of the judiciary for the purposes of state governance is, of course, the electoral structure of judges under state constitutions. Nearly all constitutional analyses of

---

27. *See* Richard Briffault, *The Item Veto in State Courts*, 66 TEMPLE L. REV. 1171 (1993).

28. *See* WILLIAMS, *supra* note 3, at 763; Jack R. Van Der Slik, *Reconsidering the Amendatory Veto in Illinois*, 8 N. ILL. U.L. REV. 753 (1988).

judicial review presuppose a judiciary that is "independent" in the sense guaranteed by Article III of the U.S. Constitution. Yet state judges are ordinarily elected and thus in a profoundly different power relationship with state legislative and executive officials. Stephen Croley, Rick Hills, and a handful of other scholars have undertaken to consider carefully the impact of the structure of state courts on the implementation of constitutional law at the state level.[29] The question is a very difficult one, as there remains much to learn about how exactly these electoral structures affect judicial elections and judicial decision making. Consider this bold conclusion from a leading legal theorist, Jeremy Waldron:

> Sometimes, however, when it is thought necessary to rebut the democratic case against judicial review, defenders of the practice will point proudly to states where judges are elected. This happens in some states in the U.S. But even where judges are elected, the business of the courts is not normally conducted, as the business of the legislature is, in accordance with an ethos of representation and accountability.[30]

On what basis can Professor Waldron make this claim? We might imagine, on the contrary, that judges believe themselves accountable to the people and, furthermore, as representatives of the public in some coherent sense. This may be true as a matter of decision-making ideology, or it may be a fact of life given the public's power over judges through the device of elections. Or we may believe with Waldron that judges conduct themselves differently in carrying out the "business of the courts." In any case, we lack a sound empirical foundation to draw anything other than the most preliminary conclusions about the motivations, incentives, and behavior of state court judges. Yet these conclusions are essential in understanding how judges participate in state constitutional governance.

Although the issues raised in the proceeding paragraphs are a good deal more complicated than the discussion here reveals, the main message I want to get across is that the structure of state power under state constitutions—a core component in state constitutionalism more generally—can be understood only when we have our minds wrapped securely around the institutions (details and all) that make up the processes of state governance. Neglecting these institutions leaves us without adequate information to make informed predictions and draw conclusions about or mount critiques of state constitutional law and politics.

B. From State Constitutionalism to State Constitutional Law

The power of judicial review can function in one or both of the ways described in Part II, that is, as a mechanism for correcting governmental errors and for

29. *E.g.*, Stephen P. Croley, *The Majoritarian Difficulty: Elective Judiciaries and the Rule of Law*, 62 U. Chi. L. Rev. 689 (1995).

30. Jeremy Waldron, *Core of the Case against Judicial Review*, 115 Yale L.J. 1346, 1363 (2006).

improving the processes of state governance. Although this is a rather abstract conception of the role of judicial review, the burden of the discussion in the several previous pages, and indeed of my analysis of state constitutional theory more generally,[31] has been to support the insight that the scope of judicial review must be yoked to the project of state constitutionalism. We are now ready to turn from state constitutionalism to state constitutional law.

State constitutional law is part of the furniture of state governance more generally. Courts ought to develop and, consistent with decision-making norms such as stare decisis and the like, apply doctrine to further the objective of active governance at the state level. The key theme here is balance. State courts are instrumental, in fact more so than their federal brethren, in assuring a balance between the very broad powers assigned to state government under the "document of limit" principle and the need to restrict appropriately the exercise of these powers to assure a proper sphere of individual liberty. Insofar as state constitutionalism negotiates between these two competing objectives and seeks to ensure a good balance, state courts ought to create a scope of review that adequately maintains this balance.

We move from these rather general observations toward the ground. Let us first disentangle the three competing approaches to the scope of review that I earlier labeled deferential, aggressive, and neutral. Taking either a deferential or an aggressive approach risks tilting the balance under state constitutionalism in one or another direction. This is a serious weakness in both approaches. For Justice Bell of the Florida Court, deference is warranted because it reinforces the active, powerful prerogatives of state legislatures and, correspondingly, protects the "popular sovereignty" underpinnings of state constitutionalism. Yet, this reinforcement is precisely the problem. Giving a Thayer/Hand-like deference to legislative judgments where the legislature is given an especially wide berth to govern furnishes an especially potent boost to an already-powerful institution. If it is error correction we are after, then the restricted power of the courts to scrutinize legislative actions that, consistent with state constitutional principles, will be far-reaching and intrusive will risk yielding more errors. And if we are interested in optimizing judicial review to improve the political process, deferential review leaves the functioning of the legislature more intact; that is, this approach defangs the judiciary in ways perhaps inconsistent with a state constitutionalism that counts on the courts to tinker usefully with the structures of governance. (On this last point especially, note that as state governance changes in important ways as a result of initiatives and other populist actions of the citizenry, we might

---

31. *See* Rodriguez, *supra* note 4; Daniel B. Rodriguez, *State Constitutionalism and the Domain of Normative Theory*, 37 San Diego L. Rev. 523 (2000); Daniel B. Rodriguez, *Turning Federalism Inside Out: Intrastate Aspects of Interstate Regulatory Federalism*, 14 Yale L. & Pol. Rev./Yale J. on Regulation 149 (1996); Daniel B. Rodriguez, *State Constitutionalism and Modern Governance: What is the Big Idea?* (manuscript, 2007).

be particularly reliant on state judges to manage the pace and strategy of these political experiments.)

Similarly, aggressive judicial review may tilt the balance in the opposite direction. The fundamental "document of limit" principle supports active lawmaking by the constitutionally authorized branches of government. Curtailing in a strong way the exercise of that power undermines this principle. Although we could imagine justifications in the context of particular state constitutions and exigencies for such a strategy of restricting state power—think, for instance, of a state whose legislature has become wholly captured by noxious private interests or so unprofessional as to be wholly incapable of wielding public power justly and efficiently on behalf of its citizens—we should be reluctant to embrace aggressive judicial review as a comprehensive solution.

Perhaps the dilemma of tilting the balance I have described is asymmetrical with regard to the choice between deferential and aggressive review. After all, can we say in earnest that state courts could, if they review state enactments aggressively, *overprotect* individual rights? Are not the consequences of deferring to broad legislative power potentially more deleterious than the consequences of securing individual rights from legislative encroachments? No, not really, for the following reasons. First, abuses of legislative power are, if not entirely self-correcting, subject to constraints other than judicial review by state courts. State legislators are subject, of course, to national constraints, whether set forth via national legislation, regulation, or the U.S. Constitution expressly. These tethers are significant and significantly different than those that limit the maneuvering room of members of Congress. Thus, while state legislative power is broad, the safety net of the national Constitution assuages some concerns about potential abuses of power. Second, and more interestingly for our purposes, we must remember from our discussion of positive rights that judicial review power is occasionally used to implement positive rights. This is not an unalloyed good by any measure. Many would regard New Jersey's long experiment with judicial management of housing policy as an expensive debacle. Similarly, judicial interventions under the rubric of state constitutions in the areas of education finance and prison reform have often yielded unintended consequences that have plagued state citizens and their pocketbooks for years. Aggressive judicial review that takes the form of broadening the scope and enforcement of positive rights, sometimes rights implied in the "penumbra" of the state constitution, have created a range of deleterious consequences. In light of these episodes and, some might suggest, the inherently problematic strategy of courts using positive rights analysis to recreate the contours of judicial policy making, the relative risks of deferential versus aggressive review are more symmetrical than we might first have thought.

Finally, aggressive judicial review limits political creativity in undesirable ways. Severe scrutiny of legislative enactments curtails legislative innovations; it undermines whatever values can be promoted through these so-called laboratories of experimentation. States can and ought to experiment with policy initiatives; the fact that states can learn from one another as they tackle similar problems means that the room for policy innovation is especially critical. Where such experimentation fails miserably and, indeed, where such efforts threaten core interests and citizens' rights, the federal government can and does intervene. Federal law, constitutional and otherwise, is a handy, ubiquitous backstop for state policy innovations. Aggressive judicial review may pretermit policy experimentation by stopping bold initiatives in their tracks. The consequences of judicially imposed limits on regulatory innovation may be quite bad.

The third approach to judicial review is what I previously labeled, perhaps somewhat colloquially, as "neutral." To put any concern immediately to rest, I well understand that no approach to review can truly be labeled neutral in the sense of utterly agnostic about process and outcomes. Of course, any approach to judicial review contemplates that certain doctrines will have both intended and unintended consequences. By "neutral," I just mean the absence of a thumb on the scale generally in favor or against judicial review. I mean judicial review that is not the result, as Justice Bell and some other judges would have it, of a particular conception of state constitutionalism. Neutrality is not an objective in and of itself; it has no special pedigree in constitutional analysis writ large; and it is subject to myriad familiar objections, the most compelling of which is that it appears to view courts as standing outside the political process and looking at judicial review from the vantage point only of what is good for the judiciary and what is proper behavior for judges in construing legislation. It is vastly more useful to view judicial review as a functional device—one instantiated, to be sure, in our constitutional tradition and beyond cavil a requisite of our written constitutions at the national and state levels—that aims to accomplish key objectives. I have reduced these objectives to only two, error correction and incentive creation, but I will gladly accept the much more complicated accounts of judicial review's purposes in the far-flung constitutional theory literature. The point remains that the practice of judicial review needs to track the constitutional project at issue. The U.S. Constitution has a distinct project, one forged through our nation's history, our structure of government at the federal level, the imperatives of citizenship in the United States, and other important considerations. The fifty constitutions of the American states have their own projects, some elements of which overlap with the project of the federal constitution and some of which are distinct. Turning state constitutionalism into state constitutional law requires attention to this distinct project. My preliminary assessment is that this project of state constitutionalism cannot support the case for either a very deferential or very aggressive scope of judicial review. Neutrality is not particularly appealing as a template for interpretation. What we need, and what this chapter merely points to, is a state constitutional law tethered more thoroughly to state constitutionalism.

V. CONCLUSION

Despite the much-vaunted nationalization of American political identity, states remain important loci of governance in the modern administrative state. Armed with the police power, a power unique to state government, states and their designated sub-state agents oversee vast swaths of individual and corporate behavior. The challenge for state constitutional theory is to create a framework—or perhaps better yet, a series of frameworks—for the creation and implementation of legal rules and strategies that facilitate governance at the subnational level while also maintaining mechanisms, in addition to those existing at the national level, for protecting freedom from governmental interference by state and local officials.

The particular subject of this chapter has been the connection between the scope of judicial review and the objectives of state constitutionalism viewed more broadly. I have considered, if rather speculatively, various approaches to this question that have been offered up by state judges grappling with these difficult questions. Left for the most part to another occasion, though, is what an optimizing judicial review might in fact look like. I end with a preview of coming attractions. Insofar as a properly designed state constitutional law is tied more deliberately to the project of state governance under state constitutions and their basic structure and principles, judicial interventions in whatever form they take will be and ought to be more avowedly political. That is, these interventions and these doctrines should exist "inside" the political process, certainly to an extent greater than that which we expect from federal judges intervening in disputes over the meaning of the federal Constitution. In short, state constitutional law is a conspicuously political process—one that is enveloped in the structures and objectives of political decision making, and rightly so. Whatever the value of this political role with regard to the federal judiciary in American constitutional law, the foundational theory of state constitutionalism points helpfully toward a positive political theory of judicial decision making and state constitutional law that is novel, distinctly state-focused, and efficacious.

6. SAME-SEX MARRIAGE AND THE NEW JUDICIAL FEDERALISM: WHY STATE COURTS SHOULD NOT CONSIDER OUT-OF-STATE BACKLASH

NEAL DEVINS

I. INTRODUCTION

Thirty years after Justice William Brennan's call for state courts to "step into the breach" left by the U.S. Supreme Court's supposed underenforcement of individual rights protections, the contours of the "new judicial federalism" remain a mystery.[1] There is, of course, the methodological question about whether state courts should rely on state-specific sources (the text and history of the state constitution) and, in so doing, develop a "coherent discourse of state constitutional law."[2] More fundamentally, does Brennan's call for a new judicial federalism have anything to do with federalism or is Brennan simply a "false prophet," asking states to pick up the slack for a recalcitrant Supreme Court and pursuing the Warren Court's nationalistic agenda of expanding civil and individual rights protections?[3] Under this view, it simply does not matter whether state courts employ a "coherent discourse of state constitutional law"; all that matters is that state courts expand rights protections.

In sorting out whether the "new federalism" has anything to do with federalism, traditionally understood, this chapter considers recent battles over same-sex marriage. In particular, I will examine whether state courts should consider out-of-state backlash when deciding cases. For example, when assessing whether to extend marriage protections to same-sex couples, should the Massachusetts Supreme Judicial Court have taken into account the possibility that its ruling would contribute to the electoral defeat of presidential candidate John Kerry or the enactment of state constitutional amendments banning same-sex marriage? If the "new federalism" is simply a rallying call for the nationalistic expansion of rights, such out-of-state effects should matter. But if the "new federalism" is about sovereign, independent states serving as "laboratories" where new legal

1. William J. Brennan, Jr., *State Constitutions and the Protection of Individual Rights*, 90 Harv. L. Rev. 489, 503 (1977).

2. James A. Gardner, *The Failed Discourse of State Constitutionalism*, 90 Mich. L. Rev. 761, 764 (1992).

3. Earl M. Maltz, *False Prophet—Justice Brennan and the Theory of State Constitutional Law*, 15 Hast. Const. L.Q. 429 (1988).

concepts can be tried out, there is simply no principled reason for state courts to take out-of-state resistance into account.

In the pages that follow, I will argue that the new judicial federalism should be something more than window dressing for an outcome-driven nationalistic agenda. For this very reason, I will defend the decision of the Massachusetts Supreme Judicial Court to protect same-sex marriage in *Goodridge v. Department of Public Health.* Unlike critics of the decision, I will argue that the Massachusetts court did not engage in judicial overreaching by failing to take into account out-of-state backlash. At the same time, I will explain why state courts should take into account in-state backlash when deciding cases. State courts cannot serve as laboratories in a new judicial federalism if their decisions are ignored or nullified. Likewise, state courts cannot pursue doctrinal innovations if judges fail to win reelection because they pursued politically unacceptable causes. In other words, just as the U.S. Supreme Court seeks to protect its turf and maximize its influence over the other branches, state supreme courts should take implementation concerns into account.

This chapter proceeds in two parts. First, I will explain why state courts should pay attention to in-state but not out-of-state backlash. I will discuss both the need for courts to pay attention to the practical consequences of their decisions and how that need should be channeled through the lens of the "new judicial federalism." Moreover, in arguing that state courts should not consider the extraterritorial effects of their decisions, I will draw a distinction between two types of out-of-state backlash. Although state courts should not consider the potential out-of-state backlash of their decisions, it is nevertheless sensible for state courts to look to the experiences of other states in assessing whether there will be an in-state backlash. State courts, in other words, are both independent (doing right by the citizens of their state without considering negative out-of-state effects) and part of a national system (recognizing that the experiences of other states are instructive in assessing what type of decision best serves in-state interests).

Second, I will apply the principles of the first part of the chapter to same-sex marriage, focusing my attention on four states that rejected state prohibitions against it: Hawaii (1993), Vermont (1999), Massachusetts (2003), and California (2008). By looking at the state political culture at the time of the decision, I will criticize the decision of the Hawaii Supreme Court, defend the decisions of the Massachusetts and Vermont courts, and offer a mixed assessment of the California Supreme Court. In Hawaii, the state supreme court went out of its way to push its views upon a reluctant legislature and hostile electorate. In sharp contrast, courts in Vermont and Massachusetts took steps to minimize conflict and, in so doing, staved off efforts to undermine these court decisions through legislation or constitutional amendments. Vermont and Massachusetts are instructive for another reason: because it is extremely difficult to amend the state constitutions in these two states, the decisions of these courts are largely insulated from potential voter backlash. In sharp contrast, many western states facilitate voter-driven constitutional initiatives. For this very reason, the California court—while having reason to believe that its decision would be acceptable to state political leaders and perhaps a majority of California voters—should have considered delaying its same-sex marriage ruling.

II. POSITIVE POLITICAL THEORY AND THE NEW JUDICIAL FEDERALISM

State court judges should care whether people would be outraged by their rulings.[4] In part, courts have no choice but to be consequentialist. Lacking the power of the purse and the sword, a judge's power "rests on the willingness of the public, and the political actors accountable to it, to respect his independence and the decrees of the court."[5] Beyond the practical necessity of taking potential backlash into account, the new judicial federalism offers a second account of why state courts ought to consider the consequences of their decisions. The new federalism is premised on the belief that constitutionalism is not a "single set of truths" but rather an ongoing national discourse about "ideas of liberty, equality, and due process."[6] Under this view, state courts learn from each other so that one state's experience informs the decision making of another state. State courts therefore should look to other states in assessing the effectiveness of competing decisional rules. In saying that state courts should pay attention to consequences, however, the new federalism draws a sharp line between a state court learning from another state's experience and its recalibrating a decisional rule for fear of out-of-state backlash. The new federalism, properly understood, treats state courts as independent entities—not simply part of a larger national discourse.

This section will spell out these two accounts of why state courts ought to be consequentialist. First, I will detail the institutional incentives for courts, especially state courts, to take backlash into account. Second, I will discuss the "new judicial federalism," focusing on the fundamental distinction between in- and out-of-state backlash.

A. Institutional Incentives

Supreme court justices (both state and federal) have "institutional preferences that may enhance or weaken the strength of [their] ideological preferences."[7]

---

4. This sentence plays off the title of Cass R. Sunstein, *If People Would Be Outraged by Their Rulings, Should Judges Care?*, 60 Stan. L. Rev. 155 (2007). Like Sunstein's article, this section will consider both normative and consequential arguments about the relevance of backlash. Unlike Sunstein, however, I will consider this question through the lens of the new judicial federalism—where states are at once independent and part of a national dialogue about the appropriate scope of rights protections. By contrast, Sunstein's analysis seems tied to a unitary court system and is therefore most useful in thinking about U.S. Supreme Court interpretations of federal law.

5. Barry Friedman, *The Politics of Judicial Review*, 84 Tex. L. Rev. 257 (2005).

6. Paul W. Kahn, *Interpretation and Authority in State Constitutionalism*, 106 Harv. L. Rev. 1147, 1147 (1993).

7. Barry Friedman, *Legislative Findings and Judicial Signals: A Positive Political Reading of* United States v. Lopez, 46 Case W. Res. L. Rev. 757, 783 (1996).

In particular, implementation concerns sometimes figure into court decisions. This is true for the U.S. Supreme Court (where life tenure and an extremely burdensome constitutional amendment process significantly reduce the risk of backlash). And it is especially true for state supreme courts (where, in many states, there is great risk of backlash because of judicial elections, interest group-driven initiatives, and the relative ease of amending state constitutions).

In understanding why courts *should* take backlash into account, consequentialists focus their attention on whether court rulings actually advance the goals intended by the court. A second reason why consequentialists should care about backlash is the larger interest of courts to maintain judicial power in our system of divided government. Each of these arguments has common sense appeal, and each argument is tied to one of the dominant models that political scientists use to explain Supreme Court decision making (external strategic actor and new institutionalism).[8] Embracing the teachings of the external strategic actor model, consequentialists argue that judges should be both goal-oriented and strategic so that "the preferences and likely actions of other relevant actors" shape the contours of judicial decision making.[9] Under this view, judges should be policy maximizers, advancing preferred outcomes without risking a counterproductive backlash. Second, by making use of the new intuitionalism, consequentialists argue that judges seek to preserve, if not strengthen, the court's institutional capital. Specifically, the new institutionalism emphasizes that the Supreme Court has institutional as well as policy-maximizing goals. Under this view, Supreme Court justices see the Court as an institution whose identity is defined by patterns of interaction with other parts of government. Accordingly, the Court cannot lose sight of its responsibilities to "maintain a distinctive and valued presence in the political system" by advancing some "vision of the special functions that [it] should perform."[10]

---

8. A third political science model, the attitudinalist model, claims that U.S. Supreme Court justices vote their policy preferences without fear of political backlash. *See* JEFFREY A. SEGAL & HAROLD J. SPAETH, THE SUPREME COURT AND THE ATTITUDINAL MODEL REVISITED (2002). Defenders of this model contend that the U.S. Supreme Court is largely insulated from political backlash; consequently, there is no reason for the justices to calibrate their decisions in anticipation of political backlash. Although generally correct, the attitudinalist model overstates matters. As the balance of this section will demonstrate, the attitudinalist model does not extend to state supreme courts—where fears of political reprisals are often substantial.

9. Lee Epstein et al., *The Political (Science) Context of Judging*, 47 ST. LOUIS L.J. 783, 800 (2003). For a more detailed explication of this model, see LEE EPSTEIN & JACK KNIGHT, THE CHOICES JUSTICES MAKE (1997).

10. Howard Gillman, *The Court as an Idea, Not a Building (or a Game): Interpretive Institutionalism and the Analysis of Supreme Court Decision-Making*, *in* SUPREME COURT DECISION-MAKING: NEW INSTITUTIONALIST APPROACHES 85 (Cornell W. Clayton & Howard Gillman, eds., 1999).

Examples of the U.S. Supreme Court taking social and political forces into account when deciding cases are legion. Numerous studies have empirically established that the Court shapes its "decisions and methods according to their perceived vulnerability to congressional override" and that it takes "cues regarding public and political interest and acceptability of outcomes from the public and organized interests."[11]

State courts likewise take into account potential opposition to their rulings. As one state supreme court justice put it: "There's no way a judge is going to be able to ignore the political consequences of certain decisions. . . . That would be like ignoring a crocodile in your bathtub."[12] In death penalty cases, empirical studies demonstrate that "politicization of the death issue has affected state court behavior."[13] More relevant to this chapter (and something I will discuss in greater detail in the next section), the Vermont Supreme Court made explicit reference to its fear of political reprisals in explaining why there was a state constitutional right to civil unions but not to same-sex marriage.

State courts are especially sensitive to possible in-state backlash for two reasons. First, state constitutions are much easier to amend than the federal constitution. Of more than 5,000 proposed amendments to the U.S. Constitution, only seventeen have been approved since the Bill of Rights and only three amendments explicitly overruled decisions of the U.S. Supreme Court. State constitutions, in contrast, have been amended more than 5,000 times.[14] From 1996–1997, for example, forty-two states considered 233 proposed constitutional amendments, approving 178 of them.[15] Second, state judges are often subject to direct democratic control. In the majority of states, justices are either elected or subject to retention votes. Empirical studies back up the common sense notion that judicial selection methods "significantly affect judicial policy in several important areas of the law."[16] Indeed, the success of interest groups in pushing for either

---

11. Tonja Jacobi, *Sharing the Love: The Political Power of Remedial Delay in Same-Sex Marriage Cases,* 15 LAW & SEXUALITY REV. 11, 28 (2006) (citing studies). *See also* NEAL DEVINS & LOUIS FISHER, THE DEMOCRATIC CONSTITUTION (2004); Frank B. Cross & Blake J. Nelson, *Strategic Institutional Effects on Supreme Court Decisionmaking,* 95 NW. U.L. REV. 1437 (2001).

12. This quote comes from California Supreme Court Justice Otto Kaus. It is favorably quoted by Washington Supreme Court Justice Robert F. Utter in *State Constitutional Law, The United States Supreme Court, and Democratic Accountability,* 64 WASH. L. REV. 19 (1989).

13. John Blume & Theodore Eisenberg, *Judicial Politics, Death Penalty Appeals, and Case Selection: An Empirical Study,* 72 S. CAL. L. REV. 465, 503 (1999).

14. John Kincaid, *State Constitutions in the Federal System,* 496 ANNALS 12, 14 (Mar. 1988).

15. Janice C. May, *Amending State Constitutions 1996–97,* 30 RUTGERS L.J. 1025 (1999).

16. DANIEL R. PINELLO, THE IMPACT OF JUDICIAL-SELECTION METHOD ON STATE-SUPREME-COURT POLICY 130 (1996).

the election or removal of state court judges has called into question the impartiality of state court decision making and, more generally, is considered a profound threat to the independence of state court systems.

Not only are state courts less insulated from popular reprisals than federal courts, state courts are far better positioned than federal courts to weigh the costs and benefits of potential backlash: "[S]tate judges are systematically exposed to and experienced in the legal institutions of their states;" "state judges spend their professional lives dealing with state legislation and administration regulation;" "[t]hey are much more likely than are their federal counterparts to know or be able to learn readily what is out there, how it came to be, and how well or badly it works."[17]

Of course, state court knowledge of in-state traditions does not extend beyond state boundaries. State judges know about their states and can make consequentialist judgments about the potential backlash of a decision there. But state judges do not know about the on-the-ground facts and legal traditions of other states, so they cannot be expected to make informed judgments about out-of-state backlash.

Another reason that state judges ought not to think about out-of-state backlash is tied to the new judicial federalism. Although part of a national discourse, state courts must retain their essential sovereignty—an issue that I will now address.

B. The New Judicial Federalism and Out-of-State Backlash

The new judicial federalism sees the states as critical players in the shaping of national constitutional values. Although there are as many iterations of this "new federalism" as there are law professors and judges who have written on this topic, proponents generally fall into one of two camps. The fault line here is whether a state court has some obligation to undertake an independent analysis of the state's constitution or, alternatively, may it "simply disagree with contemporary Supreme Court methods or doctrines in applying its state constitution without searching for special reasons in the state's text or traditions"?[18]

Without minimizing the importance of this question, let me suggest a paradigm shift so that the focus of the inquiry becomes the implementation of a state court's preferred doctrine. This question has received no attention in the literature, even though state courts have been criticized for not taking out-of-state backlash into account. Decisions by the Hawaii and Massachusetts Supreme Court on same-sex marriage have been savaged on these very grounds (principally by supporters of same-sex marriage) as "disastrous" and "provok[ing] the

17. Lawrence Gene Sager, *State Courts and the Strategic Space between the Norms and Rules of Constitutional Law*, 63 TEX. L. REV. 959, 976 (1985).

18. Hans A. Linde, *State Constitutions are Not Common Law*, 24 RUTGERS L.J. 927, 931 (1993).

biggest anti-gay backlash since the McCarthy era."[19] In the next section, I will discuss this backlash, but for now I want to focus on whether and when state courts should think about out-of-state implementation.

Federalism assumes that states have different laws and that state supreme courts speak authoritatively about the meaning of state law. Correspondingly, in determining whether to embrace one or another legal rule, state courts have unique responsibilities to their citizens rather than to the country as a whole. In particular, state courts ought not to limit the rights of their citizens in order to stave off a potential out-of-state backlash (assuming that out-of-state backlash does not boomerang into a federal constitutional amendment or federal law that undermines a state court ruling).

There is a second reason that state courts ought not to consider out-of-state backlash. For states to serve as laboratories in a nationwide conversation about constitutional values, states must experiment. In-state backlash is relevant to these experiments, but out-of-state backlash has no bearing on them. Specifically, state courts must preserve space in which they are allowed to experiment. In-state backlash undercuts judicial authority and may limit the types of experiments that states can pursue. Out-of-state backlash is quite another matter. Assuming no in-state boomerang effect, out-of-state backlash has no bearing on in-state experimentation.

At the same time, state courts can learn from the implementation experiences of other states. If interest groups (especially national interest groups) seek to oust judges or pursue constitutional reforms in one state, there is no reason to think those groups will not seek to countermand similar decision making in other states. And if these efforts either fail or are not pursued in the first instance, state courts may have reason to think that they have greater room for experimentation. Separate and apart from direct repeal efforts, state courts may see whether those subject to a court order follow it or, alternatively, resist the ruling by either dragging their feet or ignoring it altogether. If there is some type of nonaquiescence, it may make sense to pursue a different remedial strategy.

This, of course, is what the new judicial federalism is all about—state courts learning from each other and "contributing to the larger project of interpreting shared constitutional text."[20] Sometimes state courts will be pathbreakers, pursuing doctrinal innovations that may shape decision making in other states. At other times states will wait and see if other states' approaches point to a better way of interpreting state law. Whatever role a state chooses to play, out-of-state backlash ought not to limit state innovations.

---

19. Gerald N. Rosenberg, *Courting Disaster: Looking for Change in All the Wrong Places*, 54 Drake L. Rev. 795, 812 (2006); William N. Eskridge, Jr., Equality Practice 26 (2002).

20. Lawrence Friedman, *The Constitutional Values of Dialogue and the New Judicial Federalism*, 28 Hast. Const. L.Q. 93, 137 (2000).

One final observation before turning to the same-sex marriage case study: state judges are engaged in two distinct, interrelated constitutional dialogues. To the extent that state courts pay attention to what has happened in other states and make doctrinal moves that inform the judgments of other state courts, the new judicial federalism has a nationalistic cast. Most advocates of the new federalism emphasize this side of things, talking broadly about the "values placed in a constitution" and about constitutionalism as "not a single set of truths, but an ongoing debate about the meaning of the rule of law in a democratic political order."[21] But states are not simply minions in some larger national enterprise. State courts also participate in an intrastate dialogue that includes state lawmakers and voters. They "need not apologize for undercutting national unity" if they validate the ways in which states are different from one another.[22]

III. THE NEW JUDICIAL FEDERALISM AND SAME-SEX MARRIAGE

Academic and popular commentary about state court efforts to extend marriage or civil union rights to same-sex couples has largely focused on out-of-state backlash. In particular, the Hawaii and Massachusetts supreme courts have been sharply criticized for triggering a host of anti-gay legislative enactments and constitutional amendments. These attacks have largely ignored the question of whether these courts operated within their state's social and political norms. In the pages that follow, I will address that very question.

My discussion will be organized chronologically, focusing on rulings by the supreme courts of Hawaii (1993), Vermont (1999), Massachusetts (2003), and California (2008). In so doing, I will call attention to the way state courts can learn from the experiences of other states while, at the same time, respecting essential state sovereignty by refusing to consider the extraterritorial effects of their decisions. This, as Section I details, is the core principle of the new federalism—a principle that allows states to be both independent and part of a national conversation. It is also a principle at odds with the nationalistic goals of Justice Brennan and other proponents of rights-expanding state court decision making. In particular, state courts may sometimes have good reasons (consistent with the new federalism) to expand in-state rights while simultaneously prompting an out-of-state backlash that frustrates the pursuit of a nationwide expansion of rights.

Bad Beginnings: Hawaii. The nationwide debate over same-sex marriage was triggered by *Baehr v. Lewin*,[23] a 1993 Hawaii Supreme Court decision that found

---

21. Kahn, *supra* note 6, at 1148; Robert A. Schapiro, *Identity and Interpretation in State Constitutional Law*, 84 VA. L. REV. 389, 442 (1998).

22. Linde, *supra* note 18, at 932.

23. 852 P.2d 44 (Haw. 1993).

Hawaii's prohibition of same-sex marriage to be gender discrimination. Rather than formally grant same-sex couples the right to marry, however, the court remanded the case to see if the state could demonstrate that its prohibition satisfied strict scrutiny review. Over the next five years (while the litigation worked its way back towards the Hawaii Supreme Court), Hawaii lawmakers struggled with the court's decision. On the one hand, the lawmakers reached out to gays and lesbians by enacting domestic partnership laws and, in so doing, established "the most sweeping protections ever offered to same-sex couples anywhere in the U.S."[24] On the other hand, demonstrating their commitment to traditional marriage, lawmakers both passed a law limiting marriage contracts to those between a man and woman and sent to state voters a constitutional amendment proposal that would grant the state legislature the power to outlaw same-sex marriage. In November, 1998, Hawaii voters approved that amendment by a 69 to 29 percent margin, thus mooting the *Baehr* litigation.[25]

Baehr did much more than set in motion an intrastate dialogue about same-sex marriage. After *Baehr*, "an issue that had been a curiosity became an apocalyptic sensation."[26] State lawmakers, fearing that lesbians and gays would travel to Hawaii to get married and then seek to have those marriages recognized at home, enacted legislation prohibiting recognition of same-sex marriages. Between 1995 and 2001, thirty-five states enacted nonrecognition laws.[27] For its part, Congress enacted and President Clinton signed the 1996 Defense of Marriage Act (DOMA).[28] DOMA, as the House Committee report put it, was a "response to a very particular development in the State of Hawaii."[29] Echoing the concerns of state nonrecognition laws, Congress declared that "permitting homosexual couples to marry in Hawaii threatens to have very real consequences both on federal law and on the laws (especially the marriage laws) of the various States."[30]

Baehr, it would seem, did more harm than good to the cause of same-sex marriage. Outside of Hawaii, the federal DOMA and state nonrecognition statutes were a huge setback for proponents of same-sex marriage. In Hawaii, the state constitutional amendment foreclosed court-ordered same-sex marriage; proponents of same-sex marriage would now have to convince state lawmakers to repeal existing bans on same-sex marriage. The question remains: did the

24. Martin Bowley, *Same-Sex Couples, Different Rules*, THE LAWYER, Sept. 16, 1997 at 13.

25. For a detailed discussion of the politics behind the Hawaii Marriage amendment, see David Orgon Coolidge, *The Hawaii Marriage Amendment: Its Origins, Meaning, and Fate*, 22 U. HAW. L. REV. 19 (2000).

26. ESKRIDGE, *supra* note 19, at 26.

27. Id. at 27–28.

28. Pub. L. No. 104–199, 110 Stat. 2419 (1996).

29. H.R. Rep. No. 104–664 at 2 (1996).

30. *Id.*

Hawaii Supreme Court have reason to think that its ruling would prompt a counterproductive in-state backlash and, if so, what should it have done?

To start, the Hawaii Supreme Court, by taking the lead on this issue, did not know that court-ordered same-sex marriage would prove to be a nationwide sensation. This issue was not on the national radar at the time of the decision; indeed, it was the uproar over *Baehr* that prompted Gallup to start polling on same-sex marriage in 1996. So what did the Hawaii Supreme Court know? It knew that there was nationwide hostility to President Clinton's efforts to significantly expand gay rights protections. At the very time that the Hawaii Supreme Court decided *Baehr*, lawmakers were crafting the "Don't Ask, Don't Tell" law that prevented open gays from serving in the military. The court also knew that social conservatives were paying close attention to the case. The Rutherford Institute, for example, filed an amicus brief urging the state court to reject same-sex marriage.[31] More significant, the court probably knew that Hawaii voters did not support same-sex marriage. A 1991 *Honolulu Star Bulletin* poll found that "only 34 percent [of Hawaii residents] think couples of the same sex should be allowed to marry and only 36 percent think such couples should be allowed to adopt children."[32] The court may also have known that national gay rights interest groups played no role in the filing of the lawsuit, worried that the case was coming too early.[33] And finally, the court knew that it was easy to amend the Hawaii Constitution—all that is needed to refer a constitutional amendment to a majority referendum vote is the support of a majority of lawmakers over two legislative sessions (or a two-thirds supermajority in one session).

All of these bits of information suggest that the Hawaii Supreme Court had reason to fear an in-state backlash to a decision supporting same-sex marriage. At the same time, the Hawaii Court was well aware of the "island's history of tolerance and the state's broad privacy law," that Hawaii was the first state to legalize abortion, and that close to half of Hawaii's marriages are interracial.[34] Put another way, the court knew that the people of Hawaii were more likely to accept same-sex marriage than the citizens of any other state.

Assuming that Hawaii's Supreme Court sincerely believed that same-sex marriages should be legal, the question becomes: why wait? The answer, I think, is that certain risks are not worth taking. First, by ruling that *all* same-sex classifications were subject to strict scrutiny review, the court created incentives for opponents of

---

31. Linda Hosek, *Group Says Gays Should Not Get OK to Marry*, Honolulu Star Bulletin, May 23, 1992 at A-3.

32. Linda Hosek, *Residents Draw the Line on Some Gay Rights*, Honolulu Star Bulletin, Apr. 24, 1991 at A-4.

33. Eskridge, *supra* note 19, at 16–17.

34. Linda Hosek, *Isles May Be First for Gay Marriage*, Honolulu Star Bulletin, Apr. 24, 1991 at A-1.; Sherry Jacobson, *Hawaii Debates Gay Marriage: States May Recognize Such Unions After Court Ruling*, Dallas Morning News, Sept. 17, 1993 at A-1.

same-sex marriage to harden their position and to look for ways either to argue that the same-sex prohibition satisfies strict review or to amend the Hawaii Constitution to forbid same-sex unions. Instead, the court should have looked for ways in which the state and Hawaiian people could have found a way to work within parameters set by the court. For example, the court could have signaled its willingness to consider domestic partner or civil union legislation. Hawaii lawmakers were open to such legislative outs; in the wake of *Baehr*, Hawaii lawmakers enacted sweeping domestic partnership legislation. Second, not only did the Hawaii court go too far, it went too fast. An intermediate state court had upheld the same-sex marriage prohibition. Rather than fill the breach immediately, the Hawaii Supreme Court could have declined to hear the case without expressing any opinion about the constitutionality of the marriage ban. That is precisely what the U.S. Supreme Court did in 1955 when, fearing a political backlash, it delayed ruling on a constitutional challenge to Virginia's anti-miscegenation law.[35]

Let me be clear: unlike other critics of the Hawaii Supreme Court (who point to the federal DOMA and nonrecognition statutes passed by states other than Hawaii), my criticism focuses on the state court's failure to think about in-state concerns. The Hawaii Court should have either refused to hear the appeal in this case or decided the case narrowly so as to limit backlash.

The Triumph of Minimalism: Vermont. Six years after the Hawaii court's misstep in *Baehr*, the Vermont Supreme Court took a fundamentally different approach to same-sex marriage in *Baker v State.*[36] Although finding that the Vermont Constitution guarantees same-sex couples "the common benefit, protection, and security that Vermont law provides opposite-sex married couples," the Vermont court refused to extend marriage protections to same-sex couples. The court instead ruled that Vermont's existing statute should remain in effect "for a reasonable period of time to enable the Legislature to consider and enact implementing legislation in an orderly and expeditious fashion."[37] By remanding the case to the state legislature, Vermont opened the door for state lawmakers to determine if they wanted to legalize same-sex marriage or, alternatively, enact civil union legislation that would provide "marriage protections to same-sex couples."

In explaining its refusal to extend marriage rights to same-sex couples, the court spoke openly about its fear of a counterproductive in-state backlash. Expressing its desire both to issue a remedy that would endure and to provide "[greater] protections for same-sex relationships than have been recognized by" any state supreme court other than Hawaii, the court concluded that it would be too politically risky to order the state to grant marriage licenses to same-sex couples. Indeed, the court chastised a concurring opinion that called for the

35. For a defense of the Court's decision, see ALEXANDER BICKEL, THE LEAST DANGEROUS BRANCH 174 (1962).

36. 744 A.2d 864 (Vt. 1999).

37. *Id.* at 886.

outright recognition of same-sex marriage as "significantly insulated from reality."[38]

For reasons I will soon detail, it is far from clear whether Vermonters would have repudiated a state supreme court decision ordering same-sex marriage. At the same time, the Vermont court's political calculation was eminently sensible. To start, the *Baker* decision took place against the backdrop of Hawaii's repudiation of same-sex marriage in *Baehr*. More than that, Alaska lawmakers and voters preempted an ongoing challenge to Alaska's marriage laws by approving a constitutional amendment barring same-sex marriage.[39] Specifically, in the immediate wake of a February 1998 trial court ruling that same-sex couples had a fundamental right to marry, Alaska lawmakers (in March 1998) put a constitutional amendment proposal on the November ballot. That proposal was approved by a lopsided 68 to 32 percent vote.

The Hawaii and Alaska experiences are relevant for another reason. The Alaska and Hawaii constitutional amendment fights were financed, in part, by out-of-state interest groups. The national movement to enact the federal DOMA and state non-enforcement statutes was also propelled by national interest groups. Throughout the 1990s, moreover, social conservatives had pushed (with great success) state-wide initiatives limiting gay rights in at least a dozen states. So when the Vermont Supreme Court received seventeen amicus briefs from national interest groups, it had reason to know that a decision validating same-sex marriage would trigger an intense political battle over whether Vermonters, like Hawaiians and Alaskans, should approve a state constitutional amendment banning same-sex marriage. And if that were not enough, a poll taken shortly before the release of the *Baker* decision revealed that Vermonters, by a 56 to 33 percent margin, supported a constitutional amendment proposal to "keep Vermont's definition of marriage as the union of one man and one woman."[40]

Against this backdrop, there is little doubt that judicial validation of same-sex marriage would have triggered a donnybrook. A constitutional amendment would have been introduced, and national interest groups would have invested significant time and resources in this constitutional amendment battle. At the same time, there is reason to think that a constitutional amendment proposal would have failed. National trends pointed to growing acceptance of gay rights.[41]

38. *Id.* at 888.

39. For a detailed treatment of the events leading up to the Alaska constitutional amendment, see Kevin G. Clarkson et al., *The Alaska Marriage Amendment: The People's Choice on the Last Frontier*, 16 ALASKA L. REV. 213 (1999).

40. *Take it to the People, Press Release, Support for Traditional Marriage Remains Strong in Vermont*, Dec. 16, 1999.

41. By 1999, the social conservative campaign against gay rights had slowed. A 1996 Supreme Court decision, Romer v. Evans, 517 U.S. 620 (1996), cast doubt on the constitutionality of anti-gay initiatives. A 1998 Georgia Supreme Court decision nullified—on

In Vermont, the Coalition for Lesbian and Gay Rights had scored numerous legislative successes in the early 1990s—so much so that a public relations campaign for same-sex marriage was launched in 1994.[42] And although Vermonters opposed same-sex marriage, it was far from clear that state lawmakers would pursue a constitutional amendment banning it. Vermont's constitutional amendment process is "notoriously difficult. . . . Legislators can introduce amendments only once every four years. If approved, an amendment must pass in two consecutive two-year legislative sessions. Only then can people vote on the proposal."[43]

The fact that a constitutional amendment proposal might have failed, however, does not mean that the Vermont Supreme Court erred in *Baker*. Even assuming that the court backed same-sex marriage, it had good reason to minimize very real risks. By leaving it to the state legislature to sort out how best to remedy the state's illegal discrimination against same-sex couples, the "court, in effect, forced the legislature to join it in taking responsibility for fashioning and implementing a remedy."[44] In so doing, the court shifted the debate on same-sex marriage. Instead of fighting over a possible amendment to the state constitution, the focus of the Vermont legislature was whether to enact a civil union bill or legalize same-sex marriage.[45]

By leaving "breathing space for participants in the democratic process," *Baker* was able to build on "an extended legislative willingness to recognize and protect non-traditional families, while at the same time declining to disturb the yet-to-be-repudiated view of traditional families."[46] A decision demanding marriage rights for same-sex couples would have run against the grain of Vermont traditions and facilitated adversarial politics. More to the point, *Baker* exemplifies what the new federalism should and should not be. The Vermont Supreme Court

---

state constitutional grounds—the anti-sodomy statute that the Supreme Court had upheld in Bowers v Hardwick. *See* Powell v. State, 510 S.E. 2d 18 (Ga. 1998). Public opinion polls, moreover, reveal ever-growing support of gay rights, especially among younger voters. See Jack Egan et al., *Gay Rights, in* PUBLIC OPINION AND CONSTITUTIONAL CONTROVERSY 234 (Nathaniel Persily et al., eds., 2008). There was thus less intense opposition to same-sex marriage in 1999 than there had been in 1993 (when the Hawaii Supreme Court decided *Baehr*).

42. Greg Johnson, *Vermont Civil Unions: The New Language of Marriage*, 25 VT. L. REV. 15, 25–30 (2000).

43. David Orgon Coolidge & William C. Duncan, *Beyond* Baker: *The Case for a Vermont Marriage Amendment*, 25 VT. L. REV. 61, 68 (2000).

44. Tonja Jacobi, *Same Sex Marriage in Vermont: Implications of Legislative Remand for the Judiciary's Role*, 26 VT. L. REV. 381, 403 (2002).

45. *See* William N. Eskridge, *Liberal Reflections on the Jurisprudence of Civil Unions*, 64 ALB. L. REV. 853, 870–76 (2001).

46. Gil Kujovich, *An Essay on the Passive Virtue of* Baker v. State, 25 VT. L. REV. 93, 109 (2000). *See also* Johnson, *supra* note 42.

looked to out-of-state experiences to inform its judgment about in-state concerns. And although the court may have succeeded in establishing a right to same-sex marriage, it minimized the risks of backlash while setting in motion a process of incremental reform. State lawmakers could embrace the broader right, but, if not, the court could return to the issue of same-sex marriage. That option was not available to the Hawaii Supreme Court, whose unilateralism prompted a constitutional amendment forbidding such court-ordered reform.

The Massachusetts Gamble: Judicial Hubris or the New Judicial Federalism at Work?[47] In November 2003, the Massachusetts Supreme Judicial Court ruled in *Goodridge v. Department of Public Health*[48] that the state ban on same-sex marriage was unconstitutional. Finding that the state either had to allow same-sex couples the right to marry or eliminate civil marriage altogether, the court gave state lawmakers 180 days to "take such action as it may deem appropriate in light of this opinion."[49] In February 2004, acting on a request from state lawmakers to clarify this ruling, the court said that only full and equal marriage rights for same-sex couples—not proposed civil union legislation—would satisfy the court's ruling. Three months later, Massachusetts became the first state to allow same-sex marriage.

Reaction to the Massachusetts decision was intense. Inside Massachusetts, Governor Mitt Romney pushed for a constitutional amendment to overturn the ruling. And although lawmakers did not approve an amendment, a constitutional convention was convened in February 2004, and a proposed ban on same-sex marriage passed through a first-stage vote in March 2004. After same-sex couples began marrying in May 2004, however, public opposition to same-sex marriage began to wane.[50] Indeed, state voters rewarded opponents of the proposed constitutional ban in the November 2004 election cycle: all opponents of the ban won reelection, some proponents of the ban lost reelection, and opponents of the ban won six of eight open seats.[51] By March 2005, support for same-sex marriage

47. In writing about Massachusetts, I have benefited greatly from the work of Tonja Jacobi, whose published work is cited in this section. I also benefited from a student paper I supervised in the spring 2007 semester (before Professor Jacobi's published her *Goodridge*-related scholarship). That paper was written by Matthew Koldziej, a 2007 graduate of George Washington Law School. Although I suggested the paper topic to Mr. Koldziej, my interest in writing this chapter was nonetheless spurred on by Mr. Koldziej's outstanding paper.

48. 798 N.E. 2d 941 (Mass. 2003).

49. *Id.* at 970.

50. Tonja Jacobi, *How Massachusetts Got Gay Marriage: The Intersection of Public Opinion, Legislative Action, and Judicial Power*, 15 J. CONTEMP. LEGAL ISSUES 219, 221 (2006).

51. Tonja Jacobi, *Sharing the Love: The Political Power of Remedial Delay in Same-Sex Marriage Cases*, 15 LAW & SEXUALITY REV. 11, 39–41 (2006).

among Massachusetts residents had increased to 56 percent.[52] In September 2005, lawmakers rejected a proposed constitutional ban of same-sex marriage by a vote of 157 to 39.[53] With an increasingly supportive legislature and citizenry, the campaign to ban same-sex marriage floundered. In November 2006, lawmakers refused to vote on a citizen-proposed ballot initiative. In July 2008, lawmakers repealed a state law prohibiting the issuance of marriage licenses to couples who could not marry in their home state, paving the way for same-sex couples from other states to marry in Massachusetts.

Outside of Massachusetts, *Goodridge* proved to be a lightning rod. On the one hand, the decision was part of a mix of factors that in the spring and summer of 2004 prompted city and county officials to grant marriage licenses to same-sex couples in San Francisco, California; Portland, Oregon; New Paltz, New York; and elsewhere.[54] And while state courts uniformly rejected these local initiatives as unauthorized usurpations of state law, *Goodridge* undoubtedly contributed to the willingness of gay rights interests to push for same-sex marriage. On the other hand, the collective impact of these local initiatives and *Goodridge* was to energize opponents of same-sex marriage. In an effort to appeal to their social conservative base, Republicans in Congress sought both to amend the Constitution to prohibit same-sex marriage and to enact legislation stripping the federal courts of jurisdiction in same-sex marriage cases. Although Congress did not act on either proposal, there is little question that social conservatives saw same-sex marriage as a wedge issue in the November 2004 elections. Most telling, thirteen states approved constitutional amendment proposals forbidding same-sex marriage.[55] Moreover, conservative Christians helped propel the candidacies of George W. Bush and other Republicans. In Ohio, for example, "political analysts credited the ballot measure with spurring Republican voter turnout in the socially conservative western and southern portions of the state."[56] Same-sex marriage also worked to the advantage of Republicans in U.S. Senate races, providing the margin of victory in Kentucky and South Dakota.[57]

Goodridge has been roundly criticized for prompting a national backlash against gay rights interests. Indeed, criticism of the case has almost exclusively focused on this question. The issue of in-state backlash has received, at best,

---

52. Scott S. Greenberger, *One Year Later, Nation Divided on Gay Marriage*, Bost. Globe, May 15, 2005.

53. Pam Belluck, *Massachusetts Rejects Bill to Eliminate Gay Marriage*, N.Y. Times, Sept 15, 2005 at A-14.

54. For a discussion of how these initiatives (and other related matters) shaped public attitudes towards gay rights during this time, see Egan et al., *supra* note 41.

55. *See* Michael J. Klarman, Brown *and* Lawrence (*and* Goodridge), 104 Mich. L. Rev. 431 (2005).

56. James Dao, *Same-Sex Marriage Issue Key to Some G.O.P. Race*, N.Y. Times, Nov. 4, 2004 at A-4.

57. *See* Klarman *supra* note 55, at 468–70.

scant attention. This is truly unfortunate. State courts, as explained earlier, ought not to sacrifice their essential sovereignty by taking out-of-state backlash into account and thereby limiting rights protections for their citizens. What then of potential in-state backlash at the time of *Goodridge*? That is something that the Massachusetts court should have taken into account. For reasons I will now detail, the Supreme Judicial Court had good reason to think that a decision granting marriage rights to same-sex couples would withstand in-state resistance. Furthermore, by delaying its remedial order in the case, the court successfully minimized in-state backlash.[58]

To start, the Supreme Judicial Court undoubtedly knew that its decision would prompt an outcry in Massachusetts and throughout the nation, including efforts to amend the Massachusetts Constitution. In anticipation of *Goodridge*, an initiative amendment to ban same-sex marriage was proposed in the Massachusetts legislature in the summer of 2002. Although this measure was not acted on, lawmakers promised to seek a constitutional ban on same-sex marriage if the Supreme Judicial Court found a right to same-sex marriage in *Goodridge*. The Supreme Judicial Court also knew that these efforts would be backed by many of the "[h]undreds of [interest] groups" that had signed amicus briefs in the case, including "Catholic, Protestant fundamentalist and Orthodox Jewish groups."[59]

The volatility of the same-sex marriage issue was also fueled by two June 2003 developments: Canada's granting of marital rights to same-sex couples and the U.S. Supreme Court ruling in *Lawrence v. Texas* that anti-sodomy statutes were unconstitutional.[60] *Lawrence* is especially relevant, for Justice Scalia's dissenting opinion claimed that the Court's decision paved the way for a federal constitutional right to same-sex marriage.[61] *Lawrence* fueled public repudiations of same-sex marriage by the Southern Baptist Conference and U.S. Catholic bishops.[62] It also resulted in same-sex marriage becoming *the* defining issue for social conservatives, including the Family Research Council and Focus on the Family. These groups spoke about the need "for the American people" to "rise up and defend this indispensable institution" because "the homosexual activist movement . . . is poised to administer a devastating . . . blow to the traditional family."[63]

---

58. For a detailed treatment of this issue, *see* Jacobi, *supra* note 50.

59. Kathleen Burge, *SJC Puts Off a Decision on Gay Marriage*, Bost. Globe, July 15, 2003 at A-1; Kathleen Burge, *SJC to Weigh Arguments on Gay Marriage*, Bost. Globe, Mar. 2, 2003 at A-1.

60. *See* Egan et al., *supra* note 41.

61. *See* Esther Kaplan, *The Religious Right's Sense of Siege is Fueling a Resurgence*, Nation, July 5, 2004 at 33.

62. *See* Klarman, *supra* note 55, at 460.

63. Mary Leonard, *Gay Marriage Stirs Conservatives Again*, Bost. Globe, Sept. 28, 2003 at A-1; Christopher Marquis, *U.S. Gays Who Marry in Canada Face Hurdles*, N.Y. Times, June 19, 2003 at A-8.

Finally, *Lawrence* contributed to an increase in public opposition to same-sex marriage at the very time that the Massachusetts court was set to decide *Goodridge*.

The Massachusetts court was well aware of all this. Just weeks after the U.S. Supreme Court decided *Lawrence*, the Massachusetts court announced that it would delay its decision in *Goodridge*. Three months earlier (when hearing oral arguments in *Goodridge*), justices on the Massachusetts court likewise signaled their sensitivity to the interplay between the court, the Massachusetts legislature, and the public. In particular, the justices quizzed both sides on the appropriateness of the court resolving the same-sex marriage issue and the related possibility that Massachusetts voters (through a constitutional amendment) or legislators (through civil union legislation) might be able to resolve this issue.[64] By the time the justices decided *Goodridge*, they almost certainly knew that lawmakers supported civil union legislation but not the constitutionalization of same-sex marriage.

Why then did the Massachusetts court test the limits of its authority by establishing a right to same-sex marriage? The short answer is that the justices supported a right to same-sex marriage and thought that a decision establishing such a right would stick. To start, the Massachusetts Constitution is difficult to amend. Massachusetts is one of nineteen states that has had only one constitution, and among those states, it has the lowest amendment rate.[65] Amendments must be voted on in two successive legislative sessions before being submitted to the voters. This process is, by definition, time-consuming. It is intended to ensure that there is continuing public and lawmaker support for an amendment proposal. Against this backdrop, public opinion seemed to be on the side of *Goodridge*. Opinion polls taken just before the decision revealed that Massachusetts residents supported same-sex marriage 50 to 44 percent. And although *Goodridge* might have influenced public opinion (by focusing both state and national attention on same-sex marriage), the justices had reason to think that the decision would not result in sustained support for a constitutional amendment banning same-sex marriage. In addition to somewhat favorable polling numbers at the time of the decision, public support for gay rights, including same-sex marriage, was on the rise. That trend was likely to continue as younger voters overwhelmingly supported gay rights, including same-sex marriage. More than that, the justices knew that their decision would take effect in May 2004—at least two years before a constitutional amendment proposal could make its way to voters. That would likely mitigate opposition to same-sex marriage; in particular, the burden of inertia would likely favor it. A constitutional amendment would ask voters to

---

64. *From Judges, Pointed Questions*, Bost. Globe, Mar. 5, 2003 at A-6.

65. Donald S. Lutz, *Towards a Theory of Constitutional Amendment* 248–49, *in* Responding to Imperfection (Sanford Levinson ed., 1995).

take away a preexisting right rather than (as was true in other states) back up existing state policy against same-sex marriage.[66]

The justices, moreover, took strategic steps to mitigate public and lawmaker opposition to their rulings. Rather than call for immediate implementation of court-ordered same-sex marriage, the Massachusetts court remanded the case to the legislature for 180 days. At the same time, by ruling on "basic premises of individual liberty and equality of the law," the court also made clear that same-sex couples had a constitutional right to marry (strongly suggesting that civil union legislation would likewise be unconstitutional).[67] This legislative remand suggests one of two things. First, it created an escape hatch so that the court could embrace civil union legislation if the in-state backlash against its decision were truly severe. Second, the court—albeit with a wink and a nod—returned the issue to the democratic branches to build public and lawmaker support for same-sex marriage. Not only did the court signal that the "legislature retains broad regulatory power over civil marriage," it sought to facilitate legislative support of same-sex unions (or at least diminish legislative opposition to same-sex marriage). For their part, Massachusetts lawmakers took up a civil union bill and asked the court if such a bill would satisfy *Goodridge*. Even though the Massachusetts court turned down this request, the stay succeeded in drawing lawmakers into the process and, in so doing, changing the baseline about same-sex unions away from legislative opposition and toward some form of legislative acceptance.[68]

For a court interested both in advancing its vision of constitutional truth and maximizing its power, *Goodridge* is a masterstroke. The court had good reason to think its decision would not be overturned by a constitutional amendment; the court facilitated public and legislative acceptance of its decision by delaying the effective date of the remedy and remanding the case to the state legislature; and the court created a remedial delay that allowed it the opportunity to back away from its ruling if there were severe public and legislative opposition. Also, as justices on the Massachusetts Supreme Judicial Court are not subject to recall election, there was no risk of the decision limiting their ability to stay on the court.

California: A Calculated Risk that Backfired. On May 15, 2008, the California Supreme Court overturned the state's ban on same-sex marriage.[69] At that time,

---

66. It is also possible that public awareness of same-sex couples who marry might mitigate opposition to same-sex marriage. This would be especially true if there were favorable newspaper and television coverage about the same-sex couples who choose to marry. As it turns out, opposition to same-sex marriage did wane after same-sex couples began to marry. *See* Jacobi *supra* note 51.

67. Goodridge v. Dept. of Public Health, 798 N.E.2d 941, 958 (Mass. 2003).

68. For a more detailed presentation of this idea, see Jacobi, *supra* note 51, at 28–38.

69. *In re* Marriage Cases, 43 Cal. 4th 757 (2008).

the justices had good reason to think that their decision both matched prevailing social and political forces and was especially vulnerable to political attack. On the one hand, public opinion polls, the action of state lawmakers and Governor Schwarzenegger, and editorial commentary by the state's leading newspaper all suggested that California was ready to embrace gay marriage. On the other, anti-gay marriage groups had mobilized after the court agreed to decide the case so that California voters would have an opportunity to vote on a proposed constitutional amendment that would ban same-sex marriage. On November 4, 2008, California voters narrowly approved this amendment.[70]

Therefore, the California Supreme Court was simultaneously sensitive and tone deaf to the central lessons of this chapter. By granting certiorari to hear this case in December 2006, the California court paid insufficient attention both to the risks of in-state backlash and to the out-of-state backlash that followed *Goodridge*. When deciding the case, however, the court had good reason to strike down the state prohibition of same-sex marriage. At that time, the risks of in-state backlash, while substantial, did not warrant the court's retreat from its preferred position in the case.

When agreeing to rule on the constitutionality of same-sex marriage, the California Supreme Court was certainly aware of the backlash against same-sex marriage that followed *Goodridge* and the contemporaneous efforts of localities, most notably San Francisco, to recognize it. Indeed, the case was an appeal by San Francisco of a state appeals court ruling that nullified San Francisco mayor Gavin Newsom's efforts to grant marriage licenses to about 4,000 same-sex couples. More than that, the court knew that post-*Goodridge* efforts to constitutionalize same-sex marriage had failed. In 2006, two state supreme courts, Washington and New York, reaffirmed state prohibitions on same-sex marriage and a third state supreme court, New Jersey, concluded that the state must allow for civil unions but not same-sex marriage.

The California court also knew that well-funded Christian conservatives were poised to put an initiative against same-sex marriage on the 2008 ballot. With 2006 public opinion polls showing that Californians opposed same-sex marriage by a 50 to 44 percent margin, the court had good reason to fear that a decision legalizing same-sex marriage would be turned back by voters. In particular, the California Constitution is far easier to amend then most state constitutions. A constitutional amendment initiative is placed on the ballot after 8 percent of the total voters in the last gubernatorial race sign a petition calling for the amendment. And once on the ballot, a simple majority is sufficient to amend the Constitution. For this very reason, the California Constitution is routinely amended—so much so that at eight times the length of the U.S. Constitution, it

70. In May 2009, the California Supreme Court upheld Proposition 8 while simultaneously declaring it did not nullify same-sex marriages performed before its enactment.

has been labeled a "bloated mishmash" filled with "obfuscation, clutter and dysfunction."[71]

Put another way: California was no Massachusetts. Unlike the Massachusetts court, the California court could not escape the fact that its Constitution was especially vulnerable to amendment and that a decision backing same-sex marriage might well be turned back by California voters.[72] The California court, moreover, was well aware of on-the-ground facts that cut against its recognizing a right to same-sex marriage. Not only were opponents of same-sex marriage poised to launch an initiative drive, voters in thirteen states, responding to the efforts of the Massachusetts Supreme Judicial Court and Mayor Newsom, had in 2004 approved constitutional amendment initiatives outlawing same-sex marriage. And while the pendulum of public opinion was shifting in favor of same-sex unions, there was little reason for the California court to think that public opposition to same-sex marriage would turn into voter support for it during the window between December 2006 (when the court agreed to hear the case) and November 2008 (when California voters would almost certainly be asked to approve a constitutional ban on it).

Lessons from other states as well as in-state political realities suggest that the California court jumped the gun. The court should have held off on deciding this question for a few more years, when public support for same-sex marriage was likely to command clear majority support among California voters. In making this point, I do not mean to suggest that when granting certiorari in this case, the court should have known that a decision legalizing same-sex marriage was doomed to fail. Leading state newspapers supported same-sex marriage, state lawmakers approved a bill legalizing same-sex marriage in September 2005, and Governor Schwarzenegger's veto of that bill signaled that he too would support a court ruling backing same-sex marriage rights. In particular, the governor's veto message said that the power to negate California's law banning same-sex marriage (passed by a 2000 voter initiative) was reserved to state courts (which could declare the initiative unconstitutional) or "another vote of the people of our state."[73] Also, by December 2006, Massachusetts voters and lawmakers had rallied behind same-sex marriage, suggesting that the political landscape of 2004

71. Edward L. Lascher Jr. et al., *It's Too Easy to Amend the California Constitution*, L.A. Times, Feb. 4, 2009.

72. In drawing a comparison between the constitutional amendment process in California and Massachusetts, this discussion assumes that the nullification of state court decisions by voter initiatives is the very type of backlash that state courts should seek to avoid. With that said, a competing argument can be made—namely, that states with easy-to-amend constitutions should engage voters in constitutional dialogues by staking out positions that voters and lawmakers might not independently pursue.

73. Michael Finnegan & Maura Dolan, *Citing Prop. 22, Gov. Rejects Gay Marriage Bill*, L. A. Times, Sept. 8, 2005 at 1.

might give way to increasing public, elite, and lawmaker support. In other words, the California court may have taken a strategic gamble: thinking it could make history by riding the crest of a growing wave in support of same-sex marriage rights.

One final comment about the California Supreme Court's decision to hear the same-sex marriage case: in determining whether it should run risks in order to recognize a state constitutional right to same-sex marriage, the court may have considered two other variables. First, even if the court refused to hear this case, it is quite possible that opponents of same-sex marriage would have pushed for a ballot initiative amending the state constitution. Second, unlike Vermont, there was little to be gained by staking out a middle-ground position by establishing a right to civil unions. California's then-existing domestic partnership laws granted domestic partners most of the same rights and responsibilities as marriage under California law. These laws, moreover, were politically popular—a 2003 effort to repeal these laws through a state-wide initiative did not attract enough signatures even to make it to the ballot. For this reason, the same-sex marriage issue was largely symbolic.[74]

When the California court issued its decision in May 2008, elected officials, leading newspapers, and California voters supported same-sex marriage. A May 2008 Field Poll found that California registered voters supported same-sex marriage by a 51 to 42 percent margin.[75] For their part, state lawmakers reenacted a bill legalizing same-sex marriage in 2007. And although Governor Schwarzenegger vetoed that bill, the governor had also declared one month before the court's ruling that efforts to amend the state constitution to ban same-sex marriage were a "total waste of time" and that he would "fight against that." Mayors of California's three largest cities (Los Angeles, San Diego, and San Francisco) all backed same-sex marriage as did nearly all of the state's leading newspapers.

Against this backdrop, the California Supreme Court, having already spurred on a voter initiative by agreeing to decide the case, had no reason to back away from its preferred position on this issue. The fact that California voters rejected same-sex marriage does not undercut this conclusion; instead, the populist repudiation of same-sex marriage underscores the fact that states with easy-to-amend constitutions should be especially sensitive to the risks of in-state backlash. In other words, it was not enough that voters, the media, and the political establishment in California were more supportive of same-sex marriage than in other states. The California Court, when agreeing to decide the same-sex marriage issue,

---

74. When upholding Proposition 8, the California Supreme Court emphasized that Proposition 8 did not fundamentally change the legal rights of same-sex couples, which suggests the Court might have reached a different conclusion if Proposition 8 meaningfully curtailed fundamental rights. Strauss v. California, 46 Cal.4th 364 (2009).

75. Bill Ainsworth, *51 percent Support Same-Sex Marriage*, THE SAN DIEGO UNION-TRIBUNE, May 28, 2008 at A1.

should have paid more attention to the risks of in-state backlash—risks amplified by nationwide resistance to same-sex marriage after *Goodridge*.

IV. CONCLUSION

State courts can and should participate in a nationwide conversation about constitutional values. State courts must also operate as independent sovereigns and, consequently, cannot consider the extraterritorial effects of their decisions. This chapter has suggested that state courts can thread this needle by paying attention to the experiences of other states in sorting out whether their rulings may prompt a counterproductive in-state backlash. In this way, state courts simultaneously operate as independent sovereigns while participating in a nationalistic conversation about core constitutional values—values that transcend any one state.

The ongoing battle over same-sex marriage exemplifies the ways states can retain their sovereignty while simultaneously learning from the experiences of other states. The on-the-ground facts of same-sex marriage changed dramatically from 1993 to 2008. State courts should have paid attention to those changes, especially the intra- and interstate ramifications of other state court decisions. In so doing, state courts could have learned effectively to marshal resources and render decisions that would prove politically acceptable to voters and elected officials in their states. Needless to say, profound differences among state court systems allow some states to recognize rights claims that other states cannot. Most significant, states with easy-to-amend constitutions need to be especially sensitive to the risks of counterproductive populist attacks on their decision making.

State courts should pay attention to the ways in which they are both similar and different from each other and, in so doing, participate in a nationwide conversation about rights. For this very reason, state supreme courts should recognize that justice delayed may not be justice denied. By paying attention to in-state but not out-of-state backlash, state courts can respect their essential sovereignty while being a part of the new judicial federalism.

7. INTERJURISDICTIONAL ENFORCEMENT OF RIGHTS IN A POST-*ERIE* WORLD

ROBERT A. SCHAPIRO

I. INTRODUCTION

The United States may be the first modern federation, but federalism has since been widely copied elsewhere,[1] and no longer stands as a unique feature of the U.S. political structure. An aspect of U.S. federalism that remains distinctive, however, is its fully developed dual court system in which a national judiciary with trial and appellate courts coexists with state judiciaries having trial and appellate benches. Judges in the national courts are chosen by national bodies in accordance with national rules, while judges in state courts are chosen in accordance with each state's rules.

The existence of such parallel judicial structures is unusual among federalist nations. Most federalist systems rely on a single set of lower courts, commonly identified with the subnational units, to apply both national and subnational law. Australia, Canada, and Germany, for example, generally follow this alternative model.[2] In accordance with the Madisonian Compromise, the U.S. Constitution permitted that kind of arrangement in this country.[3] The Constitution contemplates the possibility of a system of lower state courts without lower federal courts. Congress, however, always has exercised its power to maintain a dual court system.

In view of the existence of parallel state and federal judicial tracks, the allocation of issues between state and federal courts becomes an important concern. The different structural features of state and federal courts in the United States magnifies the importance of the choice. The electoral accountability of most state but not federal judges may give the state and federal courts different perspectives, particularly on issues relating to hotly contested matters of public policy.[4]

---

1. Ronald L. Watts, Comparing Federal Systems 2, 3 (2d ed. 1999).

2. Ronald L. Watts, *Foreword: States, Provinces, Länder, and Cantons: International Variety among Subnational Constitutions*, 31 Rutgers L.J. 941, 955 (2000).

3. U.S. Const. art. III ("The judicial Power of the United States, shall be vested in one supreme Court, and in such inferior Courts as the Congress may from time to time ordain and establish.").

4. *See* Robert A. Schapiro, *Polyphonic Federalism: State Constitutions in the Federal Courts*, 87 Cal. L. Rev. 1409, 1453–54 (1999).

A dual court system creates the possibility of allocating cases based on the law at issue. Federal questions could be sent to federal court and state questions to state court, though of course cases raising both kinds of issues would pose allocational difficulties. Instead, in the United States, the jurisdictions of the state and federal courts overlap extensively. Issues of state law commonly arise in and are adjudicated by federal courts; issues of federal law commonly arise in and are adjudicated by state courts.

Such intersystemic adjudication, by which I mean the interpretation by a court of one political system of laws of another political system, occurs in all federalist polities. Indeed, the absence of dual judiciaries necessitates the practice. If all lower courts are subnational courts, much application of federal law will take place outside national courts. Judicial federalism entails some degree of intersystemic adjudication. The existence of a dual judicial system with largely overlapping jurisdiction, however, gives a distinctive cast to intersystemic adjudication in the United States. The same issue may arise in state and in federal court, and litigants have the ability to choose their preferred forum.

This chapter seeks to situate intersystemic adjudication within the larger framework of federalism in the United States. Federalism today is characterized by a sharing of state and federal power rather than by a rigid division between state and federal authority. Dual federalism, the idea that the states and the national government each enjoy independent and largely autonomous spheres of authority, has given way to other visions of federalism that contemplate a greater sharing of authority.[5] Elsewhere, I have developed the concept of "polyphonic federalism" to describe the appropriate understanding of federalism in the contemporary United States.[6] Polyphonic federalism understands the state and federal governments to be sources of power that are distinctive, but not mutually exclusive. State and federal governments serve as alternative mechanisms for accomplishing ends that legitimately lie within the prerogative of either system. Although conceptions of federalism have changed over time, its basic goals have remained stable. One of the key purposes of federalism is to offer enhanced protection for individual rights.[7] This chapter explores how intersystemic adjudication provides a way for state and federal courts to work together to safeguard important liberties.

Many scholars of federal jurisdiction treat intersystemic adjudication as a necessary evil. The verbal formulas vary somewhat, but these scholars express a

---

5. For a classic discussion of the decline of dual federalism, see Edward S. Corwin, *The Passing of Dual Federalism*, 36 VA. L. REV. 1 (1950).

6. *See* Schapiro, *supra* note 4; ROBERT A. SCHAPIRO, POLYPHONIC FEDERALISM: TOWARD THE PROTECTION OF FUNDAMENTAL RIGHTS (2009).

7. DAVID SHAPIRO, FEDERALISM: A DIALOGUE 36 (1995); Barry Friedman, *Valuing Federalism*, 82 MINN. L. REV. 317, 402–05; Andrzej Rapaczynski, *From Sovereignty to Process: The Jurisprudence of Federalism after* Garcia, 1985 SUP. CT. REV. 341, 380–89.

preference for the courts of a particular legal system interpreting the law of that jurisdiction.[8] Contrary to that general critical backdrop, this chapter offers a limited defense of intersystemic adjudication. Specifically, I make two primary arguments in support of intersystemic adjudication. First, I contend that intersystemic adjudication sometimes proves beneficial to the enforcement of rights—not always, but sometimes. Second, I defend intersystemic adjudication as a legitimate exercise of judicial power in our constitutional system. The arguments are related, but distinct. A judicial practice may fail the test of legitimacy, but still offer pragmatic advantages to the defense of rights. Such practices may be difficult to sustain once their illegitimacy becomes patent, but they can persist for a long time in a latency phase. This chapter argues that intersystemic adjudication can be both beneficial and legitimate.

The distinction between the law and its judicial interpretation figures prominently in my argument. Courts certainly make law. Nevertheless, a difference remains between the view that courts make law and the view that the law is only what the courts say it is. Attacks on intersystemic adjudication often conflate these two propositions. In practical terms, this debate focuses on the status of the ruling of the authoritative judicial interpreter. Does it make sense to say that the highest judicial authority erred in its interpretation of the law? The appreciation of error constitutes an important component of the argument for intersystemic adjudication. A defense of intersystemic adjudication also must confront the interpretation of the seminal case of *Erie Railroad v. Tompkins*.[9] In one reading of *Erie*, the U.S. Supreme Court sought to cabin intersystemic adjudication to limit the creative abilities of federal court judges. *Erie*, I will argue, does stand as a defining moment in the history of federalism in the United States, but does not constitute a general critique of intersystemic adjudication.

To provide an understanding of the framework in which intersystemic adjudication operates, Part II sketches the key characteristics of federalism in the United States and examines its distinctive dual judicial system. Part III explores the role of intersystemic adjudication within that framework. Drawing on conceptions of federalism, Part IV explores the benefits of intersystemic adjudication and assesses the potential disadvantages. Part V defends the legitimacy of intersystemic adjudication and acknowledges the tension between intersystemic adjudication and the spirit, if not the holding, of *Erie*. I argue, however, that *Erie* is best understood as unleashing state and federal governmental power so as to protect individuals. *Erie* heralds the development of cooperative judicial federalism; it does not represent the last gasps of dual federalism. This interpretation of *Erie* fully accords with the exercise of intersystemic adjudication. Part VI concludes by providing some more general thoughts about the role of intersystemic

---

8. *See, e.g.*, Barry Friedman, *Under the Law of Federal Jurisdiction: Allocating Cases between Federal and State Courts*, 104 COLUM. L. REV. 1211, 1236 (2004).

9. 304 U.S. 64 (1938).

adjudication as a second-best tool for enforcing rights in a system characterized by imperfection.

II. FEDERALISM AS POLYPHONY

To understand the role of intersystemic adjudication in protecting rights, it is necessary to situate the practice within the scheme of federalism in the United States. The interaction of state and federal governments constitutes a core element of contemporary federalism. Intersystemic adjudication is an application of that interactive model to the characteristic issues of judicial federalism in the United States.

A. From Dual Federalism to Cooperative Federalism to Interactive Federalism

Federalism in the United States is entering a third phase. Dual federalism provided the dominant conception of federal-state interaction into the twentieth century. In this model, sometimes termed dual sovereignty, the states and the national government exercised authority over distinct and mutually exclusive realms.[10] Federal power began where state authority ended, and the U.S. Supreme Court enforced a firm border between the two.

The First and Second World Wars, along with the Great Depression, transformed federalism. Driven by the perceived need for concerted action to address a variety of national problems, the federal government expanded its authority over social and economic matters. After initial resistance, the U.S. Supreme Court eventually blessed the enlarged view of federal power.[11] Scholars have dubbed the succeeding era a time of "cooperative federalism" in which the states and the federal government worked together to solve problems. State and federal authority no longer corresponded strictly to particular areas of regulatory activity. The states and the national government served as partners without rigid lines of demarcation. In the paradigmatic instance of cooperative federalism, the federal government designed regulatory goals and the states implemented regulations in accordance with the overall federal plan.[12]

---

10. Robert Post, *Federalism in the Taft Court Era: Can it be "Revived"?*, 51 Duke L.J. 1513, 1526–27 (2002).

11. *See, e.g.*, NLRB v. Jones & Laughlin Steel Corp., 301 U.S. 1 (1937); Wickard v. Filburn, 317 U.S. 111 (1942); United States v. Darby, 312 U.S. 100 (1941).

12. Roderick M. Hills, Jr., *Federalism in Constitutional Context*, 22 Harv. J.L. & Pub. Pol'y 181, 190 (1998); Philip J. Weiser, *Towards a Constitutional Architecture for Cooperative Federalism*, 79 N.C. L. Rev. 663, 665 (2001); Philip J. Weiser, *Federal Common Law, Cooperative Federalism, and the Enforcement of the Telecom Act*, 76 N.Y.U. L. Rev. 1692, 1697–1703 (2001).

Some have declared the end of the era of cooperative federalism.[13] Others have merely called for its demise.[14] Commentators have expressed concern that cooperative federalism lacks the competitive dynamic that can stand as an important feature of federalism. Along these lines, scholars have emphasized the importance of meaningful decentralized decision making rather than simple implementation of centrally decreed plans.[15] No one forecasts a return to dual federalism. The new phase of federalism, though, may present more occasions for competition and even confrontation among the states and between the states and the national government. The key principle shared among the somewhat divergent understandings of contemporary federalism is that the goals of federalism are best achieved not through the quixotic attempt to separate state and federal spheres, but through embracing the interaction of state and federal governments. Intersystemic adjudication can play a vital role in implementing this conception of interactive federalism.

B. A Federalism of Shared Values

Another important component of contemporary federalism stems from the relative homogeneity of values in the United States today. Dual federalism accepted the possibility that states might reach radically different conclusions about fundamental social issues. It addressed this potential by erecting barriers between state and federal domains, and then protecting each state from interference with its policy choices. Polyphonic federalism corresponds to a more cohesive understanding about fundamental values—an assumption of basic consensus on the outlines of human rights. Variations among regions, as well as within states, undoubtedly exist. Nevertheless, people in the United States agree on a shared core of values.

Greater communication and transportation among states has reduced cultural distinctiveness. Like The Gap and Starbucks, an appreciation of basic human rights seems ubiquitous. The second half of the twentieth century witnessed the effort to declare universal human rights throughout the world.[16] If the world can profess acceptance of certain core principles, it seems likely that the people in the United States could reach a similar consensus. Further, the U.S. Supreme Court has established a uniform floor of rights that must be protected in each state. Each state has its own constitution with its own understanding of fundamental rights. The specific contours of the rights may differ among states,

---

13. John Kincaid, *From Cooperative to Coercive Federalism*, 509 Annals Am. Acad. Pol. & Soc. Sci. 139, 150 (1990).

14. *See* Michael S. Greve, *Against Cooperative Federalism*, 70 Miss. L.J. 557, 559 (2000).

15. Michael C. Dorf & Charles F. Sabel, *A Constitution of Democratic Experimentalism*, 98 Colum. L. Rev. 267, 314–326 (1998).

16. Universal Declaration of Human Rights, G.A. Res. 217, U.N. GAOR, 3d Sess., U.N. Doc. A/810 (1948).

and state and federal constitutions may enshrine somewhat different formulations. Nevertheless, the rulings of the U.S. Supreme Court on issues of fundamental rights have been extremely influential in the development of state constitutional standards, and state constitutional decisions have figured in those rulings.[17]

This state-federal dialogue reflects a general convergence of views on fundamental principles of individual rights. Given that broad consensus, federalism is best understood as ensuring the existence of dual modes of realizing largely shared goals. The means may be state or federal; the ends are not.

III. INTERSYSTEMIC ADJUDICATION IN THE UNITED STATES

The dual judicial system of the United States makes intersystemic adjudication a significant feature of legal interpretation. A comparative perspective provides a valuable starting point. Federalism has become a common form of political organization in the world.[18] The United States, however, is quite unusual in maintaining a fully developed dual court system. Much more common is a single set of lower courts, generally identified with the subnational units, which hear cases raising issues of national or subnational law.[19]

A. Dual and Unitary Systems of Judicial Federalism

The U.S. Constitution did not mandate a dual court system, but Congress quickly implemented its authority to create lower federal courts.[20] Members of Congress apparently felt it prudent to establish trial courts to further the purposes of the Article III grants of federal jurisdiction, including uniformity in admiralty law, the enforcement of federal law and the collections of federal revenue, and the provision of more impartial tribunals for disputes between different states and their citizens.[21] Ensuring the enforcement of national law represents an important concern in federal systems generally. Rather than setting up a dual court system, other countries have addressed this problem by alternate methods such

17. *See* James A. Gardner, *State Constitutional Rights as Resistance to National Power: Toward a Functional Theory of State Constitutions*, 91 GEO. L.J. 1003, 1037–43 (2003).

18. DANIEL J. ELAZAR, FEDERAL SYSTEMS OF THE WORLD: A HANDBOOK OF FEDERAL, CONFEDERAL AND AUTONOMY ARRANGEMENTS xi–xv (2d ed. 1994).

19. Daniel J. Meador, *Transformation of the American Judiciary*, 46 ALA. L. REV. 763, 765 (1995).

20. ERWIN CHEMERINSKY, FEDERAL JURISDICTION § 1.2, at 9 (2003).

21. CHARLES ALAN WRIGHT & MARY KAY KANE, LAW OF FEDERAL COURTS § 1, § 23, at 3, 143–44 (2002); Henry J. Bourguignon, *The Federal Key to the Judiciary Act of 1789*, 46 S.C. L. REV. 647, 687 (1995).

as establishing some specialized federal courts, exercising control over the selection of provincial judges, or providing a right of appeal to a federal court.[22]

In light of the widespread current concern with ensuring the implementation of national law, it is instructive to recall that in 1789 Congress granted the lower federal courts in the United States jurisdiction over the enforcement of revenue laws and federal criminal laws, but not generally over cases arising under federal law.[23] An embrace of intersystemic adjudication thus dates from the birth of federal courts. Citizens from different states could bring their state-law disputes into federal court, and disputes involving issues of federal law would commonly begin in lower state courts.

The distinction between the dual judicial system of the United States and the more unitary judicial systems of other federalist nations becomes even more stark when viewed from the top of the judicial pyramid. The U.S. Supreme Court stands as the ultimate interpreter of federal law, reviewing issues of federal law that arise in lower federal courts or in state courts.[24] In exercising its appellate authority over state courts, however, the U.S. Supreme Court does not generally review questions of state law.[25] The highest court of each state is understood to render the authoritative interpretation of that state's law.

While the U.S. Supreme Court's treatment of state-law issues arising in state courts has been fairly consistent, the treatment of state-law issues arising in federal court has been a focus of substantial controversy. A fair summary would be that federal courts long have understood state courts to be the authoritative interpreters of state law. The main historical debate focused on what counted as state law. State constitutions, state statutes, and state laws governing local matters, such as property disputes, generally fell safely within the category of state law.[26] The highest state court served as the definitive interpreter of these matters. Federal courts were bound to follow these precedents. *Swift v. Tyson*[27] held that other matters of nonfederal law, especially in commercial areas, would be treated not as a species of local law, but as a kind of general common law. State courts did not serve as the definitive interpreters of this general, nonfederal law, and federal courts could reach an independent construction of these matters.[28]

---

22. K.C. (Kenneth) Wheare, Federal Government 66–68 (4th ed. 1964); Richard C. Risk, *The Puzzle of Jurisdiction*, 46 S.C. L. Rev. 703, 711–15 (1995).

23. Bourguignon, *supra* note 21, at 694.

24. Martin v. Hunter's Lessee, 14 U.S. (1 Wheat.) 304 (1816).

25. Murdock v. City of Memphis, 87 U.S. (20 Wall.) 590 (1875).

26. Green v. Neal's Lessee, 31 U.S. (6 Pet.) 291 (1832).

27. 41 U.S. (16 Pet.) 1 (1842).

28. Tony Freyer, Harmony & Dissonance: The *Swift* & *Erie* Cases in American Federalism 15–16 (1981).

In *Erie Railroad v. Tompkins*[29] the U.S. Supreme Court ended this trifurcated regime of federal law, general law, and state law. All nonfederal law became state law, subject to authoritative construction by the highest state court. For matters of state law, then, the U.S. Supreme Court is not supreme. Judicial interpretive supremacy rests with the highest court of each state.

In Australia and Canada, by contrast, a federal high court serves as the ultimate interpreter of both national and subnational law.[30] Commentators credit the existence of a single final interpreter with creating a greater sense of the unity of the law.[31] Statutory law does differ in the different states and territories, but the federal high court serves as a unifying force. The absence of parallel court systems decreases the possibility of interpretive divergence between state and federal tribunals, and the single high court structure diminishes the distinctions between the law in the various states.

B. Allocating Issues between Parallel Court Systems

Unlike these other models, the system of judicial federalism in the United States involves parallel state and federal interpretive tracks, and no single court exercises interpretive authority over both. This arrangement enhances the importance of the choice of forum, and the extensive areas of overlapping jurisdiction makes forum choice common. The state and federal paths lead to different destinations. Eventually, the authoritative interpreter—either the U.S. Supreme Court or the highest court in the state—will resolve contested issues, and that determination will enjoy binding authority in both systems. That definitive resolution, however, may be a long time in coming. Doctrines must determine in which of the independent available tracks the case will proceed.

For the most part, subject matter jurisdiction is a matter of legislative right, not judicial grace. A federal court cannot refuse to hear a properly filed state-law diversity case, nor may a state court close its doors to a federal question. Congress exercises its discretion in deciding how much of the constitutionally defined federal judicial power it will confer on the lower federal courts and how much concurrent jurisdiction will be permitted to the state courts. Once that decision is made, courts exercise their statutorily granted jurisdiction. Congress, not the courts, holds the keys to the federal courthouse, but to a large extent, Congress has lent those keys to the litigants. In matters in which state and federal courts enjoy concurrent jurisdiction, either litigant generally may opt for the

---

29. 304 U.S. 64 (1938).

30. *See* AUSTL. CONST. § 73; W.M.C. Gummow, *Full Faith and Credit in Three Federations*, 46 S. C. L. REV. 979, 989 (1995).

31. Herbert A. Johnson, *Introduction*, 46 S.C. L. REV. 641, 645 (1995); Brian R. Opeskin, *Federal Jurisdiction in Australian Courts: Policies and Prospects*, 46 S.C. L. REV. 765, 771 & n.28 (1995); L.J. Priestley, *A Federal Common Law in Australia?*, 46 S.C. L. REV. 1043, 1065–73 (1995).

federal forum.[32] The plaintiff may file in state or federal court, and the defendant may exercise the right to remove a case from state court to federal court. Judges must accept the cases properly brought before them.

Within the broad scope of federal jurisdiction, though, doctrines do exist to allow federal courts to have some say over the allocation of state and federal issues. Particularly intricate questions arise when a single case involves both state and federal elements. The resolution of a state-law question may serve as a necessary prerequisite to a federal claim. A plaintiff, for example, may assert that a state statute violates the federal Constitution. A federal court would have to decide the meaning of the challenged enactment before it could assess its constitutionality. Alternatively, a state-law claim for recovery might come within the supplemental jurisdiction of the federal court.[33] Under the current supplemental jurisdiction statute, as well as under prior judicially crafted rules, a plaintiff filing a federal claim in federal court may include any state-law claims that arise from the same transaction or occurrence as the federal claim. Supplemental jurisdiction allows for the efficient packaging of related claims and helps to preserve the availability of a federal forum for a federal claim. In the absence of supplemental jurisdiction, a plaintiff would face the choice of filing the state and federal claims together in state court or of splitting the claims between state and federal court. The claim-splitting alternative could be costly and could occasion preclusion obstacles as parallel issues were adjudicated in the two proceedings. Supplemental jurisdiction allows a federal forum for the federal claim without the hazards of parallel litigation.

IV. THE VALUES AND COUNTER-VALUES OF INTERSYSTEMIC ADJUDICATION

This part explores the potential advantages and disadvantages of intersystemic adjudication. To illustrate the principles involved, it focuses on federal court interpretation of state constitutions. I have chosen this example for several reasons. The analysis here builds on an earlier doctrinal study.[34] Further, federal court interpretation of state law presents the most contested instance of intersystemic adjudication, and federal court interpretation of state constitutions introduces yet another level of controversy. Courts understand state constitutions to enjoy an especially intimate connection to the state. Federal interpretation of the state charters thus may appear as the height of federal intrusion. To defend intersystemic adjudication in this context is to confront the most serious arguments against the interpretive practice.

---

32. 28 U.S.C. § 1441.
33. 28 U.S.C. § 1367.
34. *See* Schapiro, *supra* note 4.

A. Doctrinal Background of Dual Constitutional Claims

For cases raising claims under both the state and federal constitutions, the current jurisdictional rules give no clear guidance. Because of concerns for separation of powers and federalism, cases raising dual constitutional challenges implicate a complex thicket of doctrines. These doctrines reflect varying attempts to harmonize three sometimes conflicting principles: (1) courts should avoid federal constitutional rulings when possible (the "avoidance" principle); (2) state courts should be the primary interpreters of state law (the "local interpretation" principle); and (3) no barriers should impair the availability of a federal forum for federal claims (the "open door" principle). Complying with any two of the principles does not pose much problem. Following all three proves much more difficult.

Consider the first two principles. To honor the avoidance principle, federal courts should base their rulings on the state claim, not the federal constitutional issue. In accordance with the local interpretation principle, federal courts should not themselves adjudicate the state issue, but should instead seek the guidance of state courts. The doctrine of *Pullman* abstention allows the federal court to achieve these goals. *Pullman* abstention comes into play when novel or unsettled questions of state law arise in a federal constitutional case. In these circumstances, the federal court can require the claimant to file a suit in state court to seek clarification of state law. The federal suit remains in abeyance while the claimant proceeds with the state court litigation. After the state-law issue is clarified, the claimant can return to federal court for adjudication of any federal issues that remain. State certification statutes provide a speedier alternative to abstention. These provisions allow federal courts to refer state-law issues directly to state courts for resolution rather than forcing the claimant to initiate an independent lawsuit.[35]

Although *Pullman* abstention vindicates the avoidance and local interpretation principles, the open door policy does not fare as well. Routing dual constitutional challenges through state court delays the adjudication of the federal claim, thereby burdening access to the federal forum. Certification, when available, ameliorates but does not wholly obviate the problem of delay. The delay entailed in abstention or certification provides a powerful incentive for the plaintiff to submit state and federal claims to the state court for resolution.

Alternatively, under the doctrine developed in *Siler v. Louisville & Nashville R.R. Co.*,[36] federal courts could first adjudicate the supplemental state-law claims so as to avoid reaching, if possible, the federal constitutional issue. If the state-law ground disposes of the case, then the court has succeeded in resolving the

---

35. CHEMERINSKY, *supra* note 20, §§ 12.2–12.3, at 763–75, 789–91; Jonathan Remy Nash, *Examining the Power of Federal Courts to Certify Questions of State Law*, 88 CORNELL L. REV. 1672 (2003).

36. 213 U.S. 175 (1909).

dispute without the potential rigidity of federal constitutional adjudication. This procedure also avoids burdening access to the federal forum. The plaintiffs might or might not prevail on the state claim, but if unsuccessful, they could expect a simultaneous ruling on the federal claim, avoiding the delays of certification or abstention. This approach complies with the avoidance and open door principles but at the cost of violating the local interpretation principle. It is the federal court that is adjudicating the state claim.

Finally, the federal court could rule first on the federal constitutional claim. If that claim fails, the court could turn to the state claim, or it could even refuse to decide the state-law issue. Under the supplemental jurisdiction statute, as well as under previous case law, a court retains some discretion to dismiss supplemental claims. In the current statutory version, § 1367(c) lists potential grounds for dismissal, including that "the claim raises a novel or complex issue of State law."[37] If the federal claim raised a federal constitutional issue, dismissing the supplemental state claims would necessitate deciding, rather than avoiding, the federal constitutional issue. Beginning with the adjudication of the federal constitutional claim neither imposes a barrier to the federal forum nor transgresses the local interpretation principle. What suffers is the canon of avoiding federal constitutional adjudication.

The three principles evade easy harmonization. If one cannot satisfy all three, the question is which principles should take priority. With regard to the specific kind of state constitutional provisions on which this chapter focuses, provisions that mirror the federal Constitution but have not been interpreted to duplicate the federal version, current doctrine offers no definitive guidance.

B. Protecting Individual Rights through Intersystemic Adjudication

Having reviewed the doctrinal landscape, I turn to an evaluation of intersystemic adjudication. The "local interpretation" rule discussed above counsels against intersystemic adjudication. The following section takes issue with that principle. This section examines intersystemic adjudication by focusing on three overlapping values—plurality, dialogue, and redundancy—and on the corresponding set of counter-values that intersystemic adjudication may hinder: uniformity, finality, and hierarchical accountability. My argument is not that federal courts always should adjudicate state constitutional claims within their jurisdiction, but that federal courts sometimes should do so rather than adopt the avoidance techniques discussed above.

1. Plurality/Uniformity State individual rights guarantees may be subject to several interpretations. Federal court adjudication of state constitutional claims allows for additional exploration of their meanings. The federal court never will

---

37. 28 U.S.C. § 1367(c)(1). As I have discussed elsewhere, this ground appears to overlap with the bases for *Pullman* abstention. *See* Schapiro, *supra* note 4, at 1420.

provide the definitive interpretation of the state provision. The federal court interpretation may be helpful, however, in contributing to the discussion of the best way to realize the underlying constitutional value. Federal judges can contribute to a plurality of legal meaning, which provides a rich background for the investigation of fundamental rights.

Federal judges are rooted in a different institutional context from state judges. They are chosen by different means and enjoy tenure on different terms from state judges. Federal judges will thus be able to offer a perspective that differs from that of state judges. A useful dialogue may ensue between state and federal judges over the proper interpretation of a fundamental right. Immersion in state constitutional debates also may prove useful to federal judges in interpreting the federal Constitution. Examining state precedent may enrich a court's understanding of the sources and meaning of fundamental rights that exist in both state and federal documents.[38] State and federal courts can thus engage in a valuable dialogue over the meaning of state and federal constitutional guarantees.[39]

Plurality does come at a cost. Uniformity in interpretation also serves as an important value.[40] When a federal court interprets the state constitution, it creates the possibility of multiple meanings. The state constitution will have an interpretation in the federal system but may have a different one in the state system until the state supreme court resolves the conflict. This plurality could be unsettling and confusing. Parties may win or lose depending on the forum hearing the case. This kind of disparate result is the price of pluralism. Is the game worth the candle? Justice Sandra Day O'Connor commented on the similar problem that arises from diverse interpretations of federal law:

> While uniformity is a necessary and desirable goal, its immediate achievement is not always possible. Nor is immediate action necessarily desirable. Part of the beauty of our federalism is the diversity of viewpoint it brings to bear on legal problems. State court judges may have a different approach to a problem than might a federal judge. . . . Under our system, the 50 state supreme courts, 13 U.S. Circuit Courts of Appeals, and countless trial and intermediate appellate courts may bring diverse experiences to bear on questions that, because of the Supremacy Clause, they must answer in common.
>
> When those courts encounter an unresolved question of federal law, their differing perspectives may lead them to different conclusions. The resulting divergence provides a valuable moment in the law—a moment of dialogue

38. *See* Gardner, *supra* note 17, at 1037–43.

39. *See* Donald H. Zeigler, *Gazing into the Crystal Ball: Reflections on the Standards State Judges Should Use to Ascertain Federal Law*, 40 Wm. & Mary L. Rev. 1143, 1181 (1999).

40. *See, e.g.*, Evan H. Caminker, *Why Must Inferior Courts Obey Superior Court Precedents?*, 46 Stan. L. Rev. 817, 849–54 (1994).

> among different jurists in which they may share their views on a common issue. There can be no doubt that the dialogue is a profitable one or that the Court on which I sit listens to the voices in the debate. Indeed, it is not all that infrequent that the Supreme Court will, despite the existence of a conflict on an issue of federal law, decline to review a case so that other voices may be heard on the subject before the issue is resolved once and for all. The benefits of dialogue can, for at least a limited time, outweigh the immediate need for uniformity.[41]

In recognizing the benefit of interpretive plurality, I am assuming that state and federal constitutional rights share important features. When a state constitution and a federal constitution both talk about due process or equality, those meanings might be distinct; that is a premise of allowing the state provision to be interpreted independently of the federal.[42] The meanings, however, are not incommensurable. The state and federal charters invoke shared values. The contours of the specific rights may vary, but the ideals the provisions embody are sufficiently similar so that federal and state courts may engage in a profitable dialogue. The dual federalist premise of separating areas of state and federal regulation might suggest a fundamental divide about fundamental values. Dual federalism protected states from federal intrusion into such areas. In this framework, perhaps the states and the national government had little to share about safeguarding important liberties. The more one recognizes a move from dual federalism to cooperative or interactive federalism, the more likely that dialogue will be helpful.

2. Dialogue/Finality A related paired opposition that Justice O'Connor's comments invoke is that of finality and dialogue. Finality is a significant legal value. The law has an important settlement function. Sometimes it is more important that a matter be settled than that it be settled right. A federal court's interpretation of a state constitution will never carry that guarantee of final resolution. The same issue might arise in a different case in state court, and the federal court's interpretation of the state constitution will have no binding effect.

The flip side of lack of finality is the possibility of dialogue. What makes a conversation possible is the absence of a final authority. The federal courts can express their opinions on state constitutions and lower state courts can express their opinions. They can listen to and learn from each other. The state supreme court can learn from the dialogue until it decides to end the discussion by rendering an authoritative interpretation. The perils of finality are reflected in part in the doctrine of seeking to avoid federal constitutional adjudication. It is well

41. Sandra Day O'Connor, *Proceedings of the Middle Atlantic State-Federal Judicial Relationships Conference*, 162 F.R.D. 173, 181–82 (1994).

42. Robert A. Schapiro, *Identity and Interpretation in State Constitutional Law*, 84 Va. L. Rev. 389, 441–42 (1998).

established that courts will not rely on federal constitutional grounds if other grounds are available.[43]

It is useful to remember that the power of the state high court to give a definitive opinion does not mean that the court will necessarily give the best interpretation. Sometimes finality is more important than correctness, but that possibility recognizes the distinction between the last word and the best word. Justice Jackson's famous caution in *Brown v. Allen* seems apt here: "We are not final because we are infallible, but we are infallible only because we are final."[44] Justice Jackson referred to the U.S. Supreme Court, but the observation applies more generally to ultimate interpreters, be they state or federal high courts. When the necessarily fallible state high court does give the last word, it can benefit from other views on the topic.

3. Redundancy/Hierarchical Accountability To place the same opposition in a kind of organizational perspective, when federal courts interpret state law, hierarchical accountability will always be absent. On the organizational chart of the interpretation of state law, the state's highest court sits at the top. Its authority is ultimate. Federal courts stand outside this chain of command in the sense that no appeal lies from their decisions to the ultimate interpreters. Once the state supreme court speaks, the federal court must listen. With regard to the decision in the particular case at issue, however, the state court will never speak. From an organizational perspective, this arrangement frustrates authoritative interpretation.

The federal courts might incorrectly construe the state charter. Correction of such an error may take some time and will provide no relief to the parties in the first litigation. It is worth contemplating the possibility of error. Of course, the problem of error is pervasive. The state court or the federal court may misinterpret the state constitution. The comparison of these problems raises difficult questions. One concern is the qualitative characteristic of the error. For reasons of federalism, a federal court's misinterpreting the state constitution might be an error of a categorically greater magnitude than the state court's doing so. Scratching the paint on my neighbor's car may be more serious than putting a big dent in mine. This kind of categorical concern relates to the legitimacy of the overall enterprise of federal court interpretation of state law, a subject that I address below. Inherent in the process of interpretation is the possibility of error. If the enterprise of federal court interpretation of state constitutions is legitimate, then errors are no greater a threat here than in other forms of interpretation.

Is a federal court more likely than a state court to misinterpret the state constitution? Again, it is important to distinguish between deviation from what the

---

43. Ashwander v. Tennessee Valley Auth., 297 U.S. 288, 346–47 (1936) (Brandeis, J., concurring); Siler v. Louisville & Nashville R.R. Co., 213 U.S. 175, 193 (1909).

44. Brown v. Allen, 344 U.S. 443, 540 (1953) (Jackson, J., concurring in result).

state high court might eventually hold and incorrect interpretation. The more one understands federalism to protect distinctive state enclaves, the more federal court interpretation of state constitutions appears problematic. How can a federal court really understand the spirit of the state community? If one rejects this kind of romantic nationalist view of the state and thinks of a state constitution as more about achieving widely shared values, then the risk of error diminishes.

Moreover, this organizational structure enables a different organizational virtue: redundancy.[45] The existence of parallel, non-intersecting lines of authority means that a blockage or error in one will not affect the other. If one path for realizing state constitutional rights does not work, an alternative path exists. If for some reason, the lower state courts do not properly recognize a state constitutional right, resort may be had to the federal courts. This kind of redundancy is one of the chief results of the system of judicial federalism in the United States.

The different institutional structures of the state and federal courts may enhance the value of redundancy. State and federal courts differ in many ways. Extensive debates have focused on whether this organizational variation hinders state courts in the enforcement of fundamental rights. Evidence appears to support the conclusion that electoral pressures render state courts less sympathetic to specific kinds of individual rights claims.[46] Other scholars argue that state courts may be more receptive to certain kinds of arguments about individual rights.[47] From the perspective of redundancy, the key issue is that federal and state courts differ. Redundancy allows parties to enjoy the potential benefits of both.

V. LEGITIMACY OF INTERSYSTEMIC ADJUDICATION

So far, this chapter has explained some of the practical benefits of intersystemic adjudication in general and of federal courts interpreting state constitutions in particular. In addressing these topics, it is necessary to confront the argument that intersystemic adjudication runs counter to central organizing principles of

---

45. For discussions of the role of federalism in providing redundancy, see DANIEL J. ELAZAR, EXPLORING FEDERALISM 30 (1987); Erwin Chemerinsky, *Federalism Not as Limits, But as Empowerment*, 45 U. KAN. L. REV. 1219, 1234 (1997); Robert M. Cover, *The Uses of Jurisdictional Redundancy: Interest, Ideology, and Innovation*, 22 WM. & MARY L. REV. 639 (1981); Robert M. Cover & Alexander Aleinikoff, *Dialectical Federalism: Habeas Corpus and the Court*, 86 YALE L.J. 1042 (1977).

46. *See* Schapiro, *supra* note 4, at 1453–54.

47. *See, e.g.*, William B. Rubenstein, *The Myth of Superiority*, 16 CONST. COMMENT. 599, 622 (1999).

our constitutional system. Another way of posing the objection would be to say that the foregoing account details some of the strategic advantages that a federal forum may bring to certain parties, but that underlying postulates of the constitutional system in the United States undermine the legitimacy of these arguments.

A. Challenges: Spirit of *Erie*

The decision of the U.S. Supreme Court in *Erie* has served as a focus of scholarly resistance to intersystemic adjudication. *Erie* directly rejected one form of intersystemic adjudication that had arisen—federal courts independently interpreting state common law. More generally, commentators have found *Erie* to embody three principles that individually and in combination could be taken to oppose intersystemic adjudication: positivism, realism, and federalism.[48]

On one level, *Erie* held that in cases in which federal law did not supply a rule of decision, federal courts were bound to apply the common law as it would be applied by state courts. After *Erie*, federal courts could no longer apply general common law in preference to the common law of the particular state. The holding of *Erie* and its overruling of *Swift v. Tyson* do not directly relate to federal court interpretation of state constitutions. In all of the discussions of the role of federal courts in interpreting state constitutions, no one doubts that federal courts must follow the rulings of the highest court of the state. The state high court definitively interprets state law, including the state constitution, and the federal courts are bound to follow that construction. Indeed, even before *Erie*, federal courts were theoretically required to follow state courts' interpretations of positive enactments, such as state constitutions.[49] Only with regard to state common law did federal courts enjoy the prerogative of independent interpretation. In fact, federal courts sometimes did not defer to state court interpretations of the state constitution, but no one suggests a return to such infamous cases as *Gelpcke v. City of Dubuque*.[50]

What stands in the way of intersystemic adjudication is not *Erie*, but the larger jurisprudential commitments that *Erie* has been understood to embody. Critics of intersystemic adjudication rely in particular on certain versions of legal positivism

48. The relative significance of positivism, realism, and federalism for the *Erie* decision remains a subject of dispute. *See, e.g.*, Bradford R. Clark, *Ascertaining the Laws of the Several States: Positivism and Judicial Federalism after Erie*, 145 U. Pa. L. Rev. 1459, 1479–84 (1997); Michael C. Dorf, *Prediction and the Rule of Law*, 42 UCLA L. Rev. 651, 708 (1995); Jack Goldsmith & Steven Walt, Erie *and the Irrelevance of Legal Positivism*, 84 Va. L. Rev. 673 (1998); George Rutherglen, *Reconstructing* Erie: *A Comment on the Perils of Legal Positivism*, 10 Const. Comment. 285 (1993).

49. Green v. Neal's Lessee, 31 U.S. (6 Pet.) 291 (1832).

50. 68 U.S. (1 Wall.) 175 (1863); *see also* Township of Pine Grove v. Talcott, 86 U.S. 666, 677 (1873).

and legal realism that *Erie* arguably presupposes. The positivist theme is that all law must have a foundation in some identifiable authority. *Erie* identified as a central flaw in the pre-existing *Swift* system the existence of general common law that was in some sense neither state law nor federal law. After *Erie*, common law is either state or federal law and is authoritatively construed by state courts or by the U.S. Supreme Court, respectively.

The legal realist component of *Erie* recognized that judges make law as much as they "find" it. Accordingly, the law reflected in state court decisions is the law of the state as much as it is the product of the legislature. Both legislatures and courts make law, and it makes no sense for federal courts to distinguish between these different kinds of law when determining the content of nonfederal law.

The federalism theme emphasizes the corresponding point that while state courts are agents of the state government, federal courts are agents of the federal government.[51] For federal courts to impose their interpretation of common law principles in preference to state court interpretation represents the federal government invading the domain of the states. Federalism entails an allocation of authority between the state governments and the federal government. The *Swift* era practice of federal courts independently interpreting general common law constituted an intrusion by the federal government into an area properly belonging to the states.

Some scholars have combined these principles into an indictment of intersystemic adjudication. They argue that federal courts interpreting state law represents exactly the kind of federal intrusion into state affairs that *Erie* sought to end. Intersystemic adjudication in this view is equivalent to the federal government setting up mini-federal legislatures to create state law. Bradford Clark, for example, has stated that a federal court's interpreting state law is like the *Swift*-era practice of federal courts making general common law: "In either case, a federal court's practice of 'indulg[ing] in lawmaking by decisions' necessarily interferes with the sovereign prerogative of the states to decide both whether and how to regulate the conduct of the parties."[52] This argument would apply equally to state court interpretation of federal law. State courts interpreting federal law would be setting themselves up as mini-Congresses engaging in the illegitimate creation of federal law. What this parallel suggests is that the force of Clark's argument lies not in whether a court's rulings have a lawmaking effect, but rather in whether such lawmaking is authorized.

Of course, given the existence of both diversity and supplemental jurisdiction, scholars generally do not claim that federal courts should never interpret

51. Robert Post argues that before the New Deal transformation, the U.S. Supreme Court viewed itself as transcending the division of power between the states and the national government. *See* Post, *supra* note 10, at 1604.

52. Clark, *supra* note 48, at 1495 (footnote omitted), quoting Daily v. Parker, 152 F.2d 174, 177 (7th Cir. 1945).

state law. Some scholars do urge, though, that federal court interpretation of state law be minimized through devices such as abstention and certification.

B. Defense

This part defends the legitimacy of intersystemic adjudication. It agrees that *Erie* stands for a modern recognition of the insights of positivism and legal realism. It also agrees that *Erie* defines important issues of judicial federalism. I argue, however, that the critique previously developed misstates the implications of positivism, realism, and federalism.

1. Distinction between Law and Judicial Interpretation The key error of the critique of the legitimacy of intersystemic adjudication lies in its false attribution of exclusivity to the role of state courts. One can accept the realist insight that when state courts interpret state law, they in effect make law. One also can accept the positivist concern for locating the authority underlying law. The decisions of state courts are law because state courts are authorized by the lawmaking authority, the state, to make the law. In this sense, the state courts are lawmaking agents duly authorized by the states.

What about federal courts? In this realist/positivist sense, federal courts also are lawmaking agents, so authorized by the U.S. Constitution. But does that grant of lawmaking authority violate principles of federalism? Are not the federal courts usurping the authority of the state courts? Here it is important to remember the nonexclusive nature of a court's lawmaking authority. One need not equate state law with the declaration of a state court.

If one believes that the exclusive legitimate source of state lawmaking is a state court, then federal interpretation of state law is a kind of usurpation. If state law is whatever the state court says it is, then the federal courts are operating with a major legitimacy deficit. The federal courts would necessarily be derivative. State courts would be making the pure, essential state law, and federal courts would be attempting to determine its content through a glass darkly. Barry Friedman appears to take this position.[53] He criticizes an argument I had made that in certain circumstances, federal courts might render a "more impartial" reading of state law than would state courts. My argument referred to some of the fears of bias raised in the context of diversity litigation as well as to studies of political pressures experienced by state judges subject to electoral scrutiny. Professor Friedman responds, "It is difficult to know exactly what 'more impartial' means in this sentence. The only 'reading' of a state constitution that can be authoritative is that rendered by its highest court."[54] I take it that a "more impartial" reading is more likely to be correct than a "less impartial" (or more partial) reading. Professor Friedman does not deny the potential for a federal court to be

---

53. Friedman, *supra* note 8.
54. *Id.* at 1239 n.72.

more impartial, nor does he deny the link between impartiality and correctness. Instead, he asserts that only the highest state court can be "authoritative." But it is this equation of "authoritative" and "correct" that I seek to challenge.

The interpretation of state law rendered by the state's highest court must be followed by state and federal courts. Nevertheless, that interpretation may not be the best construction of the provision at issue. Fear of electoral repercussions, for example, might shape a state court's interpretation of the law. The opinion of a federal court interpreting the same item might provide a useful perspective, perhaps compensating for the perceived unpopularity of following a particular course. Potential bias does not make a decision less authoritative; it just makes it less likely to be correct. Federal courts also are subject to political pressures and have no monopoly on interpretive skill. The different perspective of the federal court, though, might assist the state court in its search for the best interpretation.

If instead of equating state law with the opinion of the state court, one takes the slightly more modest position that state courts participate in the creation of state law, then there is nothing necessarily illegitimate about federal courts also participating in the process. This argument applies to state common law but applies with even more force to state constitutional law.

In interpreting the state constitution, it seems much more apt to say that a state court participates in the making of the law than to say that the state constitution is nothing more than what the state court says it is. The literature on constitutional interpretation outside the courts is large and growing. The main thrust of this scholarship, which has focused on the federal Constitution, is that one need not understand courts to be the exclusive interpreters of the federal Constitution. Other governmental officials interpret the Constitution as well.[55] A great deal of what the U.S. president does is interpret the Constitution. It keeps the Office of Legal Counsel busy. A great deal of what Congress should do is to interpret the Constitution. In the federal constitutional context, the main debate is about supremacy. Should the U.S. Supreme Court be supreme in the interpretation of the federal constitution? In the state court/federal court context, supremacy is not at issue. With regard to the state constitution, the state high court is supreme, at least with respect to federal courts.

---

55. All state and federal officials take an oath to uphold the Constitution, which seems to imply some duty in addition to obeying a judicial order in a particular case. U.S. CONST. art. VI, cl. 3. For a discussion of each branch's duty to interpret the Constitution, see Frank H. Easterbrook, *Presidential Review*, 40 CASE W. RES. L. REV. 905 (1990); Michael Stokes Paulsen, *Protestantism and Comparative Competence: A Reply to Professors Levinson and Eisgruber*, 83 GEO. L.J. 385 (1994); Michael Stokes Paulsen, *The Most Dangerous Branch: Executive Power to Say What the Law Is*, 83 GEO. L.J. 217 (1994); David S. Strauss, *Presidential Interpretation of the Constitution*, 15 CARDOZO L. REV. 113 (1993).

The debate about exclusivity recognizes conceptual space between the constitution and what the court says it means. It is not conceptually incoherent to say that the U.S. Supreme Court misinterpreted the Constitution. In the case of state constitutions, plural interpretation seems an even greater practical necessity. Given the long, complex nature of state constitutions and the many activities of state government, state constitutional issues arise with great frequency. The interpretation of state attorneys general and other state officials will in many areas determine the meaning of the state constitution with practical finality. Given the necessarily plural nature of state constitutional interpretation, a federal role does little to diminish the goals of finality and uniformity.

Thus I reject the view that the decision of the state court, as reviewed through the state appellate system, actually defines the contour of the state constitutional right. In this view, it is paradoxical to speak of state courts underprotecting the rights of individuals, for it is the courts that establish the breadth of the right. Disparity between the state and federal courts necessarily evidences error by the federal tribunal.

Once one recognizes that the state high court does not enjoy the exclusive authority to interpret the state constitution, the role of the federal court comes into focus. Federal intervention can contribute to an understanding of the meaning of the state constitution. The federal court is not an outsider, an interloper. Rather, federalism gives to the federal court the ability to speak about the state constitution as well as, under current understandings, the obligation to follow the state supreme court once that interpretation has been established.

In sum, *Erie* clarified that the state high court was the supreme interpreter of state law. This result followed from particular understandings of federalism, probably buttressed by jurisprudential commitments to realism and positivism. Positivism meant that all law was state law or federal law. General common law was therefore really state law. Realism reinforced that conclusion. If common law was state law, then the state high court enjoyed the right of authoritative interpretation. However, neither *Erie* nor a broader notion of the spirit of *Erie* made the state supreme court the exclusive interpreter of state law. So when a federal court interprets a state constitution, it does not usurp state authority. As with other instances of polyphonic federalism, the federal and state courts can participate together in the protection of fundamental rights.

2. *Erie* and the New Deal This understanding of *Erie* and of the kind of judicial federalism implied by *Erie* finds support in the larger federal context of 1938, when *Erie* was decided. *Erie* stands as part of the moment that witnessed the end of dual federalism. During this period, the Supreme Court recognized the difficulty in distinguishing categorically between national and local affairs, and largely stopped trying to do so.[56] Decisions from this period such as *Darby*[57] and *Wickard*[58] unleashed the federal government to pursue a wide variety of aims that might at one point have been understood to be within the exclusive province of the states. *West Coast Hotel*[59] allowed the state and federal governments to pursue social welfare aims that previously had been denied them.

Some of the social goals were being advanced by state courts through the course of common law progression. Using their power to declare general common law, the federal courts sometimes had impeded these state-law developments. *Erie* was an effort to prevent the federal courts from interfering with the social policy being developed by the state courts. *Erie* then is really about empowering states and state courts.

Erie raises as well the issue of the appropriate separation of the state and federal court systems. The decision certainly responded to a perception of excessive federal court meddling in matters appropriately decided by state courts. The grounds of complaint, though, related not to federal courts adjudicating state-law issues, but to the nondeferential manner with which federal courts treated state court precedents. *Erie* need not stand for the necessity of rigidly separating the appropriate domains of state and federal courts. *Erie* came at a time when dual federalism was being rejected in favor of more cooperative models. *Erie* need not be understood as enforcing a regime of dual judicial federalism. With the decline of dual federalism, the state and federal governments exercised overlapping regulatory authority. Intersystemic adjudication represents an overlap of judicial authority. Just as state and federal governments may take up cooperative, competitive, or even conflictual relationships, so may state and federal courts. *Erie* did not mandate the end of such judicial interaction.

VI. RIGHTS AND REMEDIES IN AN IMPERFECT WORLD

My goal in this chapter has been to defend intersystemic adjudication in a particularly controversial setting. Intersystemic adjudication can be a valuable way to pursue a variety of goals. Certainly intersystemic adjudication contravenes important values in the legal system. Uniformity, finality, and hierarchical accountability all represent significant principles, and intersystemic adjudication undermines all of them to some extent. As against these losses, intersystemic adjudication promotes the values of plurality, redundancy, and dialogue. These principles are important as well.

---

56. Edward A. Purcell, Jr., Brandeis and the Progressive Constitution 134–36 (2000); Corwin, *supra* note 5, at 17.

57. United States v. Darby, 312 U.S. 100 (1941).

58. Wickard v. Filburn, 317 U.S. 111 (1942).

59. West Coast Hotel Co. v. Parrish, 300 U.S. 379 (1937).

The relative weight of these two sets of significant values depends on the relevant conception of federalism. Both sets remain important, but their relative value rises or falls in accordance with one's understanding of the relationship among the states and the federal government. One could adopt a dualist perspective, viewing federalism as concerned primarily with dividing power into separate spheres. Alternatively, one could understand federalism as promoting interaction among political or judicial systems that recognize largely shared goals. In this latter framework, plurality, dialogue, and redundancy would serve especially valuable roles. This interactive or polyphonic conception of federalism aligns with the benefits that intersystemic adjudication promotes.

One's view of intersystemic adjudication may reflect as well one's assessment of relative risks. If one fears that a strict division of authority may lead to error, a sharing may reduce the peril. As between "two heads are better than one" and "too many cooks spoil the broth," two heads may well seem less risky. This assessment may turn on one's appreciation of the risk of governmental error. To the extent that state or federal governments fail in their role of protecting vital liberties, the availability of a backup power becomes critical. An interactive understanding of federalism and an acceptance of intersystemic adjudication facilitates this fail-safe option.

In several settings, intersystemic adjudication may provide for remedies that are unavailable within a unitary framework. This analysis has focused on federal court adjudication of state constitutional claims, but the implications are broader. Not only may federal courts participate in the enforcement of state rights, but state courts may participate in the enforcement of federal rights. By way of illustration, I will touch briefly on two situations in which state courts can fill remedial gaps in the application of federal law. Both sovereign immunity and federal justiciability requirements present instances in which intersystemic adjudication can realize the role of federalism in protecting rights.

Federal statutes provide extensive protection for individual rights against threats from private parties or from states. Doctrines of sovereign immunity, however, may impair the full enforcement of these rights against states. As a matter of federal constitutional law, individuals generally may not seek monetary redress from states for the violation of their federal rights.[60] Decisions of the U.S. Supreme Court have created a right without a remedy, at least on the federal level.

Federalism has a response: state courts may enforce the federal right against states. Federal law may not be able to require states to provide such remedies, but state constitutions can. Indeed, in some situations, state "right to remedy"

60. Seminole Tribe of Florida v. Florida, 517 U.S. 44 (1996); Alden v. Maine, 527 U.S. 706 (1999).

clauses may mandate such enforcement.[61] State constitutional principles of sovereign immunity may bar such actions, but remedial principles available in state court provide at least the possibility of a remedy for the violation of federal rights. Many have argued that the U.S. Supreme Court erred in interpreting the federal constitution to confer such immunity on states.[62] Whatever the merits of these critiques, the more general point is that error is part of any system. Through intersystemic adjudication, federalism in the United States provides a powerful way to address such errors.

Federal justiciability rules provide another example of a remedial gap. In certain areas, the U.S. Supreme Court has adopted restrictive understandings of the standing doctrine. The Court has held that the U.S. Constitution limits the ability of Congress to confer standing on plaintiffs for the enforcement of federal rights.[63] These restrictions impair the enforcement of federal statutes, particularly in the environmental context in which the harms targeted by the statute may be diffuse. Situations may arise in which Congress clearly has the authority to provide environmental protections, but cannot guarantee the enforcement of the rules.

Intersystemic adjudication again provides an answer. Plaintiffs may bring the federal claims in state courts, which need not follow federal justiciability requirements. State courts can provide the remedial structure unavailable in federal court. When state courts hear federal claims that could not be brought in federal court, complicated jurisdictional issues may arise. The state courts' interpretations of federal law may not be reviewable in the U.S. Supreme Court. For this reason, some commentators have urged that state courts be forced to apply federal justiciability rules to federal causes of action.[64] Of course federal courts' interpretations of state law are never subject to direct review by that law's ultimate interpretive body.

Unreviewable state court interpretations of federal law may impair principles of finality and uniformity in the law. For these reasons, Congress might choose

---

61. Lauren K. Robel, *Sovereignty and Democracy: The States' Obligations to Their Citizens under Federal Statutory Law*, 78 IND. L.J. 543, 544 (2003).

62. Critical analyses of the Court's sovereign immunity jurisprudence include Akhil Reed Amar, *Of Sovereignty and Federalism*, 96 YALE L.J. 1425 (1987); William A. Fletcher, *The Diversity Explanation of the Eleventh Amendment: A Reply to Critics*, 56 U. CHI. L. REV. 1261 (1989); William A. Fletcher, *A Historical Interpretation of the Eleventh Amendment: A Narrow Construction of an Affirmative Grant of Jurisdiction Rather than a Prohibition Against Jurisdiction*, 35 STAN. L. REV. 1033 (1983); Vicki C. Jackson, *The Supreme Court, the Eleventh Amendment, and State Sovereign Immunity*, 98 YALE L.J. 1, 40, 45 (1988); Vicki C. Jackson, *Seminole Tribe, the Eleventh Amendment, and the Potential Evisceration of* Ex Parte Young, 72 N.Y.U. L. REV. 495 (1997).

63. *See, e.g.*, Lujan v. Defenders of Wildlife, 504 U.S. 555 (1992).

64. William A. Fletcher, *The "Case or Controversy" Requirement in State Court Adjudication of Federal Questions*, 78 CAL. L. REV. 263, 283 (1990).

to give federal courts exclusive jurisdiction in certain cases. Instead, though, Congress may wish to take advantage of the plurality, dialogue, and redundancy offered by state court enforcement of federal law. Congress might prefer that the U.S. Supreme Court allow broader standing in federal court or that the federal executive actively enforce federal statutes. However, federalism, in the form of intersystemic adjudication, provides a vital second (or third) best solution.

In an ideal world, a unitary government could provide citizens with efficient and responsive governance. In an ideal federalist world, state courts always would protect state rights, and federal courts always would protect federal rights. In the actual world, though, intersystemic adjudication provides a valuable and legitimate way to address situations in which governments and courts fall short of this ideal.

8. DUAL CONSTITUTIONS AND CONSTITUTIONAL DUELS

JIM ROSSI

I. INTRODUCTION

With the post-New Deal growth of federal power, states increasingly are called on to implement federal programs. In a variety of regulatory contexts, ranging from health, safety, and environmental regulation to network infrastructure and transportation, Congress and federal regulators routinely look to state and local governments to implement federal programs and regulatory goals. Often the federal government offers a "carrot" for state or local action, providing federal funding for programs such as welfare, Medicaid, or public school standards and testing. And frequently state executive agencies take the bait, voluntarily agreeing to implement extensive federal programs under regulatory standards dictated by federal law.

But the mere desire of a state government to take up such a federal invitation does not necessarily confer upon the state the power to do so. Participation in a national regulatory program requires action by organs of state governance: the state legislature may be required to enact implementing legislation, and state executive agencies must adopt and enforce new policies. Yet the authority of state legislatures and executive agencies derives not from federal legislation or voluntary state-federal agreements, but from the state constitution. Consequently, a state's desire to participate directly in national programs may from time to time conflict with restraints on state power imposed by the state's constitution.

Occasionally, a state's conformance to standards and procedures laid down by national regulators may raise concerns under state constitutional rights provisions.[1] More commonly, state participation in a national program may require organs of state government to take actions that conflict with the allocation of

1. For example, following the September 11 attacks, Portland, Oregon police refused to cooperate with the FBI's attempt to interview approximately 5,000 men of Middle Eastern descent, claiming that the FBI's program resulted in a type of racial profiling prohibited by Oregon law. Fox Butterfield, *A Police Force Rebuffs F.B.I. on Querying Mideast Men*, N.Y. Times, Nov. 21, 2001, at B7. William Van Alstyne argues that state and local governments may not accept federal funds where doing so puts at risk rights that state constitutional law protects. William Van Alstyne, *"Thirty Pieces of Silver" for the Rights of Your People: Irresistible Offers Reconsidered as a Matter of State Constitutional Law*, 16 Harv. J. L. & Pub. Pol'y 303 (1993).

powers among the branches or levels of government articulated in the state constitution. These latter kinds of conflicts are the subject of this chapter. In the prototypical scenario discussed here, states are asked or voluntarily choose to adopt programs that rely on, implement, or incorporate federal statutes and regulations. In these situations, dual constitutions—federal and state—produce the prospect of dueling substantive and procedural constitutional norms between the national and state levels of government.

A frequent source of such conflicts is national programs based on principles of cooperative federalism, in which the federal government relies on states or localities to adopt or implement a federal goal. Even where Congress has not explicitly attempted to yoke state agencies to national programs, states sometimes unilaterally adopt federal standards in the interest of promoting uniformity or efficiency. For example, a state statute regulating water pollutants might rely on definitions or standards adopted by the federal Environmental Protection Agency (EPA), or may even explicitly incorporate EPA regulations or guidance documents into state law. Or a state legislature may affirmatively oppose the adoption or implementation of federal law by officials in a state executive branch, placing a state legislature in direct confrontation not only with a federal statute or regulatory program but with its own executive.

Each of these variations raises potentially difficult issues arising from the complex interplay of state and national constitutional regimes. Can a state executive agency participate in a federal program if the state legislature has not authorized it to do so? May a state legislature delegate authority to formulate specific regulatory standards not to a state executive agency, but to a federal one? Can Congress legislatively enlist the cooperation of state agencies over the opposition of the state legislature—or where forbidden by the state constitution? Many of these situations implicate separation of powers concerns under state constitutions, especially with respect to state-level nondelegation doctrines that forbid legislatures to transfer legislative decision-making authority to other bodies. For example, in formulating a state implementation plan pursuant to the Clean Air Act, a state legislature may give a regulatory agency express authority to adopt regulations that rely on definitional terms or incorporate standards in EPA guidelines. Although such a delegation seems innocuous (for example, a state legislature may just be attempting to save administrative costs by borrowing a standard from a well-informed and recognized regulatory authority at the federal level), it may run afoul of state constitutional principles of nondelegation, which are often stricter than their federal counterpart.[2]

---

2. *See* Jim Rossi, *Institutional Design and the Lingering Legacy of Antifederal Separation of Powers Ideals in the States*, 52 VAND. L. REV. 1167 (1999); John Devlin, *Toward a State Constitutional Analysis of Allocation of Powers: Legislators and Legislative Appointees Performing Administrative Functions*, 66 TEMP. L. REV. 1205 (1993); Harold H. Bruff, *Separation of Powers under the Texas Constitution*, 68 TEX. L. REV. 1337 (1990).

Cooperative federalism programs, such as those under environmental statutes and in the telecommunications context that are touted for valuing state-centered solutions to regulatory programs, present a particularly difficult challenge for state constitutions, which frequently delimit a narrow scope of authority for state and local agencies. Although a federal program may have implicitly or expressly allowed these agencies to act, a state legislature might refuse to acquiesce in the federal goals, presenting a potential conflict between federal and state legislative power.

The issues arising under the U.S. Constitution are no less complex. Federal courts might resolve such conflicts by relying on preemption analysis under the Supremacy Clause, for example, leading them to find that Congress not only allowed state regulation but effectively authorized state agencies to regulate an activity where a state legislature has failed to do so—even though regulation would otherwise violate the state's constitution.[3] Effectively, such a finding would allow the federal program to preempt state separation-of-powers jurisprudence. Even without endorsing broad federal preemption of state law, one author has drawn on political process principles to argue for a normative clear statement rule that might have implications in this context: state and local agencies might be presumptively authorized to act under federal law in the absence of a clear statement by the state legislature to the contrary.[4]

Although looking to federal law has its appeal as a solution to these conflicts, I argue in this chapter that state courts have a way of resolving such conflicts on their own terms, as a matter of state constitutional law. I concur with the general outcome of allowing state agencies to implement cooperative federalism programs and adopt federal standards, but instead of rooting federally inspired regulatory programs in federal preemption doctrine or a clear statement rule constructed by federal judges, I argue that state constitutions, properly interpreted by state courts, should be understood to allow and authorize state implementation of federal programs and standards by state executive branch agencies. In other words, the best normative interpretation of state separation of powers does not require state courts to surrender the field to federal courts to sustain cooperative federalism programs and facilitate intergovernmental collaboration. State constitutions are not rendered moot by virtue of the existence of a federal program, including one that purports to authorize state agencies to act or that provides substantive regulatory standards to state agencies. Rather than inviting broad preemption, state courts can make state constitutions more relevant to the resolution of state-federal conflicts if they take an institutionalist interpretive strategy to separation of powers in the context of federalism programs.

---

3. Washington Dept. of Game v. Federal Power Comm'n., 207 F.2d 391, 396 (9th Cir. 1953).

4. Roderick M. Hills, Jr., *Dissecting the State: The Use of Federal Law to Free State and Local Officials from State Legislatures' Control*, 97 MICH. L. REV. 1201 (1999).

Part II illustrates how cooperative federalism programs present particularly salient conflicts between state legislatures and federal goals and discusses the two predominant solutions to these conflicts in the literature. Part III sets forth the descriptive approaches state courts have adopted to deal with the problem of unconstitutional delegations by state legislatures against the backdrop of federal programs. Part IV argues that these strategies are unsatisfying, if not disingenuous. The chapter advances the argument that a state separation-of-powers jurisprudence that positions itself to address the specific institutional decision-making processes of state governments, rather than absolutist rules defining spheres of sovereignty, provides the most promising interpretive alternative for state courts to address the type of separation-of-powers problems presented in state implementation of federal programs. An institutional approach to understanding the interpretation of state constitutions in an era of national programs positions a state constitution within a dual federal-state system without making it an obstacle to a federal program or allowing federal law implicitly to preempt it.

II. DUELS BETWEEN FEDERAL REGULATORY GOALS AND STATE CONSTITUTIONS IN COOPERATIVE FEDERALISM PROGRAMS

In the past three decades, a novel approach to federalism issues has emerged as an alternative to the traditional view that federal and state governments occupy distinct spheres of legal authority. In contrast to the traditional flavor of federalism, which relegates state and federal authorities to independent jurisdictional spheres, cooperative federalism envisions overlap between federal and state regulators as a positive good. Generally, cooperative federalism has been defined as follows:

> Cooperative federalism programs set forth some uniform federal standards—as embodied in the statute, federal agency regulations, or both—but leave state agencies with discretion to implement the federal law, supplement it with more stringent standards, and, in some cases, receive an exemption from federal requirements. This power allows states to experiment with different approaches and tailor federal law to local conditions.[5]

Such an approach recognizes that state and federal regulators do not operate in hermetically sealed jurisdictional spheres; rather, the overlap in their authority is "messy and chaotic."[6] Federal and state regulators often must work together in implementing their regulatory goals.

---

5. Philip J. Weiser, *Federal Common Law, Cooperative Federalism, and the Enforcement of the Telcom Act*, 76 N.Y.U. L. Rev. 1692, 1696 (2001) (footnotes and citations omitted).

6. *Id.* at 1693.

Moreover, the cooperative federalism model sees jurisdictional overlap as a positive good. It concedes a need for federal regulation and adopts uniformity as a general goal, but also recognizes the positive contribution states can make to the regulatory process. For example, given the reduced cost of political mobilization at the state and local levels, involving states in the regulatory process may increase participation. This can have obvious payoffs for regulatory compliance, legitimacy, and efficiency. States are also more likely to experiment in their regulatory approach, trying out regulatory mechanisms that would be unlikely to be adopted without experience by Congress or federal regulators. State enforcement and state-adopted programs encourage experimentation with different approaches and allow tailoring of federal goals to local conditions.[7] Cooperative federalism is built into several federal statutes, including the major environmental statutes passed in the 1970s and the Telecommunications Act of 1996.[8]

One novel and fundamental question about such programs is how courts should resolve conflicts between federal regulatory programs and recalcitrant state legislatures that through inaction (and sometimes affirmative action) impede their implementation. For instance, if a state legislature refuses to authorize its state regulatory agency to embrace a competitive approach to local telephony, federal and state regulators may find themselves at odds. The only way state regulators can break the impasse is by ignoring state law, including the constitutional allocation of powers delimited in a state constitution. Commentators have proposed two main solutions to this problem.

The first solution relies on the Supremacy Clause of the U.S. Constitution, which allows Congress and federal agencies to preempt "any state law" that contravenes a federal state or regulation. That Congress and federal agencies have the power to override state executive decisions has long been recognized by federal courts. For instance, in *State of Washington Department of Game v. Federal Power Commission*, the U.S. Court of Appeals for the Ninth Circuit required the State of Washington to accept a hydro license for the City of Tacoma over the objections of the Washington State Attorney General, who opposed the project.[9] Even though the City of Tacoma had not obtained a permit from the Washington State Supervisor of Hydraulics, as was required under a statute passed by the Washington legislature, the court held that "the Federal Government's power over navigable waters is superior to that of the state."[10] Relying on the Supreme Court's decision in *First Iowa Hydro-Electric Cooperative v. Federal Power*

---

7. Philip J. Weiser, *Towards a Constitutional Architecture for Cooperative Federalism*, 79 N.C. L. Rev. 663 (2001).

8. *See, e.g.*, Clean Water Act, 33 U.S.C. § 1370; Comprehensive Environmental Response, Compensation and Liability Act, 42 U.S.C. § 9614(a); AT&T v. Iowa Utilities Bd., 525 U.S. 366, 385 n.10 (1999).

9. 207 F.2d 391 (9th Cir. 1953).

10. *Id.* at 396.

Commission,[11] the Ninth Circuit reasoned that any other result would give a state veto power over a federal hydro project, thereby destroying the effectiveness of the hydroelectric licensing scheme laid out in the Federal Power Act.[12]

On the federal preemption view, a federal assertion of power is justified under obstacle preemption analysis pursuant to the Supremacy Clause, however crude Congress's delegation to the federal agency or the federal regulatory action may be. The federal regulatory action is supreme notwithstanding the contrary wishes of a state legislature or a state executive. Further, the federal assertion of power prevails over, or preempts, any allocation of power between the branches and between state and local governments laid out in a state constitution. In a dissent to *First Iowa*, Justice Felix Frankfurter argued that applicants for Federal Power Commission licenses should be required to follow state procedural requirements, even though this might delay approval of a project, because the measure of "justice" is "deliberate speed."[13] The Court, however, appears to have rejected Frankfurter's view to the extent that the federal preemption approach to validating cooperative federalism programs is effective only if courts are extremely receptive to finding federal preemption of such programs, thus elevating regulatory expediency over state constitutional procedural requirements.

The continued vitality of the preemption approach to validating state and local agency implementation of cooperative federalism goals may be questionable in light of recent U.S. Supreme Court cases that limit federal power. *New York v. United States*[14] and *Printz v. United States*[15] both struck down federal laws that imposed duties on nonfederal officials. As Roderick Hills observes, however, the Court's anti-commandeering decisions are not necessarily fatal to the federal preemption approach to upholding the implementation of cooperative federalism programs by states:

> Federal law does not require anyone to *do* anything when it preempts state laws that limit the power of state or local officials. At most, such laws simply require the state to *remove* certain restrictions on the power of subordinate officials so that those officials can *voluntarily* assume federal duties.[16]

So long as some state or local official voluntarily attempts to assume federal duties, Congress has not forced state or local action, and no commandeering threat is present.

A second approach does not imply preemption broadly, but uses judicially created clear statement rules to favor cooperative federalism approaches—or at

---

11. 328 U.S. 152 (1946).
12. 207 F.3d at 296.
13. 328 U.S. at 188.
14. 505 U.S. 144 (1992).
15. 521 U.S. 898 (1997).
16. Hills, *supra* note 4, at 1211.

least to require recalcitrant state legislatures to reject them more affirmatively and explicitly. In one of the leading articles on the architecture of cooperative federalism programs, Professor Roderick Hills argues that federal authorities have the power to "delegate" federal powers to specific state and local institutions even where the state legislature has itself declined either to make or to authorize such a delegation.[17] Professor Hills rejects as unpersuasive the absolutist "state supremacy" position as a barrier to the exercise of federal power through state institutions. Instead, drawing on political process concerns, he embraces a general presumption in favor of delegating power to nonfederal governmental institutions for the purpose of promoting local self-governance.[18] His approach, a presumption in favor of the exercise of local power absent state legislative authorization to the contrary, is also compatible with allowing cooperative federalism programs to operate within a state.

Both the federal preemption approach and a judicially constructed presumption in favor of local authority allow state and local agency implementation of cooperative federalism programs even against the backdrop of contrary state laws, including state constitutions that might limit local power or legislative delegations to executive agencies. Yet both approaches leave little role for state constitutions in a cooperative federalism environment. Under the preemption view, federal law crudely overrides state constitutions even where federal law is vague. Under the state autonomy view, courts are to construct a presumption that favors local power over centralized state legislative authority, notwithstanding contrary state constitutional law. Thus, in both cases state constitutional law is effectively overridden—and thus rendered superfluous—as a matter of federal law. Both of these approaches pose a substantial threat to state constitutions as an independent set of legal restraints on state-level allocations of powers.

Perhaps the laudable ends of federal programs justify the means of overriding state constitutions in the cooperative federalism context. But there is an odd irony to these methods of sustaining cooperative federalism goals. Both rely on constitutional norms imposed on states from the "outside," not on legal norms recognized as legitimate within a state's own constitutional system. For any approach to regulation that purports to value local participation and political processes—as cooperative federalism does—bluntly overriding the primary source of legal legitimacy for the state's system of government seems to be a high cost to pay.

---

17. *Id.* Hills includes in his analysis not only the scenario where a state has refused to authorize a state agency to implement federal law, but also where a state legislature has prohibited a state agency from acting in accordance with federal law.

18. *Id.* at 1215–22.

III. INTERPRETIVE EFFORTS TO RETAIN THE RELEVANCE OF STATE CONSTITUTIONS AGAINST THE BACKDROP OF FEDERAL PROGRAMS

Despite efforts to find solutions to potential conflicts from outside the state, state courts have developed their own methods for approaching federal programs from the inside—i.e., as a matter of state constitutional interpretation. State constitutions are frequently embraced as a source of legitimacy for local solutions to regulatory programs. State constitutions are desirable framework mechanisms for governance in three main respects. First, state political processes, governed primarily by state constitutions, are more likely to allow regulatory solutions to adapt to local circumstances and needs.[19] Second, state political processes, spelled out in state constitutions, are more likely to provide for adaptation and experimentation rather than the one-size-fits-all approach more common at the national level.[20] Third, to the extent that state political processes are more easily accessible to interest groups than the national political process, a state constitution is a framework for political legitimacy that might hold greater promise than the national Constitution for formulating legitimate political solutions. State constitutions are more likely to reflect the unique institutional issues affecting state and local governments and thus yield legitimate solutions to regulatory problems, particularly when compared to a single, one-size-fits-all solution forced onto a state from outside.[21]

With these benefits to state-based political processes in mind, many commentators embrace what has come to be known as "independent state constitutionalism" as a way for state courts (and federal courts borrowing from or applying state law) to stay true to the origins, purposes, and structure of unique constitutional documents.[22] An independent state constitutionalism is a challenge, as fifty state judicial systems attempt to parse meaning from fifty different

---

19. *See* Deborah Jones Merritt, *The Guaranty Clause and State Autonomy: Federalism for a Third Century*, 88 COLUM. L. REV. 1, 7–9 (1988).

20. "It is one of the happy incidents of the federal system that a single courageous State may, if its citizens choose, serve as a laboratory; and try novel social and economic experiments without risk to the rest of the country." New State Ice Co. v. Liebemann, 285 U.S. 262, 311 (1932) (Brandeis, J., dissenting). *Cf.* Michael C. Dorf & Charles F. Sabel, *A Constitution of Democratic Experimentalism*, 98 COLUM. L. REV. 267 (1998).

21. *See* James D. Heiple & Kraig James Powell, *Presumed Innocent: The Legitimacy of Independent State Constitutional Interpretation*, 61 ALB. L. REV. 1507 (1998); Daniel B. Rodriguez, *State Constitutional Theory and Its Prospects*, 28 N.M. L. REV. 271 (1998); Robert F. Utter, *State Constitutional Law, The United States Supreme Court, and Democratic Accountability: Is There a Crocodile in the Bathtub?*, 64 WASH. L. REV. 19, 46–47 (1989); Robert F. Williams, *In the Supreme Court's Shadow: Legitimacy of State Rejection of Supreme Court Reasoning and Result*, 35 S.C. L. REV. 353 (1984).

22. Lawrence Friedman, *The Constitutional Value of Dialogue and the New Judicial Federalism*, 28 HAST. CONST'L L. Q. 93 (2000); Williams, *supra* note 21.

constitutional texts, but an independent state constitutionalism may allow articulation of a set of trans-state constitutional norms independent of the federal constitution.[23] It is important, though, to recognize what an independent state constitutionalism does and does not require. As an interpretive task, independent constitutionalism requires state courts to make sense of a state constitution on its own terms. Independent constitutionalism does not, however, commit every state to a view of independent constitutional power. State power, in other words, does not exist solely to serve the state polity; it also exists to protect individuals from tyrannical acts on the part of both state and national governments, and may also exist as a type of "cog" in the machine of a broader, more national political process.[24]

A. State Separation of Powers Limits on Legislative Delegations

State courts seem to recognize that while an independent interpretive method is important, state power does not exist in complete isolation from the federal system. Scholars have suggested that state constitutional rights are not entirely independent of the U.S. Constitution's rights protections.[25] The same may also be said of structural provisions of state constitutions, such as separation of powers.

State judicial applications of the nondelegation doctrine in the context of state implementation of federal law are particularly telling. Whereas federal constitutional law embraces a relaxed nondelegation doctrine,[26] the separation of powers doctrine applied to legislative delegations by many state courts is much more rigid.[27] Florida courts, for example, endorse a strong nondelegation doctrine in interpreting the Florida Constitution, sharply limiting the power of Florida's legislature to pass laws that give other branches of government, particularly the executive branch, the power to make fundamental policy choices. The text of Florida's constitution states: "The powers of the state government shall be divided into legislative, executive, and judicial branches. No person belonging to one branch shall exercise any [of the] powers appertaining to either of the other branches unless expressly provided herein."[28] Florida courts rely on this text for the doctrine that the legislature may delegate legislative power to the executive branch only through specific, constraining standards and guidelines.

The key modern nondelegation case in Florida constitutional law, *Askew v. Cross Key Waterways*, held unconstitutional an environmental statute delegating

---

23. *See* Chapter 5.

24. *See, e.g.*, James A. Gardner, *State Constitutional Rights as Resistance to National Power: Toward a Functional Theory of State Constitutions*, 91 Geo. L.J. 1003, 1005 (2003).

25. *Id. See also* Chapter 4.

26. Kenneth Culp Davis, *A New Approach to Delegation*, 36 U. Chi. L. Rev. 713 (1969).

27. *See* Rossi, *supra* note 2.

28. Fla. Const. art. II, Section 3.

to the Florida Administration Commission the authority to designate geographic areas of critical state concern and, in certain instances, to adopt land use regulations.[29] The statute enunciated several limitations on agency designation of areas, allowing the "critical state concern" designation only if: (1) the area contains or has a significant impact upon "environmental, historical, natural, or archeological resources of regional or statewide importance"; (2) the area is "significant(ly) affected by, or (has) a significant effect upon, an existing or proposed major public facility or other area of major public investment"; or (3) the area has major development potential, such as the proposed site of a new community.[30] Despite these limits on agency discretion in the statute, the Florida Supreme Court struck down the statute as unconstitutional on nondelegation grounds. Although the court acknowledged a need for an agency to "flesh out" policy, it also noted that this is "far different from that agency making the initial determination of what policy should be."[31] Based on a somewhat formalistic interpretation of Florida's strict separation of powers clause, the court rejected a procedural safeguards approach, holding that the Florida Legislature is required, at a minimum, to provide some standards or guidelines to aid the agency in exercising its discretion. The court also acknowledged how the presence of such standards or guidelines aids judicial review.[32] Since *Askew*, the Florida Supreme Court has had several occasions to revisit the doctrine and has consistently reaffirmed the need for specific standards and guidelines in legislation to validate a delegation of legislative authority to an agency.[33]

Another example is a Texas Supreme Court case, *Texas Boll Weevil Eradication Foundation, Inc. v. Lewellen* (*Boll Weevil*).[34] A 1993 Texas statute empowered the Commissioner of Agriculture to certify a nonprofit organization representing cotton growers to create a private entity called the "Official Cotton Growers' Boll Weevil Eradication Foundation" (Foundation). The Foundation was authorized to propose geographic eradication zones and to conduct referenda in each zone to establish whether local cotton growers wished to establish an official boll weevil eradication zone. If an official zone was established, the Foundation proposed assessments for cotton growers to pay subject to the growers' approval in a subsequent referendum. The Foundation was also given broad powers to impose penalties for late payment of assessments and to recommend to the Department of Agriculture that nonpaying growers' crops be destroyed.

29. Askew v. Cross Key Waterways, 372 So.2d 913 (Fla. 1979).

30. *Id.* at 914.

31. *Id.* at 920.

32. *Id.* at 920–25.

33. *See, e.g.*, B.H. v. State, 645 So.2d 987, 993–94 (Fla. 1994); Chiles v. Children, 589 So.2d 260, 266–67 (Fla. 1991); *but see* Florida Gas Transmission Co. v. Public Serv. Comm'n, 635 So.2d 941, 944 (Fla. 1994).

34. 952 S.W.2d 454 (Tex. 1997).

The statute contained few checks on the Foundation's powers apart from referenda and a requirement that the Commissioner of Agriculture certify the organization petitioning to become the Foundation.

The court invalidated the statute on the grounds that the Texas Legislature had unconstitutionally delegated power to the Foundation in violation of the separation-of-powers clause of the Texas Constitution. After summarizing dissenting and concurring U.S. Supreme Court opinions and scholarly criticism endorsing a revival of the nondelegation doctrine, the court observed that "[s]tate courts may have less need to reinvigorate the doctrine, since they have historically been much more comfortable with striking down state laws on this basis than their federal counterparts."[35]

In terms of their results, these cases illustrate how state separation of powers doctrine constrains the power of state agencies in more rigid ways than federal separation of powers doctrine constrains federal agencies. In reaching these results, state courts rely overwhelmingly on the texts of state constitutions. As commentators have previously concluded, however, the judicial approach to state separation of powers doctrine is not dictated exclusively by the texts of individual state constitutions.[36] States with similar textual language reach very different results, and states with different constitutional language sometimes reach the same results.[37] Thus, something other than constitutional text has to be driving state courts in the separation-of-powers context.

B. State Nondelegation Doctrine and State Incorporation of Federal Regulatory Standards by Reference

State courts are aware of the challenge nondelegation doctrine presents for state constitutional jurisprudence. As shown above, where a state legislature has delegated authority to a state agency to adopt federal standards or to implement a federal goal, the delegation could raise separation-of-powers concerns, especially with respect to nondelegation analysis. Nevertheless, consistent with the growth of cooperative federalism, most states allow broader legislative delegations where a state legislature has assigned policy-making authority to a federal, as opposed to a state, agency.

Although these results facilitate potentially desirable intergovernmental cooperation, state courts have tended to justify relaxation of state constitutional separation of powers constraints in ways that are at best unpersuasive, and at worst do violence to sound principles of state constitutional interpretation.

The four main explanations state courts give for upholding the adoption of federal standards in states—uniformity, proactivity, extraterritoriality, and

35. *Id.* at 468.

36. Rossi, *supra* note 2; Gary J. Greco, *Standards or Safeguards: A Survey of the Delegation Doctrine in the States,* 8 ADMIN. L.J. AM. U. 567 (1994).

37. Rossi, *supra* note 2, at 1191–1201.

political expediency—thus illustrate a familiar and more general weakness of state constitutional discourse.[38]

1. **Uniformity** Appeals to uniformity are commonplace in state decisions addressing separation-of-powers challenges to state executive branch implementation of federal programs. For example, in *McFaddin v. Jackson,* the Tennessee Supreme Court upheld a statute that made individual retirement plans taxable if subject to the federal estate tax, but exempt if excluded from the federal estate tax.[39] Articulating concerns of uniformity and administrative simplicity in conforming tax statutes, the court reasoned that the delegation was constitutional despite the legislature's failure to provide adequate standards and safeguards. Also, in Florida the Supreme Court has upheld a statute that made unlawful "unfair . . . acts or practices in the conduct of any trade or commerce" and instructed state regulators to adopt regulations consistent with those of the Federal Trade Commission.[40] The Minnesota Supreme Court implicitly endorsed uniformity when it upheld a state law incorporating the federal definition of "eligible small business" as contained in regulations of the U.S. Small Business Administration "as amended from time to time."[41] A New Jersey appellate court also cited uniformity as a basis for upholding a similar delegation.[42] The court invoked the need for uniformity in upholding media advertising classification standards for state laws and postal regulations.[43]

Commentators have also embraced the promotion of uniformity as an accepted rationale for upholding the adoption of or acquiescence to federal law in the states, notwithstanding state constitutional principles to the contrary.[44] This is perhaps the least satisfying analytical approach used by state courts for upholding state agency adoption of or acquiescence to federal law, but because it is preeminent, it warrants some evaluation. Uniformity is an undeniably valuable goal for any federal program. It advances predictability and certainty for private firms seeking compliance with the law across jurisdictions. It also reduces administrative costs for federal agencies attempting to monitor state compliance with federal standards or goals. For states too, it reduces the administrative costs of regulation to the extent that a state agency can avoid reinventing the wheel on every legal or policy issue.

Appeals to uniformity, however, seem too weak to drive the outcome of state separation-of-powers jurisprudence in this context. Unlike many rights provisions

38. *See* James A. Gardner, *The Failed Discourse of State Constitutionalism*, 90 MICH. L. REV. 761 (1992); 1 KENNETH CULP DAVIS, ADMINISTRATIVE LAW TREATISE 102 (1st ed. 1958).

39. 738 S.W.2d 176 (Tenn. 1987).

40. Dept. of Legal Affairs v. Rogers, 329 So.2d 257 (Fla. 1976).

41. Minn. Energy & Econ. Dev. Auth. v. Printy, 351 N.W.2d 319, 351–52 (1984).

42. State v. Hotel Food Bars, 112 A.2d 726 (N.J. 1955).

43. New Jersey Surburbanite Co., Inc. v. State, 381 A.2d 34, 38 (N.J. Super. Ct. App. Div. 1977).

44. *See* Arnold Rochvarg, *State Adoption of Federal Law—Legislative Abdication or Reasoned Policymaking*, 36 ADMIN. L. REV. 277, 298 (1984).

of the U.S. Constitution that are incorporated into state constitutions, federal separation-of-powers principles are not so incorporated; at best, the U.S. Constitution speaks in a "whisper" to separation of powers in the states. Thus, to the extent separation-of-power principles apply at all to the states, they emanate primarily from state constitutional law, not from the U.S. Constitution.

The very notion of an independent set of state separation-of-powers norms eschews uniformity as its primary animating principle. Further, because Congress has not legislated in the interests of uniformity—since the states themselves retain legislative power—what state courts seem to be doing in embracing uniformity is replacing Congress's failure with their own sense of what is in the interests of interstate commerce. At best, appeals to uniformity might be said to constitute an effort by state courts to elevate state legislative intent over the non-delegation doctrine where, in the court's view, the legislature intended to promote uniformity (and presumably commerce) between states. This might be good policy, and might be grounded in some implied federal preemption argument as a matter of federal law, but there is no reasonable argument that it is based in an interpretation of state separation of powers.

Further, in the context of some state legislative delegations, particularly in cooperative federalism contexts, appeals to uniformity may actually undermine the goals of federal programs. Cooperative federalism programs such as the EPA's effort to establish water standards and the FCC's effort to implement competition in local telephony embrace variation from state to state as a way of legitimating federal goals. Uniformity is a stronger interpretive basis for upholding the legal status of federal regulations. By suggesting that standards must be identical from state to state, uniformity may undermine the premise of cooperative federalism that state political processes are more likely than their federal counterparts to yield legitimate political solutions to regulatory programs and are more efficient at achieving compliance.

2. Proactivity Another way state courts attempt to preserve delegations to federal agencies is to distinguish between proactive and retroactive standards by federal agencies. These courts assume that the state legislature, in approving an agency's rulemaking or regulatory powers, implicitly had knowledge of existing federal regulations. At the same time, because the state legislature could not have known about future changes to the law, these courts limit the state agency from adopting future federal agency regulations or interpretations without new action by the state legislature.

For example, the Texas Solid Waste Disposal Act criminalizes the transportation, storage, processing, disposal, and export of "hazardous waste," defined as "solid waste identified or listed as a hazardous waste by the administrator of the U.S. EPA."[45] A Texas appellate court upheld this delegation, but only with respect

45. Tex. Health & Safety Code Ann. §§ 361.221(a)(1), (2); § 361.003(15).

to existing EPA listings. The court noted that this delegation "may be read to say the legislature has delegated to the EPA the power to define hazardous waste . . . and that the definition may change from time to time at the will of the EPA," but also observed that such a construction would "place in doubt" the constitutionality of the statute under Texas's strict nondelegation doctrine.[46] The court read the statute to incorporate by reference the EPA's definition of solid waste at the time of enactment of the Texas statute, but not modifications adopted by the EPA afterwards.[47] On a similar rationale, the Oklahoma Supreme Court rejected a legislative delegation to the U.S. Department of Labor to set future minimum wage rates in Oklahoma.[48]

While this distinction, which draws on loose constitutional due process rhetoric, might seem to promote general fairness, as a matter of constitutional interpretation it is not at all helpful to state separation-of-powers jurisprudence. It relies on a fictional account of legislative knowledge of specific federal standards at the time of the passage of state legislation. More important, as many state courts use this as a canon of construction for upholding delegations (and limiting them), it relies on the judiciary to effectively limit statutes—even when the statute is clearly to the contrary. Although many states apply a prohibition on prospective lawmaking as a canon for upholding delegations, this is not only a disingenuous interpretive technique, but also freezes the state regulatory apparatus and may contribute to gaps in regulation, thus undermining other (nonconstitutional) goals of regulation, such as uniformity. For example, if used broadly to sustain state regulatory programs, it might result in a state having systematically lower minimum wages or outdated food and drug standards in comparison to the federal system or other states.

3. Extraterritoriality State courts have also found ways to take delegation to a federal agency outside of the jurisdictional realm of the state nondelegation doctrine altogether. By characterizing the regulatory action as external fact or federal (not state) lawmaking, state courts may avoid having to confront the implications of state legislative delegation to a federal agency. A recent Michigan case took such an approach. The Michigan legislature had passed a statute limiting the liability of drug manufacturers for drugs and labeling in compliance with Food and Drug Administration standards. In reviewing a nondelegation challenge to the statute under Michigan's Constitution, the court held that, by referencing FDA conclusions regarding the safety and efficacy of a drug, the legislature was merely using factual conclusions of "independent significance" that in no way constituted a delegation of legislative authority.[49]

---

46. *Ex parte* Elliott, 973 S.W.2d 737, 740 (Tex. Ct. App. 1998).
47. *Id.* at 741.
48. Oklahoma City v. Oklahoma, 918 P.2d 26 (Okla. 1995).
49. Taylor v. Smithkline Beecham Corp., 658 NW.2d 127, 133 (Mich. 2003).

The characterization of these issues as factual is specious. Under federal law, it is well recognized that an FDA determination regarding the safety and efficacy of a drug may be based on factual findings or inferences, but is infused with legal and policy significance. Perhaps more interesting is the suggestion that because these determinations are "independent" and nationwide, they are somehow extraterritorial—outside of the jurisdiction of a state court to make a determination that they violate the separation-of-powers doctrine within the state. This is, of course, based on a false premise that federal law has any significance in this context independent of a state adopting or acquiescing in it. Moreover, as a jurisdictional or sovereignty argument, this has troubling implications. It would authorize delegations not only to Congress or to federal agencies, but to private out-of-state entities, such as national organizations and associations.

4. Separation of Powers as Raw Politics Upholding state programs that implement federal goals will frequently advance state interests. Implicit in some state court opinions is the notion that state separation of powers doctrines should be relaxed where the state stands to benefit politically. For instance, if a state does not conform its regulations to national standards, it might face a loss of a business that relies on the predictability of regulation from state to state in deciding which markets to serve. In more explicit political confrontations, a state may face a loss of federal funding if its agencies fail to conform their regulations to national standards or guidelines. This is a strong form of the uniformity argument in which uniformity is not embraced for the sake of efficiency and predictability, but to benefit a state, or interest groups within a state.

This is perhaps the most ambitious normative basis for relaxing separation of powers in the name of federal programs. But it seems to have more horsepower than it needs to deal with the specific problem of delegation of authority to adopt federal standards. It reduces much state constitutional law, and separation-of-powers doctrine in particular, to nothing more than raw politics. Indeed, many political scientists see formal divisions of governmental power as rendered irrelevant by the rise of political parties.[50] Perhaps reduction to politics is the best any theory of allocation of power between the branches of government in states might hope for, but at some level this calls into question whether we ought to continue to have separation-of-powers doctrine at all in the states. Without some principled normative basis, however, courts should not selectively reduce some separation-of-powers conflicts to political ones while treating others as legal conflicts. Although separation-of-powers principles are often contested, they play a fundamentally important role in organizing and defining the powers of state governments as well as in lending legitimacy to the internal political processes

---

50. Theodore Lowi, The End of Liberalism (2d ed. 1979); E.E. Schattschneider, The Semi-Sovereign People: A Realist's View of Democracy in America 78–96 (1960); *see also* Larry D. Kramer, *Putting the Politics Back into the Political Safeguards of Federalism*, 100 Colum. L. Rev. 215 (2000).

of states. If state constitutionalism is to have any hope as an independent interpretive enterprise, it must either make some effort to articulate the allocation of powers outside of crude appeals to politics or abandon the nondelegation doctrine altogether.

IV. A SOLUTION FROM WITHIN: SEEDS FOR AN INTERPRETIVE THEORY OF SEPARATION OF POWERS FOR SYSTEMS OF DUAL CONSTITUTIONS

The reasons state courts give for upholding state legislative delegations to agencies to implement federal programs are all based on the assumption that state constitutions are independent. They also all implicitly treat state constitutions as isolated sources of sovereign power. A more nuanced interpretive approach would not view state constitutions as isolated but as part of a complex institutional scheme in which shared authority is more commonplace.[51] If understood as responding to specific institutional problems in the design of state governments, state separation-of-powers doctrine could provide a superior interpretive starting point for state courts faced with nondelegation issues involving federally inspired regulatory programs. A normative focus on institutional issues would not relegate state constitutions to the superfluous status of the federal preemption and clear statement approaches to upholding the pursuit of federal goals and standards by state agencies.

A. Normative Foundations of the Nondelegation Doctrine

The classical liberal (or libertarian) perspective, often associated with Locke and Montesquieu, sees constitutional restrictions on legislative delegation as applying a rigid separation of functions between a legislature and other governmental branches in order to protect individual liberty. Although the classical liberal account is popular, it has also been criticized for its adherence to formal rules of separation between the branches of government without regard to function. Most contemporary liberal accounts of separation of powers, by contrast, focus on the non-rights-based functions of nondelegation, such as enhancing accountability. Some functionalist accounts emphasize how nondelegation protects legislative accountability by ensuring a tight connection to majoritarian electoral processes,[52] while other accountability advocates see more complicated links to

---

51. *See, e.g.*, ROBERT A. SCHAPIRO, POLYPHONIC FEDERALISM (2009).

52. DAVID SCHOENBROD, POWER WITHOUT RESPONSIBILITY: HOW CONGRESS ABUSES THE PEOPLE THROUGH DELEGATION (1993); David Schoenbrod, *Delegation and Democracy: A Reply to My Critics*, 20 CARDOZO L. REV. 731 (1999).

electoral values[53] or endorse a welfare-based definition of accountability.[54] Still others see separation of powers as concerned primarily with promoting efficient government.[55] Certainly, where one places the functional emphasis influences how strongly one views the role of constitutional restrictions on legislative delegations, but the nondelegation doctrine has been defended on both libertarian and functionalist grounds.

One recent functionalist account of the nondelegation doctrine creatively and usefully blends the incomplete contracts and interest group accounts of lawmaking to argue that the nondelegation doctrine enhances welfare by preserving majoritarian checks on lawmaking. Scott Baker and Kimberly Krawiec argue that legislation can be understood as a type of incomplete contract between legislators and interests groups participating in the lawmaking process.[56] In their view, the nondelegation doctrine can be understood as a type of penalty default rule, in which courts declare unconstitutional statutes that are passed by a legislature to shift or avoid responsibility. By requiring majoritarian processes (i.e., a legislative vote) to more fully constrain executive decision makers, such a penalty has the effect of limiting the manipulation of the legislative process by powerful interest groups seeking to maximize their ability to capture or control the executive branch at the cost of majoritarian processes.

Understanding nondelegation as a type of penalty default rule for interest groups in the political process assumes that lawmaking responsibility is clearly within the constitutional ambit of a single branch of government—namely, the legislature. Separation-of-powers principles delimit the respective spheres of authority for legislative and executive branches of government, but the incomplete contracts argument for a nondelegation doctrine should not be taken too far. In addition to looking at legislation as a type of incomplete contract, as do Baker and Krawiec, economists have suggested that one way to understand a constitution is as a type of incomplete contract in which elected officials are offered incentive schemes with payoffs, but in which all future states of affairs

53. Jerry Mashaw, *Prodelegation: Why Administrators Should Make Political Decisions*, 1 J.L. Econ. & Org. 81 (1985).

54. This is the view that legislative delegations "conceal political transfers from the public, making it more difficult for the public to interfere with them" at some cost to social welfare. Eric A. Posner & Adrian Vermeule, *Interring the Nondelegation Doctrine*, 69 U. Chi. L. Rev. 1721 (2002).

55. David Epstein & Sharyn O'Halloran, Delegating Powers: A Transaction Cost Approach to Delegation under Separation of Powers (1999); Jessica Korn, The Power of Separation: American Constitutionalism and the Myth of the Legislative Veto (1996); John A. Rohr, To Run a Constitution: The Legitimacy of the Administrative State (1986).

56. Scott Baker & Kimberly D. Krawiec, *The Penalty Default Canon*, 72 Geo. Wash. L. Rev. 663 (2004).

are not specified.[57] On this account of constitutions, separation of powers can be understood as a set of default rules designed to fill the gaps of an incomplete contract that exists between the legislature and executive. A rigid separation of powers that splits decision making between the branches, as is present in many states, might promote accountability by ensuring clarity of authority for both the legislative and executive branches. This increases the majoritarian accountability behind fundamental policy choices by the legislative branch.

At the same time, rigid separation of authority to protect a tight relationship to majoritarian elections through the institution of the legislative branch is not always sufficient to protect accountability. If branches of government with opposing interests are allowed to make independent claims on public resources without any joint decision making, common pool problems might lead to decreases in accountability. The budgeting process is a good example. Suppose that one decision-making body—the executive—has complete control over the size of the budget, while another body—the legislature—has control over its composition. In a perfect world, voters will know which branch is accountable for which decision, but informational asymmetries between legislators and voters (or between the executive and voters) can lead to informational rents that have disastrous consequences for voters. Similarly, once a legislature has made a delegation decision, authority is frequently shared between the executive branch—charged with enforcing and implementing the law—and the legislative branch—which retains authority over budget and control over statutory criteria. Features such as checks and balances can be understood as a way to elicit information from voters in democratic processes where there is a conflict between the branches.[58]

Thus, although a bargaining framework may provide some support for a nondelegation doctrine, it must also consider the role of checks and balances in a political system. Overlaps in authority between the executive and legislative branches can provide checks and balances—a type of competition that can elicit information from voters to keep executive and legislative officials more accountable. For example, even lawmaking power delegated to the executive branch may be subject to majoritarian processes in national elections for the U.S. president.[59] This may be one reason that federal courts refuse to accept the strong nondelegation doctrine that some commentators, such as Baker and Krawiec, urge as a penalty default.

B. Extending a Normative Account of Nondelegation to the States

In many state constitutional systems, however, the checks and balances counterargument against a nondelegation doctrine is weaker due to unique institutional

57. Torsten Person, Gerard Roland, & Guido Tabellini, *Separation of Powers and Political Accountability*, 112 Q. J. Econ. 1163 (1997).

58. *Id.* at 1166.

59. Jerry L. Mashaw, Greed, Chaos and Governance: Using Public Choice to Improve Public Law 152–56 (1997).

features of state governments. For example, to the extent that an executive branch is unilateral, the political process can more systematically elicit information from voters to dissipate informational rents from delegation; if, however, an executive branch is not unilateral, the political process may not naturally provide clear checks and balances. If legislators are term-limited, or legislatures meet infrequently, interest groups may be able to take advantage of informational asymmetries and persuade agencies to adopt policies with little or no scrutiny by voters. An analysis of the benefits of separation-of-powers doctrines such as the nondelegation doctrine in the states must begin by focusing on institutional features that distinguish the design of state governments from the federal government.

In the United States, the design of political institutions in many state constitutions differs fundamentally from their design in the federal Constitution. Key institutional differences between the federal and most state legislative systems suggest that at the state level, more information about executive agency regulation is likely to be hidden from voters. One difference is that state legislatures are in session for shorter periods than the U.S. Congress, and thus state legislative assemblies are likely to have less familiarity with issues and less time to evaluate bills. For example, the Texas Legislature sits for a 140-day session once every two years.[60] Florida has a sixty-day session, only about forty-five of which are working days; New Mexico's sessions are only sixty calendar days in odd-numbered years, while in even-numbered years sessions are limited to thirty days and the focus is mainly on fiscal matters.[61] Many other state legislatures have similarly short sessions.[62] Term limits, widely endorsed in states, exacerbate the effect of the information asymmetry between legislative and agency decision makers. A short legislative session might make delegation to an executive branch more practical, but most state courts have not endorsed delegation for the purpose of efficiency. Instead, state courts adhering to a strong nondelegation doctrine trade off the potential efficiencies associated with delegation to ensure that the legislature, rather than agencies, makes key policy decisions. This safeguards against lessening the accountability provided through legislative elections.

Other institutional design features also illustrate why such a safeguard on legislative accountability may be necessary in the states. Although in some states the legislative staff is extensive, most states provide members of the legislature little staff assistance in exercising their lawmaking function.[63] Also, because of geographic proximity and economic and cultural similarities, the organization

60. Tex. Const. art. III, §§ 5, 24.

61. Alan Rosenthal, The Decline of Representative Democracy: Process, Participation, and Power in State Legislatures 128 (1998).

62. *See* The Council of State Governments, The Book of the States 64–67 (1998–99).

63. *See* Alan Rosenthal, Legislative Performance in the States: Explorations of Committee Behavior 149–51 (1974).

and mobilization of interest groups, such as farming or tobacco, is much easier at the state than the national level. Given lower costs of organization and mobilization, such interest groups are more likely at the state than federal level to influence the political process. Modern state legislatures also undergo a higher degree of turnover than the U.S. Congress,[64] making it more likely that the state legislative process will produce laws that are the product of highly organized special interest groups representing a small but vocal group of the legislature's constituency.

At the federal level, delegation of decision-making authority to agency decision makers can have pro-democratic effects, in part because the unitary executive provides some degree of streamlined accountability to the U.S. president's office for agency policy decisions. Even though the president is not aware of most agency decisions—especially minor ones—the president is often held accountable by the media, Congress, and the public at large for the positions taken by agencies within the executive branch. Many suggest that the U.S. Constitution envisions a "unitary executive."[65]

Although a few states follow this approach, most do not have a unitary executive.[66] In Texas, for instance, the long ballot provides for the separate election of officials such as the lieutenant governor, the attorney general, the comptroller, the treasurer, and the land commissioner.[67] Florida also has a plural executive branch, providing for separate and independent election of a Governor and an Attorney General, a Commissioner of Agriculture, a Commissioner of Education, a Comptroller, an Insurance Commissioner, a Treasurer, and a Secretary of State.[68] Most other states have similar provisions. Among states that deviate from the unitary executive model, the governor's power to lead and supervise bureaucracy is reduced, although political scientists observe great variations in the degree of reduced leadership and supervision.[69] Regardless of the variations of degree across the various states, in most states the ability of a governor to oversee

---

64. *Id.* at 67–80.

65. *See generally*, Steven G. Calabresi & Kevin H. Rhodes, *The Structural Constitution: Unitary Executive, Plural Judiciary*, 105 HARV. L. REV. 1155 (1992); Saikrishna Bangalore Prakash, *Hail to the Chief Administrator: The Framer's and the President's Administrative Powers*, 102 YALE L.J. 991 (1993).

66. All but four states provide for independent election of lower (or coequal) executive branch officials, and many provide for popular election to executive offices. THE COUNCIL OF STATE GOVERNMENTS, THE BOOK OF THE STATES 38–40 (1998–99).

67. Tex Const. art. IV, §§ 1, 2.

68. Fla. Const. art. IV, §§ 4, 5.

69. *See* Thad Beyle, *Governors*, in POLITICS IN THE AMERICAN STATES (Virginia Gray, Herbert Jacob & Robert B. Albritton eds., 1990); Joseph Schlesinger, *The Politics of the Executive*, in POLITICS IN THE AMERICAN STATES (Herbert Jacob & Kenneth N. Vines eds., 1971); Julia E. Robinson, *The Role of the Independent Political Executive in State Governance: Stability in the Face of Change*, 58 PUB. ADMIN. REV. 119 (1998).

executive policy making is weak relative to the U.S. president's. From an accountability perspective, this makes delegation more suspicious at the state rather than the federal level.

Because of institutional design differences between the federal system and that of many states, and the way these differences reduce majoritarian checks on delegations, state courts have stronger accountability-based reasons for endorsing the nondelegation doctrine than their federal counterparts. In the states, delegation is more likely to result in informational asymmetries that hide policy choices from voters and majoritarian processes. State legislatures—and often agencies—are more prone to faction than the U.S. Congress or federal agencies. As has been recognized since James Madison wrote *Federalist No. 10*, the costs of organizing and mobilizing local factions are lower at the state level than in national politics. Moreover, state legislatures, in session for very limited terms, are not as effective as Congress at providing political oversight for agency policy decisions. In addition, at the state level agencies are less accountable to an executive leader than federal agencies, and judicial review of agency decision making is much less rigorous at the state than at the federal level.

Combined, such factors allow state political processes to send less complete informational signals to voters than may occur at the federal level. The nondelegation doctrine may help to clarify these signals. At the state level, this doctrine may play a more important role in minimizing the ability of interest groups to persuade a legislature to delegate primary policy decisions to the executive branch. The nondelegation doctrine serves to focus these interest groups, and voter attention more generally, on the legislature. Delegation is a terrific strategy for any private interest group that is not successful in obtaining what it wants from the legislature. Even if an interest group can obtain what it wants from the state legislature, it might prefer an agency solution to a legislative solution (perhaps due to lower transparency and greater future control). Because in states there is less direct electoral accountability in the executive branch, interest groups may be able to extract informational rents from the executive that are not available from the legislature. Separation of powers and the nondelegation doctrine might thus be understood as responding to this particular governance failure in state democracies. By contrast, in the federal system where national elections for U.S. president serve to promote executive accountability and interest groups that are successful in states lack power or cancel each other out in the federal lawmaking process, the need for a nondelegation doctrine is less acute.

When compared to competing explanations, this account provides a superior method for understanding the outcomes of constitutional challenges to state delegations in the context of federally-inspired regulatory programs—including the adoption of federal standards and cooperative federalism goals—than the competing explanations provided in the written judicial opinions of state courts. Separation of powers in the states serves to enhance the accountability of the legislative process by eliciting information about important policies from voters and minimizing the opportunities for rent-seeking by interest groups. The information that can be gained from voters in the states by invalidating delegations is more likely to be useful to the state legislative process than it is to the U.S. Congress. Further, as political scientists have recognized since the time of Madison, the costs of organizing and mobilizing interest groups are lower at the state as opposed to the federal level. While a powerful interest group with parochial interests may be successful in influencing policy at the local or state level, in national politics that same interest group may have little or no power, or its influence may be diffuse. Thus, there is little need for a nondelegation doctrine to be applied to a state legislature's delegation to a federal agency. In such a context, there is a clearer majoritarian check on the federal executive than would have generally existed had the state executive adopted the same standard. Further, because interest groups are more diffuse and thus far less likely to play a major role in federal regulatory processes, there is nothing to be gained by a nondelegation doctrine limiting interest group domination of legislative bargaining at the state level. Put simply, state separation of powers in such contexts has little or no purpose, and its application should be suspended to the extent it poses any conflict.

The relaxation of the nondelegation doctrine in the context of state acquiescence in or adoption of federal programs can thus be understood within state separation of powers itself—not by making some broad policy appeal to uniformity, creating a legislative fiction, redefining law or policy as fact, or turning separation of powers into nothing more than a political bargaining chip. Such an analysis would suggest that state legislatures may delegate to state agencies the power to adopt ready-made federal standards without regard to retroactivity concerns. To be sure, states might make such delegations for a variety of different policy reasons, including some that might not be geared towards national uniformity or administrative efficiency. Some interest groups may even be organized around federal programs from which they benefit, and they would be encouraged to lobby state legislators for their adoption. A state political process—not nondelegation doctrine—would be the most effective way to guard against interest group politics in such delegations. Adding an executive branch role in their implementation would enhance rather than reduce the chances of publicly transparent reasons for adopting the federal standards.

Cooperative federalism programs often involve a fundamentally different kind of delegation—from Congress to a state agency—but they also frequently depend on affirmative state legislative support. Recalcitrant state legislatures can serve as barriers to the implementation of such programs, and a similar set of state nondelegation concerns exacerbates their influence. The institutional design account of state separation of powers suggests that state courts can find a normative constitutional solution for cooperative federalism programs from within a state, rather than ceding to federal courts the preemption or political process override of a state's constitution.

This approach does not have the superfluous horsepower of the raw politics assessment of separation of powers. Rather, it would give courts a more principled basis for recognizing when the raw politics assessment of separation-of-powers doctrine might have a useful role to play in the states. Although an institutional design account is deferential to national politics, and thus consistent with efforts to introduce humility and deference into public law,[70] it also recognizes—as do state courts in their interpretive practices—that state constitutions do not always require deference to the legislature on issues of delegation; this gives them some principled basis for understanding when deference is appropriate. Politics has a place in state and national processes, but the institutional design account also allows state constitutions some modest role in constraining it and provides a baseline for delimiting when politics might eclipse legal constraints. In states that do not endorse the nondelegation doctrine as a matter of state constitutional interpretive practice, it would seem that the political process has completely supplanted any legal restriction on legislative delegation of authority to adopt federal standards or to implement cooperative federalism programs.

An institutional design account of state separation of powers is very much in line with what other commentators have urged in this unique constitutional interpretation context. G. Alan Tarr, for instance, has argued that given unique features of state constitutional structure, states require a "distinctive" separation of powers jurisprudence.[71] Dan Rodriguez has argued for a "trans-state" constitutionalism. In echoing these efforts, I do not intend to contend that a one-size-fits-all approach to legal doctrine on all nondelegation constitutional questions is appropriate. Rather, the challenge for separation of powers is to identify what makes it distinctive from the federal system in normative ways that might be generalizable across some, if not all, states. Political science provides a fertile starting place for any such interpretive theory; specifically, a study of the power and effects of interest groups in state political processes provides the seed for a theory of state separation of powers that is both distinctive from federal political processes and generalizable across states. Such an account requires careful study of how interest group participation in state politics, and in the unique institutional settings of state government, might call for a different allocation of powers than other institutional settings, such as our federal system of government. Although this chapter applies this insight to separation of powers between state legislative and executive branches, such a project may even have implications for other structural doctrines of state constitutional law that balance or mediate participation in state and federal political processes, such as the political question doctrine and standing.

---

70. Michael A. Fitts, *The Vices of Virtue: A Political Party Perspective on Civic Virtue Reforms of the Legislative Process*, 136 U. Pa. L. Rev. 1567 (1988).

71. G. Alan Tarr, Understanding State Constitutions 7–8 (1998).

V. CONCLUSION

Echoing prominent appellate lawyer John Frank, who describes state constitutional law as "a sort of pallid me-tooism,"[72] Dan Rodriguez suggests that state constitutional law in its present state is but a minor part of our national constitutional order.[73] Appeals to federal preemption and clear statement rules in federal courts as a way of overcoming the obstacles posed by state constitutions in a dual constitutional lawmaking structure threaten to reduce its role even further.

Yet federal programs need not render moot the legal status of state constitutions. As many state courts recognize, state constitutions continue to play an important role in organizing political processes in the adoption of federal standards. Their role is equally, if not more, important where state agencies are implementing federal programs of a cooperative federalism nature. A more sophisticated federalism would not see all decentralized power as homogenous, but would recognize distinctive features of state and local power, which are often in conflict. Particularly where states implement federal goals or simply borrow federal standards, a more sophisticated account of state power would recognize that state legislatures and executive officers also have distinctive features and frequently conflict over implementation issues. For state constitutions to retain their relevance against the backdrop of such conflicts, a more nuanced interpretive account is needed. The challenge is for state courts to develop an interpretive strategy for preserving their own state-specific constitutional values while also recognizing the larger objectives of federal regulatory programs and goals. For state systems, an institutional account of separation of powers holds greater promise than its competitors as an interpretive strategy for state courts as they struggle with this task.

---

72. *See* John P. Frank, *The Emergence of State Constitutional Law*, 63 TEX. L. REV. 1339, 1340 (1985).

73. Rodriguez, *supra* note 21, at 272; *see also* Chapter 5.

9. STATE COMMON LAW AND THE DUAL ENFORCEMENT OF CONSTITUTIONAL NORMS

HELEN HERSHKOFF

I. INTRODUCTION

Imagine a worker who is fired from her job. The employee has received consistent satisfactory evaluations; indeed, her supervisor informally had told her to expect a promotion. Yet instead of receiving a pay raise, she gets a pink slip. If the employee worked for the government, she could try to find out the reasons for the dismissal by filing a challenge under the Due Process Clause of the U.S. Constitution.[1] A private employee has no such constitutional right; other than the Thirteenth Amendment's prohibition on slavery, the federal Constitution applies only to governmental conduct.[2] Although critics have urged eliminating state action as a condition for constitutional enforcement, the federal Constitution generally protects against public but not private abuses of power.

A different story emerges when we turn from federal to state constitutional practice. State courts are not required to apply the federal state action doctrine; moreover, not all state constitutions contain a state action limitation.[3] A workplace's nongovernmental status thus does not inevitably foreclose a state court from subjecting an adverse job action to constitutional review. The state court practice of extending constitutional protection into the private realm, while both important and controversial, has tended to eclipse an even more significant aspect of state constitutionalism: the use of state common law as a modality for elaborating and enforcing state constitutional norms in private domains located beyond federal constitutional regulation.

In contrast to federal doctrine, state judicial practice embraces an interpretative fluidity that hurdles the formal boundaries of private and public law. As former Chief Judge Judith Kaye of the New York Court of Appeals explains, "[W]hile federal constitutional law is cabined by the text of the Constitution, state courts move seamlessly between the common law and state constitutional law, the shifting ground at times barely perceptible."[4] Indeed, even in states that

1. *E.g.*, Perry v. Sindermann, 408 U.S. 593 (1972).

2. The Civil Rights Cases, 109 U.S. 3 (1883).

3. *See* John Devlin, *Constructing an Alternative to "State Action" as a Limit on State Constitutional Rights Guarantees: A Survey, Critique and Proposal*, 21 Rutgers L.J. 819 (1990).

4. Judith S. Kaye, *State Courts at the Dawn of a New Century: Common Law Courts Reading Statutes and Constitutions*, 70 N.Y.U. L. Rev. 1, 15 (1995).

adhere to a state action requirement—and so limit the direct enforcement of state constitutional norms to government actors—state common law doctrines of contract, tort, and property provide a pathway for the interpretation and application of constitutional norms in private disputes. Through actions such as the public law tort or the implied covenant of good faith, state courts transport state constitutional values into areas of private life that are outside the reach of federal constitutional protections. These common law doctrines provide an important complementary site for generating public norms that are vital for securing individual dignity in the varied domains of modern day life.

State courts—more explicitly than federal courts—draw from diverse sources of authority in their common law decision making, including foreign legal principles.[5] The state judicial practice of indirectly enforcing constitutional norms through common law pathways invites comparison with practices abroad, where courts, unlike U.S. federal courts, deal explicitly with the "horizontal" enforcement of constitutional rights in areas considered private and so beyond constitutional regulation. Courts abroad speak of the possibility of human rights in the private sphere,[6] and they recognize claims that permit the third-party application of constitutional rights.[7] International judicial practice provides an illuminating interpretive frame that is salient in uncovering and appreciating the ways in which state common law supports public values and encourages social commitments by serving as a vehicle for interpreting and adapting constitutional norms in nongovernmental settings.[8]

This chapter thus is fundamentally concerned with the principles that join private and public law together in the project of dual constitutional enforcement. The point is not to merge common law with constitutional law, but to highlight the private law portals through which constitutional values infuse and influence areas of life traditionally deemed private. Part II provides the comparative frame by identifying judicial techniques used by foreign courts in adapting constitutional norms to private disputes that engage nongovernmental actors. I then take a domestic turn and look at state court practice. As in legal systems outside the United States, state courts in a surprising range of cases effectively resolve private disputes in light of constitutional norms although these norms do not

5. Renáta Uitz, *Yet Another Revival of Horizontal Effect of Constitutional Rights? Why? And Why Now?—An Introduction, in* THE CONSTITUTION IN PRIVATE RELATIONS: EXPANDING CONSTITUTIONALISM (András Sajó & Renáta Uitz eds., 2005).

6. ANDREW CLAPHAM, HUMAN RIGHTS IN THE PRIVATE SPHERE (1993).

7. *See* Lorraine E. Weinrib & Ernest J. Weinrib, *Constitutional Values and Private Law in Canada, in* HUMAN RIGHTS IN PRIVATE LAW 43, 44 (Daniel Friedmann & Daphne Barak-Erez eds., 2002).

8. *See* Margaret H. Marshall, *"Wise Parents Do Not Hesitate to Learn from Their Children": Interpreting State Constitutions in an Age of Global Jurisprudence*, 79 N.Y.U. L. REV. 1633, 1641 (2004).

always give rise to a direct cause of action in private relations. Even where state constitutional doctrine bars a private litigant from enforcing a constitutional right directly against a nongovernmental actor, state courts rely on constitutional norms as a source of interpretative authority to reshape common law relations in ways that effectuate the underlying public right in the context of private activity. Part III locates state common law interpretive practice in the theory of federalism, sovereignty, and judicial capacity that supports the project of dual constitutional enforcement described in this volume. I also address whether concerns about horizontal constitutional enforcement abroad and in Article III courts has the same traction when undertaken by state common law courts. Part IV draws on private and public law interpretive theory to conceptualize state judicial practice within the project of dual constitutional enforcement. A brief conclusion urges greater attention to the democratic implications of recovering the accepted tradition of a "common law infused with constitutional values."[9]

II. FRAMING THE EXTENSION OF CONSTITUTIONAL NORMS TO PRIVATE CONDUCT

The common law, standing for private law doctrines of contract, tort, and property, governs relations among individuals in activities that are consensually organized and said to be free of government coercion. Public law, by contrast, refers to constitutional and administrative law and regulates relations between individuals and the government. The doctrinal division maps the classical distinction between the private, conceived (at least before the Legal Realists) as a domain of prepolitical ordering immune from governmental restraint, and the public, viewed as a realm of political choices supported by government force.[10] Limiting constitutional enforcement to "state action" reinforces the public/private distinction and relieves aspects of the common law from constitutional scrutiny. Constitutional analysis thus starts from an unspoken baseline of common law entitlements said to be located in an autonomous sphere that is distinct from the public and is constrained by the market and other extra-legal expressions of private preference.[11]

Some states, whether in their constitutions or through their judicial practices, take a different approach to the public/private divide: in these legal systems, a doctrinal fire wall does not separate the public values of constitutional law from

---

9. Judith S. Kaye, *Foreword: The Common Law and State Constitutional Law as Full Partners in the Protection of Individual Rights*, 23 RUTGERS L.J. 727, 738 (1991–92).

10. *See* Robert L. Hale, *Coercion and Distribution in a Supposedly Non-Coercive State*, 38 POL. SCI. Q. 470 (1923).

11. *See* Cass R. Sunstein, *Lochner's Legacy*, 87 COLUM. L. REV. 873, 874 (1987).

the common law decisions that support private ordering.[12] From an international perspective, the interpretive practices of these state courts resemble those of jurisdictions abroad, such as India and South Africa, in which courts achieve the horizontal application of constitutional norms in disputes involving nongovernmental actors using the pathways of private law doctrine.[13]

A. Foreign Models of Horizontal Constitutional Application

Georg Nolte writes, "Over the past few years . . . European constitutional theory and practice is becoming aware that it has developed certain rules and possesses certain properties which are characteristically different from US constitutionalism and vice versa."[14] One such practice, in Europe and elsewhere, reflecting a confluence of factors involving constitutional text, legal culture, and political ideology, concerns the enforcement of constitutional rights in private disputes between nongovernmental litigants. Variously called the *horizontal* or *third-party* application of constitutional rights (the different terminology tends to track the divide between common law and civil law systems), the practice has drawn a great deal of attention as commentators seek to identify and justify the ways in which constitutional norms might be enforced in private disputes. The literature includes a variety of models; as the South Africa Court emphasized in *Du Plessis v. De Klerk*, "there is no universal answer to the problem of vertical or horizontal application of a bill of rights."[15] Differences reflect not only the particularistic divergence typical of comparative analysis, but also fundamental disagreements about the role of the private in civil society and of maintaining plural sites in which norms are elaborated and respected. These disagreements also implicate questions of democratic legitimacy and individual autonomy within different political regimes. Just as withholding constitutional review in cases involving nongovernmental activity fails to protect against abuses of private power in areas of critical significance to the individual, so a different set of problems might arise if constitutional law is permitted, in Dean Derek Van Der Merwe's provocative phrase, to colonize the common law.[16]

I set out here a synthetic approach to the issue of horizontal constitutional application that draws mainly from the writings of retired Justice Aharon Barak, former

12. *See generally* Ellen A. Peters, *State Constitutional Law: Federalism in the Common Law Tradition*, 84 MICH. L. REV. 583 (1986).

13. *See, e.g.*, Helen Hershkoff, *Transforming Legal Theory in the Light of Practice: The Judicial Application of Social and Economic Rights to Private Orderings*, *in* COURTING SOCIAL JUSTICE: JUDICIAL ENFORCEMENT OF SOCIAL AND ECONOMIC RIGHTS IN THE DEVELOPING WORLD 268–302 (Varun Gauri & Daniel M. Brinks eds., 2008).

14. Georg Nolte, *European and US Constitutionalism: Comparing Essential Elements*, *in* EUROPEAN AND US CONSTITUTIONALISM 3 (Georg Nolte ed., 2005).

15. Du Plessis v. De Klerk, 1996 (3) S.A. 850 at 871 D–E (Kentridge A.J.).

16. Derek Van Der Merwe, *Constitutional Colonisation of the Common Law: A Problem of Institutional Integrity*, 2000 J. S. AFR. L. 12 (2000).

President of the Supreme Court of Israel.[17] Justice Barak identifies four models distinguished along three matrices: the rights to be enforced (constitutional or nonconstitutional), the status of the defendant (governmental or nongovernmental), and the procedural pathway (direct constitutional cause of action or indirect common law cause of action). Justice Barak explains: "The first model designates that constitutional human rights—which were defined and determined by the constitution or in a basic law—apply directly in private law, and directly influence private relationships (direct application model)."[18] The second model is the mirror image of the first, and withholds direct application of constitutional rights in private disputes on the view that constitutional rights apply only against the government. Justice Barak describes the third and fourth models as "mid-points between the two extreme models," and they are most relevant to the common law practices of some state courts in the United States.[19] The third model, referred to as the indirect application model, uses common law doctrines (e.g., the doctrine of good faith) to enforce constitutional norms through a process Justice Barak calls "public law 'absorption.'"[20] At least one commentator suggests that the distinction between direct and indirect horizontal application makes a practical difference in those cases in which the existing common law doctrine does not provide a cause of action or afford some other procedural pathway for constitutional enforcement.[21] Finally, the fourth model, parallel to the second, assumes that constitutional rights apply only against government actors, but assimilates the courts to other state institutions for state action purposes. Most similar to the theory informing *Shelley v. Kraemer* in U.S. doctrine,[22] this model assumes that "the judiciary is prohibited from developing common law . . . or granting relief in a specific case . . . that harms a constitutional right."[23]

B. Horizontal Application by State Courts Using Common Law Pathways

Turning from foreign to U.S. state courts, I put to the side those models that look to the direct application (or not) of constitutional rights in private settings, and instead focus on instances in which public norms operate indirectly on nongovernmental actors through the pathways of the common law. I survey here three techniques used by state courts, each of which has parallels in foreign practice

17. Aharon Barak, *Constitutional Human Rights and Private Law*, 3 Rev. of Constitutional Studies 218 (1996); Aharon Barak, *Constitutional Human Rights and Private Law*, *in* Friedmann & Barak-Erez, *supra* note 7, at 13.

18. *See* Barak, *Constitutional Human Rights and Private Law*, *supra* note 17, at 225.

19. *Id.* at 255.

20. *Id.* at 226.

21. Johan van der Walt, *Progressive Indirect Horizontal Application of the Bill of Rights: Towards a Co-Operative Relation between Common-Law and Constitutional Jurisprudence*, 17 S. Afr. J. on Hum. Rts. 341, 343 (2001).

22. 334 U.S. 1 (1948).

23. Barak, *Constitutional Human Rights and Private Law*, *supra* note 17, at 226.

and effectively achieves horizontal constitutional enforcement: enforcing constitutional norms through existing common law causes of action, elaborating common law doctrines in the light of constitutional norms, and developing common law defenses informed by constitutional norms.

1. Invigorating Private Causes of Action: The Public Policy Tort Consider the woman who faces sexual harassment in the workplace. She complains to a supervisor and is fired for insubordination. Because the workplace is private, the federal Equal Protection Clause provides her no remedy; if the workplace has only eight employees, federal antidiscrimination law likewise offers no relief.[24] Similarly, many state equal rights amendments, although specifically aimed at gender discrimination, stop short of private market activity.[25] In each of these settings, we may say either that the lack of government involvement blocks constitutional enforcement or that the substantive scope of the equality right leaves intact the American common law rule of at-will employment, a rule that relieves employers of having to justify terminating a worker who has been hired for an indefinite period. State courts have applied the at-will rule since at least the last quarter of the nineteenth century when it was first announced.[26]

Beginning in 1959, some state courts began to modify the at-will rule by recognizing the "public policy tort."[27] Today, the majority of state courts permit recovery where "the discharge of the employee contravenes a clear mandate of public policy."[28] Generally, the tort covers a termination in one of four situations: (1) "for refusing to commit an illegal act"; (2) "for performing a public duty or obligation"; (3) "for exercising a legal right or privilege"; and (4) "in retaliation for reporting employer misconduct, i.e., whistleblowing."[29] Whether the public policy must involve third-party effects remains an open question in some states.[30]

Constitutional norms provide state courts with guidance in assessing whether a public policy exists and whether the employee's termination violates that policy.[31] The Washington Supreme Court explains, "In determining whether a clear mandate of public policy is violated, courts should inquire whether the employer's

---

24. *See* Title VII of the Civil Rights Act of 1964, 42 U.S.C. § 2000e-2(a) (2007).

25. Wolfgang P. Hirczy de Miño, *Does an Equal Rights Amendment Make a Difference?*, 60 Alb. L. Rev. 1581, 1597–98 (1997).

26. H.G. Wood, A Treatise on the Law of Master and Servant § 134, at 272 (1877).

27. *See* Petermann v. Int'l. Bhd. of Teamsters, Local 396, 344 P.2d 25, 27 (Cal. Dist. Ct. App. 1959).

28. Henry H. Perritt, Jr., Employee Dismissal Law and Practice § 1.07 (5th ed. 2007).

29. Gardner v. Loomis Armored, Inc., 913 P.2d 377, 379 (Wash. 1996).

30. Stewart J. Schwab, *Wrongful Discharge Law and the Search for Third-Party Effects*, 74 Tex. L. Rev. 1943 (1996).

31. Brock Rowatt, *The Public Policy Exception to Employment at Will: Can Judicial Decisions be Used as a Source of Public Policy?*, 62 UMKC L. Rev. 325, 331–32 (1993).

conduct contravenes the letter or purpose of a constitutional, statutory, or regulatory provision or scheme."[32] Illinois echoes this approach:

> But what constitutes clearly mandated public policy? There is no precise definition of the term. In general, it can be said that public policy concerns what is right and just and what affects the citizens of the State collectively. It is to be found in the State's constitution and statutes and, when they are silent, in its judicial decisions.[33]

State courts have located public policy in a number of state constitutional provisions. In an early case recognizing the public policy tort, the Supreme Court of Oregon affirmed a verdict for an employee terminated for serving jury duty.[34] The court looked first to the Oregon Constitution's guarantee of trial by jury, which provides civil litigants and criminal defendants a right to a jury trial. Oregon statutes governing excuse from jury duty also establish that jurors are to serve without interference. These constitutional and statutory sources convinced the court to find that discharging an employee for serving jury duty was "a socially undesirable motive" that demanded deterrence through the tort system. "If an employer were permitted with impunity to discharge an employee for fulfilling her obligation of jury duty," the court explained, the "jury system would be adversely affected. The will of the community would be thwarted."[35] The public policy tort effectively placed the worker in the role of a private attorney general: the tort provided individual compensation and also protected the public's collective interest in the jury system that the employer's private conduct threatened. Although the litigation did not involve a public actor, the court recognized that failing to enforce the constitutional norm would generate negative social externalities that would undermine important public values.

State courts also have found a clear public policy in state constitutional equality provisions. *Roberts v. Dudley*, decided in 2000 by the Washington Supreme Court, offers an example of this approach.[36] Plaintiff claimed that she had been fired because she was pregnant and challenged her dismissal on grounds of sex discrimination. The state equal rights amendment did not apply to private employment; similarly, state antidiscrimination law did not govern because of the size of the employer's work force. Nevertheless, the court located in state

---

32. Thompson v. St. Regis Paper Co., 685 P.2d 1081 (Wash. 1984) (quoting Parnar v. Americana Hotels, Inc., 652 P.2d 625, 631 (Haw. 1982)). Courts also look to constitutional amendments; *see, e.g.*, Brockmeyer v. Dun & Bradstreet, 335 N.W.2d 834, 840 (Wis. 1983).

33. Palmateer v. Int'l. Harvester Co., 421 N.E.2d 876, 878 (Ill. 1981); *see also* Novosel v. Nationwide Ins. Co., 721 F.2d 894, 897–98 (3rd Cir. 1983).

34. Nees v. Hocks, 536 P.2d 512 (Or. 1975).

35. *Id.* at 515–16.

36. 993 P.2d 901, 911 (Wash. 2000).

judicial decisions interpreting the Washington Constitution and state antidiscrimination law a clear "public policy against discrimination" that could be enforced as a matter of contract.[37] Although state antidiscrimination law limited the availability of statutory remedies against an exempt employer, the court held that having identified a "public policy against employment discrimination," it retained common law power to remedy private employment practices that undermined the constitutional norm.[38]

Similarly, in *Phillips v. St. Mary Regional Medical Center*,[39] the California Court of Appeal reversed the trial court's dismissal of a retaliation claim brought by a private employee who alleged he had been fired for having filed an unsuccessful discrimination claim against his employer. Defendant, a nonprofit religious organization, enjoyed immunity in the discrimination suit under a statutory exemption. Nevertheless, the court held that the California Constitution reflects a "fundamental and firmly established public policy against employment discrimination based on certain classifications including race and sex," which could be enforced through a public policy tort. Limiting the tort to policies located in the constitution or statute "strikes the proper balance," the court explained, "among the interests of employers, employees and the public." Not only does the tort action protect the private interest of the worker to be free from discrimination, but also the tort serves "society's interests . . . through a more stable job market, in which its most important policies are safeguarded." The court insisted that recognizing the tort would impose "no impediment" on even exempt employers, for they are "bound, at a minimum to know the fundamental policies of the state and nation as expressed in their constitutions and statutes" and so bound by equality norms.[40]

Some state courts also recognize a public policy tort action based on state constitutional privacy provisions. Alaska is one of eleven states extending constitutional protection to privacy, which has been interpreted as affording a broader substantive right than the Fourth Amendment's search-and-seizure clause.[41] Although the Alaska court has declined to enforce the privacy right directly against nongovernmental actors, the public policy tort indirectly achieves horizontal enforcement through a common law pathway.[42] Liability in the tort action

---

37. *Id.* at 901. The Washington Constitution art. XXI, § 1 (amend. 61) prohibits sex discrimination.

38. *Roberts*, 993 P.2d at 908.

39. 96 Cal.App.4th 218 (2002).

40. *Id.* at 227 (internal citations omitted).

41. The states are Alaska, Arizona, California, Florida, Hawaii, Louisiana, Montana, South Carolina, Texas, and Washington. Reginald C. Govan & Freddie Mac, *Workplace Privacy, Practicing Law Institute 34th Annual Institute on Employment Law*, PLI Order No. 6740 (Sept–Nov. 2005).

42. *See, e.g.*, Luedtke v. Nabors Alaska Drilling, Inc., 768 P.2d 1123, 1133–36 (Alaska 1989).

turns on a balancing test that weighs the worker's interest in privacy against the public's interest in health and safety. Thus, in assessing whether an oil rigger's privacy interest was violated by his employer's requiring a drug test to assess use of marijuana in off-duty activities, the court emphasized that "work on an oil rig can be very dangerous" and declined to order relief.[43] Similarly, the New Jersey Supreme Court has refused to enforce that state's constitutional search-and-seizure provision directly against private employers, but recognizes a public policy tort that balances private and public interests and indirectly enforces the public norm.[44]

2. Informing Common Law Liability Rules: The Implied Covenant of Good Faith State courts also look to constitutional norms for guidance in construing contract terms. The implied covenant of good faith offers perhaps the most notable common law pathway for achieving constitutional enforcement horizontally. Through this doctrinal channel, state courts consider a variety of constitutional norms that effectively set objective parameters for private agreements.[45] The Restatement (Second) of Contracts defines the implied covenant as imposing on "each party a duty of good faith and fair dealing" in the performance of a contract.[46] The Restatement makes clear that it is impossible to identify all the forms of prohibited bad faith behavior,[47] and some state courts—admittedly only a few among the minority of courts that even embrace the doctrine of implied covenant—define bad faith in the light of state constitutional norms.[48]

For example, in *Toussaint v. Blue Cross & Blue Shield of Michigan*, the Michigan Supreme Court enforced the implied covenant where the employer not only had assured an at-will employee that he would not be dismissed "as long as [he] did [his] job," but also reinforced the expectation of job security by giving the worker a copy of the company personnel manual, which stated "it was the 'policy' of the company to release employees 'for just cause only.'"[49] The Michigan court found that firing an employee without good cause after making such a promise

---

43. *Id.* at 1136.

44. *See* Hennessey v. Coastal Eagle Point Oil Co., 129 N.J. 81 (1992). New Jersey also recognizes the tort of "unreasonable intrusion upon seclusion" in the private workplace setting, for which the courts use a balancing test to assess competing factors. Gregory T. Alvarez & Jason E. Ruff, *Private-Sector Employees and Workplace Privacy in the Electronic Era*, 247 N.J. LAW MAG. 24 (Aug. 2007).

45. *See* Guy Mundlak, *Human Rights and the Employment Relationship: A Look through the Prism of Juridification*, *in* Friedmann & Barak-Erez, *supra* note 7, at 298.

46. RESTATEMENT (SECOND) OF CONTRACTS § 205 (1979).

47. *Id.* at § 205 cmt. d.

48. *See, e.g.*, Magnan v. Anaconda Industry, Inc., 429 A.2d 492 (Conn. 1980); Fortune v. Nat'l Cash Register Co., 364 N.E.2d 1251 (Mass. 1977); Gates v. Life of Mont. Ins. Co., 638 P.2d 1063 (Mont. 1982); Monge v. Beebe Rubber Co., 316 A.2d 549 (N.H. 1974), modified in Howard v. Dorr Woolen Co., 414 A.2d 1273 (N.H. 1980).

49. 292 N.W.2d 880, 885 (Mich. 1980).

contravened Michigan public policy; the employer had secured for itself a cooperative and loyal work force while depriving the employee of the security he deserved to receive in exchange. In reaching this conclusion, the court looked to the U.S. Supreme Court's decision in *Perry v. Sindermann*, in which a public employer's interest in continued public employment was found to be legitimate—and so protected as a matter of procedural due process—where the expectation of job security could be traced to "rules and understandings, promulgated and fostered by state officials" despite the absence of a tenure system.[50] The Michigan court comfortably extended this precedent without even mentioning the lack of state action: "if there is in effect a policy to dismiss for cause only, the employer may not depart from that policy at whim simply because he was under no obligation to institute the policy in the first place."[51]

3. Creating Common Law Defenses: Balancing Property and Speech Rights Finally, state courts look to constitutional norms in recognizing defenses that effectively reshape common law entitlements in light of public values. A key example of this technique involves state judicial reliance on free speech and association norms in elaborating the appropriate scope of property rights in trespass cases. Property rights conventionally are understood as the power to exclude.[52] Private property owners have no obligation to permit outsiders to enter their grounds or to facilitate relations between outsiders and persons who have been invited onto the premises. As the U.S. Supreme Court has emphasized, "an uninvited guest may [not] exercise general rights of free speech on property privately owned."[53] However, when the government is in the position of property owner (for example, of parks or streets), the judicially created public forum doctrine constrains the unfettered right to exclude: speech rights "supersede the 'property rights' of the state" and require the government to "'subsidize' speech by allowing individuals to use publicly owned property for speech purposes."[54]

A few state courts—far fewer than those that recognize the public policy tort—interpret a property owner's common law right to exclude uninvited guests from the premises in the light of a countervailing policy that favors certain kinds of speech, associational, and other expressive activity. *State v. Shack* offers an early iteration of this approach in the context of a criminal trespass action brought on behalf of a farm owner who employed migrant workers housed on his property.[55] A lawyer from a nonprofit organization sought access to the workers in

50. 408 U.S. 593, 603 (1972).

51. *Toussaint*, 292 N.W.2d at 895.

52. *E.g.*, Adderley v. Florida, 385 U.S. 39, 47 (1966).

53. Lloyd Corp. v. Tanner, 407 U.S. 551, 568, 567 (1972).

54. Geoffrey R. Stone et al., The First Amendment 295 (2d ed. 2003).

55. State v. Shack, 277 A.2d 369 (N.J. 1971). *See* Helen Hershkoff, *The New Jersey Constitution, Positive Rights, Common Law Entitlements, and State Action*, 69 Alb. L. Rev. 553, 556–58 (2006).

their lodgings to discuss how they could obtain government services such as medical and legal assistance. The New Jersey Supreme Court rejected defendant's effort to treat the farm as a company town, and so as a state actor for constitutional purposes. The court further rejected defendant's argument that under the federal Supremacy Clause, the Sixth Amendment barred enforcement of the state trespass statute. Instead, the court construed the scope of the farmer owner's common law property right, finding that the trespass statute did not apply to defendant's action: the farm owner's property right did not include authority to bar a lawyer from meeting with workers in their lodgings to discuss government services. "The policy considerations which underlie that conclusion," the court explained,

> may be much the same as those which would be weighed with respect to one or more of the constitutional challenges, but a decision in nonconstitutional terms is more satisfactory, because the interests of migrant workers are more expansively served in that way than they would be if they had no more freedom than these constitutional concepts could be found to mandate if indeed they apply at all.

While recognizing the farm owner's right to run his business without interference, the court emphasized that a "right in . . . real property of course is not absolute." The court declined "to open the employer's premises to the general public if in fact the employer himself has not done so." But the court found it to be "unthinkable that the farmer-employer can assert a right to isolate the migrant worker in any respect significant for the worker's well-being."[56]

Whether the common law permits a property owner the absolute right "to exclude anyone at all for any reason" was again at issue in *Uston v. Resorts International Hotel*, raising a wholly different factual context: a casino owner's right to bar a "card counting" patron from the blackjack table.[57] In deciding whether the property owner could exclude the guest, the New Jersey court drew an analogy to a state constitutional decision finding it unreasonable for Princeton University, a private institution, to exclude individuals who wanted to leaflet on campus. The court explained: "Property owners have no legitimate interest in unreasonably excluding particular members of the public when they open their premises for public use."[58] Drawing no distinction between political and nonpolitical speech, the court treated the casino as a common carrier with a right to exclude guests who pose a security risk because intoxicated or physically threatening, but not, absent administrative regulation, those who play blackjack in a particular way.

---

56. *Shack*, 277 A.2d at 371–73.
57. Uston v. Resort Int'l Hotel, Inc., 445 A.2d 370, 373 (N.J. 1982).
58. *Id.* at 375.

Probably the most famous example of a state court's adapting common law property entitlements in the light of constitutional norms concerns whether individuals may leaflet and engage in other expressive activity on the grounds of a private shopping mall. Some commentators liken a shopping mall to the modern-day public square—"the focus of what little social life many of us share with others"; others see it as a contemporary "homestead."[59] *Lloyd Corp. v. Whiffen* involved efforts by individuals to solicit signatures for initiative petitions at a shopping mall in Oregon.[60] The shopping center included "more than 66 blocks of publicly owned sidewalks"; a public park and public bus stops were adjacent to the center. The center's owner barred all solicitation of any kind on the premises and publicized the ban in large notices posted at all of the center's twenty-five entrances. The Oregon court expressly declined to treat the dispute as a constitutional matter, instead turning to a common law solution: "Avoiding needless constitutional rulings is not a technical nicety of judicial etiquette," the court explained. "This rule prevents premature foreclosure of opportunities for legislators who are better equipped to consider and choose among different policies." But the court added that in applying a common law rule or devising an equitable order, a court "must observe constitutional principles as much as a legislative or administrative body." Looking to state constitutional provisions that protect the right "to collect signatures to initiate public lawmaking," the court emphasized that "[t]he signature-gathering process for political petitions is a form of political speech and no one contests that free speech is one of our society's most precious rights." The property owner's right to exclude thus could not be interpreted to allow a wholesale exclusion of such speech. On the other hand, although the court deemed the mall to be "the antithesis of a private place," it underscored the importance of reducing uninvited interference with the running of a business and so imposed "reasonable restrictions" on the requested speech activity (including limits on the setting up of card tables in walkways or other places).[61] As in the public policy tort cases, the signature-solicitors functioned as private attorneys general seeking to enforce not only their only right to political speech, but also the public's right to open discussion, thus protecting against negative social externalities that would undermine the strength of the constitutional right.

C. Reconfiguring Private Relations in Light of Constitutional Values

The cases surveyed do not conform to the typical dualisms of federal constitutional practice—most notably between state action and private action, between

59. Sarah G. Vincent, *The Cultural Context of the Shopping Mall: Tension Between Patron's Right of Access and Owner's Right to Exclude*, 37 UWLA L. Rev. 221, 221 (2004); *compare* Uston, 445 A.2d. at 239.

60. 773 P.2d 1294 (Or. 1989).

61. *Id.* at 1295–96, 1297 (citations omitted), 1299, 1300–01.

public regulation and private ordering, and between judicial supremacy and democratic accountability. In place of these binary divisions, state judicial decision making emphasizes the interconnection of legal categories: public values interpenetrate forms of private ordering that nevertheless remain distinct from the public; constitutional concepts affect judicial interpretation even as the court disavows making a constitutional decision; and the court's decree resolves a specific contextualized dispute while leaving open the possibility of revision from legislative or other actors. These interpretative characteristics reflect the often-praised features of the common law approach[62]—as Justice Souter has described, a process that avoids an "all-or-nothing analysis that tends to produce legal petrification instead of an evolving boundary between the domains of old principles."[63]

If these state practices differ from the federal, they also diverge somewhat from the academic models earlier identified as channeling enforcement of constitutional rights horizontally. The state courts surveyed take constitutional norms into account, but they do not frame the question as whether a private actor has violated a constitutional right owed to another private actor; to the contrary, the state courts examined have avoided using the language of rights and duties and instead focus on a discrete relation that is reconfigured in light of the public value. The constitutional norm is thus acknowledged to apply to all legal actors, but not to impose specific obligations on a private litigant.[64] Thus, for example, in public policy tort cases involving termination for having served on a jury, the courts have relied on the constitutional norm to reorder the workplace relation to protect the integrity of the jury system and respect the "will of the community."[65] Arguably, the courts adhere to a private law model in which government intervention is justified only where negative externalities threaten third parties—here the third-party interest in preserving the vitality of constitutional values. Of course, disputes presenting contested values involve more difficult line drawing, but this problem is not unique to instances of indirect horizontal enforcement.

III. IMPLICATIONS FOR FEDERALISM, SOVEREIGNTY, AND JUDICIAL PRACTICE

This part briefly makes the case for explicitly harnessing state common law practices in the project of dual constitutional enforcement, situating them within its

62. *See, e.g.*, W. J. Waluchow, A Common Law Theory of Judicial Review: The Living Tree 231–32 (2007).

63. Washington v. Glucksberg, 521 U.S. 702, 770 (1997) (Souter, J., concurring).

64. *Cf.* Gunther Teubner, *The Anonymous Matrix: Human Rights Violations by "Private" Transnational Actors*, 69 Modern L. Rev. 327, 329 (2006).

65. Nees v. Hocks, 536 P.2d 512, 516 (Or. 1975).

theory of federalism, sovereignty, and judicial capacity. I also explore whether concerns about horizontal application in the context of Article III and foreign judiciaries have as much traction in the state court context.

A. Harnessing Common Law Practices in the Project of Dual Enforcement

The theory of dual enforcement makes three important claims about federalism, state sovereignty, and judicial capacity. Alone and together, these claims are consistent with the state court practice of interpreting and enforcing constitutional norms through common law pathways. Above all, they recognize that it is impossible conceptually to segregate aspects of U.S. law or legal institutions from the whole of which they are a part. All function within the orbit of constitutional norms that influence social relations even outside the mechanistic channels of direct constitutional enforcement. Nor is this influence unidirectional; rather, state court interpretation at the periphery affects the shape and content of constitutional meaning at the federal core. Although well-known institutional reasons may caution against having Article III courts generally subject common law decisions to constitutional review, the national aim of constructing constitutional meaning surely benefits from state common law decisions that rely on state constitutional law as a source of interpretive authority.

1. Federalism The project of dual enforcement sets to rest any notion "that states and federal government (should) operate in different, mutually exclusive spheres."[66] Federalism from this perspective does not connote separate spheres of national and state power, nor does it embrace top-down enforcement of norms centrally constructed and imposed hierarchically on subordinate actors. The approach as elegantly described by Robert A. Schapiro instead is "polyphonic," drawing creative energy from "the existence of multiple, independent sources of political authority" marked by interconnection as well as competition.[67] Although the polyphonic approach generates occasional dissonance,[68] it resists blockading any aspect of state power from the national collaborative enterprise: again, as Schapiro puts it, "Full concurrent power is the norm."[69] Within this framework, state common law offers a localized, decentralized, experimental approach that is coextensive with national authority and competent to collaborate in the construction of complementary as well as critical constitutional meaning.[70] Although state

---

66. Roderick M. Hills, Jr., *Against Preemption: How Federalism Can Improve the National Legislative Process*, 82 N.Y.U. L. Rev. 1, 4 (2007).

67. Robert A. Schapiro, *Toward a Theory of Interactive Federalism*, 91 Iowa L. Rev. 243, 248–49, 285 (2005).

68. *See* Hans A. Linde, *The State and Federal Courts in Governance: Vive La Différence!*, 46 Wm. & Mary L. Rev. 1273 (2005).

69. Schapiro, *supra* note 67, at 285.

70. Helen Hershkoff, *Positive Rights and State Constitutions: The Limits of Federal Rationality Review*, 112 Harv. L. Rev. 1131, 1196 (1999).

decision-making processes enjoy constitutional protection, a state's "particular outputs" are "not assured of supremacy"; to the contrary, they may be required to yield under national pressure.[71]

2. State Sovereignty In addition, the dual enforcement project ascribes a normative content to state sovereignty that Lawrence Sager refers to as the promotion of "moral progress." Even during the nineteenth century regime of dual federalism, states experimented with "maverick ideas," whether because of alternative sensibilities, economic imperative, or institutional necessity, which eventually propagated, consolidated, informed and even displaced competing national commitments.[72] We need not embrace the wholesale optimism of this analysis to recognize that states at different times in our nation's history have pushed forward what Sager calls a "moral frontier" located beyond the border of federal constitutionalism. State common law, as an aspect of state sovereignty, helps to publicize issues, transcend boundaries, and test the constitutional waters by offering case-by-case elaborations of constitutional norms in discrete situations.

3. State Judicial Capacity Finally, the special capacities of state courts as common law courts sit comfortably with the project of dual enforcement. State courts are not bound by Article III or constrained by federal separation-of-powers doctrine. They hold concurrent jurisdictional authority over all matters federal unless specifically withdrawn by Congress.[73] In addition, state courts have experience in consulting multiple and open-textured sources for legal guidance; they comfortably consult "related rulings from other jurisdictions when analyzing issues arising under the law of their own jurisdictions . . . provided those rulings are given only the weight to which their persuasive value entitles them," and are familiar with federal and constitutional sources in their decision making.[74] Finally, the common law approach allows state courts to move in classic "molecular motions" before undertaking more radical moves under federal or state constitutions.[75] The conditional nature of common law decision making—and the possibility of reversal from many different pressure points—opens up rather than shuts down discussion with other legal actors, thereby contributing to the overall project of elaborating constitutional norms within different loci of power.

B. Concerns about State Judicial Use of Common Law for Horizontal Enforcement

So far the discussion has assumed the beneficial aspects of using common law pathways to extend constitutional rights into private settings. However, commentators raise a number of concerns about enforcing constitutional rights horizontally.

71. Schapiro, *supra* note 67, at 286–87.

72. *See* Chapter 2.

73. Helen Hershkoff, *State Courts and the "Passive Virtues": Rethinking the Judicial Function*, 114 Harv. L. Rev. 1833, 1877–1904 (2001).

74. *See* Chapter 4.

75. Southern Pacific Co. v. Jensen, 244 U.S. 205, 221 (1917).

Two arguments predominate: that eliminating the state action requirement could deprive private law of integrity; and that extending constitutional rights to private activity will have the perverse effects of diluting constitutional protection and of diminishing individual liberty. In this chapter I cannot address all of these concerns as applied to Article III and foreign judiciaries. However, in this section I suggest two arguments that potentially mitigate these concerns in the state common law context: the institutional position of state courts within the federal system, and the "dynamic effects" of state common law decision making within a national framework.[76]

1. Preserving Common Law Integrity Some commentators argue that the horizontal enforcement of constitutional norms involves the "colonization" of private decision making by forms of public discourse that are and ought to remain distinct. Rhetorically, the term *horizontal enforcement* assumes a set of public norms, essentialized in character, that are exogenous to the common law because they are rooted in constitutional sources. This description, however, does not accurately map interpretive practice. State courts do not mechanistically enforce idealized constitutional rules in a private setting; rather, they filter constitutional principles using "normative resources" indigenous to state common law analysis.[77] As Peter Benson explains in the analogous international context:

> It should be emphasized that the realization of human rights via private law channels does not mean merely that private law provides a remedy for breach of a right that is worked out independently of and apart from it. . . . Rather, the indirect application model supposes that the human right which is given protection through a civil action and remedy is specified and given place from within private law itself.[78]

The examples that Benson offers from India apply equally well to the state practices surveyed: enforcement of the constitutional norm occurs through common law doctrines that establish the liability of the defendant (e.g., the implied covenant of good faith), through common law channels that reconfigure defenses available to the plaintiff (e.g., the availability of public policy as a constraint), and through hybrid pathways (e.g., the balancing of speech and property interests in the state shopping mall cases). In these cases, constitutional norms do not command, control, or displace common law practices; rather, they fortify private adjudication by providing new sources of guidance and by expanding the range of justificatory reasons for decision making.

---

76. *See* Cass R. Sunstein & Adrian Vermeule, *Interpretation and Institutions*, 101 MICH. L. REV. 885, 886 (2003).

77. Benson uses the term *normative resources*. Peter Benson, *Equality of Opportunity and Private Law*, *in* Friedmann & Barak-Erez, *supra* note 7, at 206. A similar usage appears in Weinrib & Weinrib, *supra* note 7, at 43–72.

78. Benson, *supra* note 77, at 206.

2. Maintaining Robust Constitutional Protection Commentators further warn that horizontal enforcement presents a "threat to private rights" and so predict an overall dilution of constitutional protection.[79] Boiled down, the argument forewarns that state courts, unwilling to extend the full force of constitutional values into the private sphere, will weaken public protection to put the two domains on equal footing.[80] The formal response to this concern is the familiar "national floor" argument[81]—the idea that federal constitutional law provides a protective backstop to any dilution caused by state judicial practices. One might say that this response rests on the hierarchical notion of federalism that the polyphonic conception rejects. Reconfigured, the conventional response captures an important insight built on the institutional position of the state judiciary within the national system. The location of states within the nation arguably generates competitive pressure that can be expected to protect against a downward thinning of national rights. State judicial systems operate within a complex network of other legal actors; unlike the U.S. Supreme Court, which is criticized for claiming to be final and supreme on matters of constitutional interpretation, state courts rarely have the last word on a legal issue—state common law decisions are "subject to amendment, modification, or even reversal"[82] by federal courts, administrative agencies, Congress, and local legislators and decision makers. Only if state common law decisions withstand these competitive pressures will their "molecular" actions become "molar."[83] Although these institutional arrangements may not fully protect against the "leaky floors" of a national backstop, the problem results from federalism, and not from horizontal constitutional enforcement.[84]

3. Ensuring Private Autonomous Spheres Finally, commentators warn that horizontal application—which they call "private constitutional law"[85]—causes "the constitutionalizing of a wide range of interactions between citizens" at the cost of narrowing individual liberty. Certainly a major argument in favor of retaining the state action doctrine is the concern that the cure is worse than the disease: its elimination jeopardizes aspects of private life that intuitively deserve

79. John H. Garvey, *Private Power and the Constitution*, 10 CONST. COMMENT. 311, 315 (1993).

80. *See* William P. Marshall, *Diluting Constitutional Rights: Rethinking "Rethinking State Action,"* 80 NW. U. L. REV. 558, 562 (1985).

81. Judith S. Kaye, *In Memoriam: William J. Brennan, Jr.*, 111 HARV. L. REV. 14, 17 (1997).

82. Henry P. Monaghan, *Foreword: Constitutional Common Law*, 89 HARV. L. REV. 1, 3 (1975).

83. Richard A. Posner, *The Meaning of Judicial Self-Restraint*, 59 IND. L.J. 1, 16 (1983/1984).

84. Marc L. Miller & Ronald F. Wright, *Leaky Floors: State Law below Federal Constitutional Limits*, 50 ARIZ. L. REV. 227 (2008). *See also* Justin Long, *Intermittent State Constitutionalism*, 34 PEPP. L. REV. 41, 69–70 (2006).

85. Marshall, *supra* note 80, at 560.

to be shielded from public scrutiny. However, as Richard S. Kay suggests, "the relevance of the public-private distinction need not be identical for every one of the rules of the Constitution."[86] Extending constitutional values to nongovernmental actors through the common law does not require applying constitutional rights in the same way and to the same extent as to governmental actors. Courts can respect the principles and values embraced by constitutional norms without confining them to "pre-established standards of behaviour" that apply to all actors in the same way.[87] Private action works differently from government power, and those differences matter as to how abuses are to be best regulated. The indirect application of constitutional norms in the private setting thus involves line drawing and balancing in the light of facts and circumstances—an approach traditionally associated with common law analysis.

IV. COMMON LAW AS A MODALITY FOR CONSTITUTIONAL DEVELOPMENT

The academic literature on social norms has moved constitutional analysis beyond a mechanistic command-and-control legal model toward a deeper appreciation of how law constitutes and motivates aspects of individual identity, social relations, and human agency.[88] Commentators now comfortably recognize that law in its "'symbolic,' 'expressive,' or 'meaningful'"[89] dimension affects constitutional practice, and, further, that constitutional interpretation comprises a practice not confined to the U.S. Supreme Court but rather shared with other political actors. The project of dual constitutional enforcement embraces this approach by including state courts among the actors who participate in the construction and elaboration of constitutional meaning.

A. State Constitutional Norms as an Interpretive Canon

In the weakest conception, we might characterize state constitutional norms as forming part of a background "interpretive regime" that guides but does not direct how state courts are to construe common law. The idea of background principles providing interpretive guidance is hardly novel. Philip Frickey and William Eskridge describe a system of rules of statutory interpretation as an "interpretive regime," meaning

---

86. Richard S. Kay, *The State Action Doctrine, the Public-Private Distinction, and the Independence of Constitutional Law*, 10 CONST. COMMENT. 329, 332 (1993).

87. Stephen R. Perry, *Judicial Obligation, Precedent and the Common Law*, 7 OXFORD J. OF LEGAL STUD. 215, 217 (1987).

88. *See generally* ALAN HUNT, EXPLORATIONS IN LAW AND SOCIETY: TOWARD A CONSTITUTIVE THEORY OF LAW (1993).

89. Matthew D. Adler, *Expressive Theories of Law: A Skeptical Overview*, 148 U. PA. L. REV. 1363, 1364 (2000).

> a system of background norms and conventions against which the Court will read statutes. An interpretive regime tells lower court judges, agencies, and citizens how strings of words in statutes will be read, what presumptions will be entertained as to a statute's scope and meaning, and what auxiliary materials might be consulted to resolve ambiguities.[90]

The authors explain that "constitutionally based canons . . . are vehicles for the Court to enforce values it considers important, but in a manner that does not challenge the ultimate power of a coordinate branch of government."[91] Nicholas Quinn Rosenkranz develops a similar interpretive approach in arguing that rules of statutory interpretation can be seen as a form of "constitutional common law" developed from the Constitution but not required by it, and which can be overruled by Congress.[92] Within such an interpretive regime, state constitutional provisions function as a legal norm in the Dworkinian sense, as providing "a reason that argues in one direction, but does not necessitate a particular decision" by the judge seeking to resolve a dispute.[93] In a position of interpretive equilibrium, the constitutional norm authorizes decision in no particular direction, but affects the judge's assessment of how best to fit the case at hand into the legal system overall.[94]

B. State Constitutions as Part of the "Implicit Dimension" of Private Law

The private law theory of "implicit dimension" offers additional insight into state interpretative practice.[95] "Implicit dimension" in contract theory refers to "the implicit understandings and expectations of the participants." The problem of having a court determine the "contexts and conventions" of a legally recognized relation is not confined to contract formation but rather extends more broadly to market transactions. Implicit dimensions can include customs, expectations, understandings, and knowledge of social institutions.[96] As John Wightman writes, they encompass "the background context which confers meaning on the parties' dealings." The doctrinal pathways that allow consideration of these implicit dimensions include "context-based provisions" such as the implied

---

90. William N. Eskridge & Philip P. Frickey, *Foreword: Law as Equilibrium*, 108 HARV. L. REV. 26, 66 (1994).

91. *Id.* at 68.

92. Nicholas Quinn Rosenkranz, *Federal Rules of Statutory Interpretation*, 115 HARV. L. REV. 2085, 2094–95 (2002).

93. RONALD DWORKIN, TAKING RIGHTS SERIOUSLY 26 (1997).

94. *Cf.* RONALD DWORKIN, LAW'S EMPIRE 380 (1986).

95. Hugh Collins, *Introduction: The Research Agenda of Implicit Dimensions of Contracts, in* IMPLICIT DIMENSIONS OF CONTRACT: DISCRETE, RELATIONAL AND NETWORK CONTRACTS 1–24 (David Campbell, Hugh Collins, & John Wightman eds., 2003).

96. John Wightman, *Beyond Custom: Contract, Contexts, and the Recognition of Implicit Understandings, in id.* at 143, 147.

covenant of good faith.[97] Arguably, constitutional norms reconstitute the "contexts and conventions" that must be taken into account when a court considers a contract or other common law dispute. At the least, they cannot be ignored in considering the relevant baseline assumptions on which the private relation builds. The existence of these norms thus may be said to alter a private dispute's social baseline by presenting a set of assumptions about social commitments and public values that otherwise might be absent from the court's common law decision. Treating constitutional norms as part of the common law's implicit dimension does not mandate the incorporation of rights provisions into a common law rule, but rather offers a strong source of interpretive authority that a court would not be permitted to ignore without an articulated justification.

C. State Constitutional Provisions as Common Law Default Rules

Finally, "default rule thinking" offers another way to conceptualize the influence of constitutional norms in common law decision making.[98] In the private setting, a default rule governs unless the parties choose to contract around it;[99] in the public setting, we might argue that a state constitutional norm functions as a default rule justifying an interpretive approach that the court ought to follow unless the political branches or the court speaks explicitly to the contrary. Although the state court is not obliged to enforce the norm, it must take the norm into account—what it no longer can do is ignore or simply discredit this value. Default thinking, typical of private law doctrine, has increasingly affected those aspects of public law scholarship concerned with cooperation among different government actors. For example, the Supreme Court has used default rules to encourage legislative dialogue: "Model default rules are designed to elicit a legislative response by prescribing a specific procedure to protect a given constitutional right while also inviting political actors to formulate alternative procedures to replace it."[100] They can influence the effectuation of constitutional norms that are candidates for underenforcement because of specific institutional limitations.[101] John Ferejohn and Barry Friedman categorize this form of default rule as "normative or transformative," arguing that it is enlisted most usefully when the Supreme Court's "prescriptions might leave room for other constitutional actors to take a more aggressive posture toward rights enforcement."[102]

97. *Id.* at 149, 144.

98. *See* John Ferejohn & Barry Friedman, *Toward a Political Theory of Constitutional Default Rules*, 33 Fla. St. U.L. Rev. 825, 825 (2006).

99. Alan Schwartz, *The Default Rule Paradigm and the Limits of Contract Law*, 3 S. Cal. Interdisc. L.J. 389, 390 (1993).

100. Tara Mikkilineni, *Constitutional Default Rules and Interbranch Cooperation*, 82 N.Y.U. L. Rev. 1403, 1406 (2007).

101. Ferejohn & Friedman, *supra* note 98, at 852.

102. *Id.* at 850, 853.

Thinking about state constitutional norms as default rules comports with the theory of polyphonic federalism for they serve to spur interjurisdictional dialogue and the elaboration of public values across state boundaries.

V. CONCLUSION

"[T]he best reason for adopting a particular new regime," David A. Strauss recommends, "is that the new regime had already been adopted in practice, even though it was not fully acknowledged."[103] That constitutional values pervade private law doctrines is readily apparent even if the categories of private and public law still retain heuristic importance. Nor should this interpretive practice come as a surprise. Common law and constitutional law, whether federal or state, operate within a single national culture and so share background assumptions that influence doctrine and decision making.[104] The federal state action doctrine obscures this insight by treating the rules governing private ordering as separate and immune from constitutional scrutiny and by further suggesting that the culture of private law, with its emphasis on individualism and efficiency, differs significantly from that of the public. Once we acknowledge the overlap of public and private law, the question becomes not whether, but how much and to what extent this intersection should take place.

Nearly two decades ago, Judge Kaye emphasized: "The partnership of real common law and real constitutional law holds great promise for the future."[105] Recognizing the influence of state constitutional norms on the development of common law doctrine in particular holds special importance for understanding the relation between law and social change. Constitutional scholars tend to think that socioeconomic conditions and the patterns of private life are resistant to judicial influence. Indeed, the view that constitutional litigation holds little power in revising long-lived patterns of inequality or social behavior is the mainstay of a great deal of academic writing about constitutional entrenchment.[106] But we hold an incomplete picture of law's possibility if we ignore the influence of constitutional norms on the common law principles that affect private orderings. In discrete settings, a court's enforcing such norms will influence the direction of common law doctrine and affect decisions in specific cases.

---

103. David A. Strauss, *The Common Law Genius of the Warren Court*, 49 Wm. & Mary L. Rev. 845, 859 (2007).

104. *Cf.* Paul W. Kahn, *Interpretation and Authority in State Constitutionalism*, 106 Harv. L. Rev. 1147, 1168 (1993).

105. Judith S. Kaye, *Foreword: The Common Law and State Constitutional Law as Full Partners in the Protection of Individual Rights*, 23 Rutgers L.J. 727, 752 (1992).

106. *See, e.g.*, Ran Hirschl, Towards Juristocracy: The Origins and Consequences of the New Constitutionalism 118 (2004). *But see* Hershkoff, *supra* note 13, at 302.

The common law's approach—conditional, local, and plural—forewarns that social effects are likely to be slow, uneven, and incremental. But to the extent that common law judging legitimately includes "[m]oral judgments . . . about fairness, good policy, or social utility," state courts unquestionably can consider and elaborate constitutional norms in their development of common law doctrines.[107] The private world of contract, property, and tort already functions as an inevitable partner in the elaboration of constitutional values. I have tried in this chapter to make this practice explicit and to ensure its inclusion as a full partner in the project of dual constitutional enforcement.

107. *See* David A. Strauss, *Common Law Constitutional Interpretation*, 63 U. Chi. L. Rev. 877, 900–01 (1996).

INDEX

R

S

www.ingramcontent.com/pod-product-compliance
Ingram Content Group UK Ltd.
Pitfield, Milton Keynes, MK11 3LW, UK
UKHW020923170926
475595UK00031B/34

9 780195 368321